STRETCHING THE IMAGINATION

STRETCHING THE IMAGINATION

Representation and Transformation in Mental Imagery

CESARE CORNOLDI
ROBERT H. LOGIE
MARIA A. BRANDIMONTE
GEIR KAUFMANN
DANIEL REISBERG

New York   Oxford
OXFORD UNIVERSITY PRESS
1996

Oxford University Press

Oxford   New York
Athens   Auckland   Bangkok   Bombay
Calcutta   Cape Town   Dar es Salaam   Delhi
Florence   Hong Kong   Istanbul   Karachi
Kuala Lumpur   Madras   Madrid   Melbourne
Mexico City   Nairobi   Paris   Singapore
Taipei   Tokyo   Toronto

and associated companies in
Berlin   Ibadan

Copyright © 1996 by Oxford University Press, Inc.

Published by Oxford University Press, Inc.,
198 Madison Avenue, New York, New York 10016

Oxford is a registered trademark of Oxford University Press

Library of Congress Cataloging-in-Publication Data
Stretching the imagination : representation and transformation in
mental imagery / Cesare Cornoldi . . . [et al.].
p.   cm. — (Counterpoints)
Includes bibliographical references and index.
ISBN 0-19-509947-8
ISBN 0-19-509948-6 (pbk.)
1. Mental representation.   2. Perception.   3. Imagery (Psychology)
I. Cornoldi, Cesare.   II. Series: Counterpoints
BF316.6.S77   1996
153.3'2—dc20   94-45730

1 3 5 7 9 8 6 4 2

Printed in the United States of America
on acid-free paper

Foreword

You have before you the inaugural book in *Counterpoints: Cognition, Memory, and Language*. With its publication, the academic community has gained a new forum—and a new kind of forum—for scholarly debate. The *Counterpoints* series was conceived as an opportunity for in-depth, international dialogue on topics of current concern to researchers in psychology, education, child development, linguistics, and neuroscience. Each volume consists of a seminar-like presentation of three to four major chapters that take a position on a major topic under discussion. The core chapters are preceded by a historical overview and are followed by a summary and discussion that is a collaboration of the contributors. In this way, alternative perspectives can be weighed and differences can be resolved . . . or agreed upon. We hope that as a timely and widely read forum, *Counterpoints* can serve as a catalyst for discussion and integration across diverse areas of research and theory. With both hardback and paperback editions and with multiple volumes published each year, *Counterpoints* will serve as an important research and didactic tool for students, faculty, and practitioners. We look forward to our future collaborations.

Marc Marschark, Series Editor
Rochester Institute of Technology
National Technical Institute for the Deaf

Contents

STRETCHING THE IMAGINATION

CHAPTER 1

Counterpoints in Perception and Mental Imagery: Introduction

Cesare Cornoldi and Robert Logie

The relationships among perception, representation, and mental imagery have given rise to one of the most vigorously debated areas of psychology. Research in this area has generated an abundance of theory, together with contrasting positions and heated discussion. However, the *vis polemica* present in many studies in the field apparently tends to address detailed aspects of individual studies rather than general philosophical questions or psychological theories that have their roots in the history of human thinking.

Classical and medieval thinkers, like Aristotle, Diogenes Laertius, Augustine, and Aquinas have given a central position to imagery and imagination, inspiring long-standing psychological concepts. For example, Figure 1.1 represents a typical classical view of stages of information processing from sensation to imagination, and from thinking to memory (see Clarke & Dewhurst, 1972; Mecacci, 1993). The first cell on the right, close to the sensory receptors, holds sensation *(sensus communis)*, the second cell includes fantasy and imagination, the third thinking and judgment, whereas memory is at the extreme left side.

Classical philosophers were followed by the British empiricists—Berkeley, Hobbes, and Hume—who developed the idea that knowledge is built up from mental images—that is, traces of sensory experience. These philosophers made the point particularly clear: If our knowledge is based on experience, mental representations are the result of that experience, and the representations reflect the properties of sensory perception.

We can attribute to that period one of the most salient moments of the contrast between an empirical and a "rational" theory of acquisition and organization of knowledge. However, this contrast is recurrent in the history of thinking, ap-

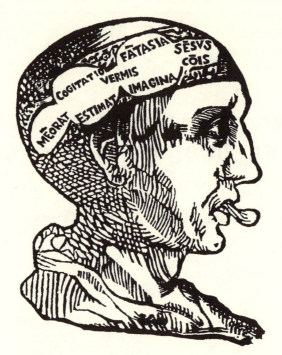

FIGURE 1.1. Medieval representation of neuropsychological functions (from Mecacci, 1993).

pearing in different guises—Aristotle against Plato, Descartes against British empiricism, and recently large groups of philosophers, psychologists, and social scientists have been debating these issues among themselves. This contrast has not necessarily involved a consideration of the origin and nature of mental images, but there are some clear implications that can be gleaned from the debate. The terminology itself was consequently adapted and modified, sometimes using the term *image* for describing the unit for the content of thinking, sometimes substituting it. Descartes used the term "idea" and the German philosopher Christian Wolff preferred the expression "representation."

When twentieth-century psychologists considered these problems, they were influenced by past philosophy and brought into the debate the passion and the radical nature inherent in the core problems in human thinking. Histories of psychology give a great deal of space to the debate between the so-called Wurzburg school and introspectionists as to whether it is possible to think without the use of images. The radical refutation of the concept of mental imagery by behaviorism dominated the western side of the Atlantic Ocean. In striking contrast, the concept of imagery was central to much of the thinking in the European cognitive tradition (e.g., Bartlett, Piaget). In the more recent past, the concept of imagery was greeted as one of the milestones of cognitive theory, but was soon exposed to the debate between "imagery theorists" and "propositionalists."

All these debates seem still to influence recent views about perception, imagery, and representation, suggesting that the major philosophical puzzles cannot be definitively solved and tend to reemerge. The essays included in the present volume testify eloquently to the continuity and the roots of this debate. In particular, Geir Kaufmann reexamines modern philosophical and psychological theories that consider the concept of imagery. Dan Reisberg, Maria Antonella Brandimonte, and Walter Gerbino explore, from different points of view, what in a mental representation is retained of the properties and of the information present in perception.

In many respects it is curious to observe that such a lengthy debate originated from the simple consideration of a single empirical phenomenon, apparently very local and specific. Often little things can produce more significant events. It is not for nothing that the Trojan War was caused by an apple or that the intense hatred between Lilliputians and their neighbors was focused on the position of an egg! An extensive debate (and a book) has arisen from a poor duck that can be mistaken for a rabbit. In fact, the starting point of the present debate is an influential experimental paper by Chambers and Reisberg (1985) showing that an ambiguous figure (a drawing which can be seen either as a duck or as a rabbit) can be reinterpreted at the perceptual level, but not at the imagery level. The implications of this result were many and important. For example, the result demonstrated that perception and imagery rely at least in part on separate mechanisms rather than the use of completely overlapping resources. This disconfirmed a typical assumption of imagery theorists. Another implication of the result concerned the demonstration of the limits in the use of imagery for discovery and creativity. This contradicted a classical view that imagery was a key medium for creative thought. This view was also found in the history of philosophy, particularly the romantic philosophers, such as Fichte and Hegel.

These wide repercussions explain why the Chambers and Reisberg study was reconsidered in an extensive series of experimental studies, conducted not only by other American experimental psychologists, but also by European researchers. Many of these studies have been discussed or criticized in the chapters of this volume. Some of these experiments were run by Reisberg, by Brandimonte, and by Kaufmann, each on the basis of different theoretical premises, but also with slightly different experimental results. The various empirical observations made by the different authors create a very particular case. In fact, we are in front of not only a strange, bizarre phenomenon, open to different interpretations, but also of an experimental situation that can produce different effects.

The three universities to which the protagonists are affiliated are spread throughout the world, in Oregon, Italy, and Norway, not only physically distant, but also separated by past tradition and current research interests. Nevertheless, we can follow a common effort of research and comparison, proof of the increasing tendency of contemporary psychology to be devoted to work in a worldwide perspective.

None of these three scientists has maintained a radical position against or in favor of the existence and the critical role of mental imagery. In fact, Reisberg, Brandimonte, and Kaufmann often have been involved in research focused on the concept of mental imagery, never denying its importance, but rather arguing for better specifications of the classical imagery theories. It is not for nothing that they had the opportunity of meeting on one of the occasions of the "Imagery and Cognition" workshops, which every other year are organized in Europe. In particular, when the last workshop was held (Tenerife, December 1992), Reisberg, Brandimonte, and Kaufmann accepted our and Marc Marschark's invitation to sit around a table and discuss their different positions. This debate is the basis for the last part of this volume. The function of this first chapter is to introduce the reader to the main theoretical and empirical problems raised in the three core chapters in which Reisberg, Brandimonte and Gerbino, and Kaufmann have presented their views.

ISSUES OF THE THEORETICAL DEBATE

The study of mental representations has two main themes. First, it addresses the definition of format and organization of knowledge stored in the mind. Second, it seeks a description of how mental representations are formed. Even if we have no empirical view of how knowledge is acquired, we cannot deny that sensory experience makes a substantial contribution to the content of mental representations. Therefore, perception is necessarily involved in some way in mental representations, but the question remains open as to the nature of its involvement. The debate on this point is complicated both by theory and by terminology. At first blush, the question is quite straightforward: How is perception involved in mental representation? However, before attempting an answer, we may simply end up generating further questions such as: What exactly is meant by "perception" and by "mental representation"? Does every sensory experience produce a "perception"? Can all perceptual experiences be understood in the same way? Is a mental representation the only possible content of mind? How is meaning represented in mind? The exercise may progress ad infinitum, but in many ways this reflects the legitimate progression of science. To answer the broad question that is unlikely to have a straightforward and simple answer, we generate more detailed questions which we attempt to answer by setting up thought experiments, theories, or real experiments. The scientific skill lies in generating those detailed questions that will be informative for the broader issues, but that will also be tractable theoretically and empirically.

The discussion on mental representations is intimately related to modern cognitive theory, but it may be ambiguous and also open to critical considerations that are present in the history of thinking and are reflected in the chapters of this book. For example, Kaufmann mentions the modern philosophers' critique of the concept of mental representation as a static entity independent from the psychological process creating it. Sometimes representations are considered like objects that can be seen, analyzed, and even measured, and thinking is considered as a process that can operate either on external objects or on internal objects—that is, on their representations. This naive realistic view facilitates reasoning about mental representations but runs the risk of focusing on the processes of perception while ignoring those characteristics that are specific to mental representations.

Perception and Representation

The present volume is especially concerned with those mental representations that are strictly connected with the physical world and that may directly inform theories of the relationship between perception and representation. These representations are often considered as having a specific imaginal format and have been discussed with reference to a few key questions such as: Are they analogs of perception? Do they share the same psychological processes as perception?

The present book has the fortune of being born during a new phase in the study of imagery. This phase is characterized by a more problematic and sophisticated view of the relationship between perception and imagery. As has been observed elsewhere (e.g., Marschark & Cornoldi, 1990), imagery theorists from the late 1950s on necessarily responded to critics who denied the existence of functional value of imagery as a phenomenon or as a construct. This required well-supported arguments and lucid specifications that could be derived from cases where images have a clear role and profile—that is, as complete analogs of perceptions. As a result, there was little attention paid to the unique properties of imaginal representations, which clearly demonstrate ways in which images are not direct analogies of perception.

If we review the main experimental and theoretical contributions of the 1970s and of the early 1980s, we consistently find a preoccupation with demonstrating the analogy. In retrospect, such demonstrations accumulated into rather tedious collections of mental representations, which appeared to have characteristics that were identical to those of perceptions. These demonstrations failed to tell us anything new and simply suggested that imagery researchers were attempting to import, unabridged, what was already known about perception.

It is worth noticing that a weakening of the "analogical" postulate coincides with a loss of interest in the ontological affray between propositional and imagery theorists. The debate had already lost some impetus when it began to be apparent that it was ultimately irresolvable and untestable (e.g., Anderson, 1978). Furthermore, the spread of more critical considerations concerning similarities and differences between perception and imagery had the effect of surrendering arguments to the anti-imagery theorists. Intons-Peterson and McDaniel (1990) have reviewed cases illustrating asymmetries between imagery and perception, as distance estimations, magnitude estimations, brightness contrast, some aspects of mental rotation, and mental scanning. In particular, mental scanning of an image tends to take longer than does visual scanning of a physical stimulus. They also argued that images are knowledge-weighted. That is, they include conceptual information generally absent during the visual perceptual experience. For example, Intons-Peterson and Roskos-Ewoldsen (1989) have shown that the time taken to imagine walking between two locations while carrying an object is affected by the weight of the object and by the familiarity of the environment. Neither factor could be obtained directly from the visual percept of the object.

An important contribution to the demise of the analogical postulate comes from research on the reinterpretation of mental images. Everyone knows that we visually perceive things we did not or could not see at a first glance. With extended viewing of the stimulus, perception can offer the ability to see embedded figures, to operate perceptual reversals between figure and ground, or to "see" a complete pattern when not all parts of the scene are visible. Is imagery able to do the same? Imagery research has often considered this problem, sometimes showing the capacity of mental imagery to reinterpret images (e.g., Anderson & Helstrup, 1993; Finke & Slayton, 1988). In these cases mental imagery and perception behave in a similar fashion, and in ways that are more powerful than other forms of mental processing. However, the case does not seem to be general. The opposite view also can be found in the early cognitive literature on mental representations. For example, Reed (1974) observed that students had difficulty in detecting imagined parts embedded in previously seen patterns. Similarly, Hinton (1979) observed that people were able to point to the positions in space of various parts of a perceived wire cube, but that the same task was very difficult in its imaginal form.

In 1985 Chambers and Reisberg published a paper offering further evidence concerning the asymmetries between perception and imagery. If people see a pattern that, depending on the interpretation of its parts, can appear like a duck or a rabbit, they do not meet particular difficulty in reversing the interpretation. On the other hand, such a reversal becomes impossible if it relies on the memory representation of the pattern. The Chambers and Reisberg data appear clear and conclusive, suggesting, first, that imagery does not allow reinterpretation of a representation, and second that imagery and perception are completely different processes. However, as is well illustrated in this book, the story is much more complicated, raising doubts about both points. The first claim is challenged by the observation that imagery seems better able to reconstrue representations than was argued from the original data.

The second claim is complicated by questions such as what do we mean when we say that perceptual experience is involved. For example, it can be argued that the original perceptual experience was of only one interpretation of the drawing, and since the original percept did not include the second interpretation, then the mental representation of that percept did not include the second interpretation either. That is, the mental representation is a representation of a percept. This argument additionally distinguishes between the phenomenal object or percept and properties of the physical object that include all the information necessary for successful reinterpretation. In our view, when we consider the similarities and differences between perception and representation we must focus on the properties of the experience related to the percept rather than to the properties of the physical object. It is true also that the properties of the physical object are not the properties of the world, but sample the world in a way in which it can be experienced by humans. It is equally true that at any one moment, not all of these properties are included in the percept.

Physical Objects and Percepts

In the last 20 years many disciplines and many areas of psychology have contributed to the development of a cognitive theory of mental images. However, the contribution of the psychological study of perception has been less systematic than we might wish.

The chapters by Reisberg and by Brandimonte and Gerbino in this volume offer a very nice illustration of how perception research could be used for the study of mental images. Between them, only Walter Gerbino can be considered a specialist in visual perception. The other authors, however, have successfully combined their cognitive background with a review of the perception literature, exploring how studies on the formation of the phenomenal object can be used for examining the formation and characteristics of the image of the object. Gerbino, who prepared the later sections of Chapter 2, has anchored his analysis to the classical Italian tradition in the study of perception, inspired by Gestalt and Gibsonian theories.

In general, both chapters share some critical points. For example, they distinguish between the physical object and the object as it is seen by us. Furthermore, they try to identify the main mechanisms of perceptual analysis and organization, like the reference frame; the perceptual center; selected, focused, attentively processed elements; and elaboration priorities. It is suggested that, if these principles are operating on perception, a fortiori they will be operating on mental imagery.

There is an abundance of evidence that we perceive objects not as they are, but as we interpret them. Consequently, perception does not maintain all the characteristics of the physical object and cannot run all the operations that are possible only when we have available the physical object. This argument raises the doubt that a negation of the analogy between perception and imagery simply should be due to an incorrect comparison between operations possible on an image and operations possible on a physical object, rather than on a percept. Chapters in this volume help us consider this issue. However, they suggest that this is not the only perspective from which to consider the issue.

In fact, the asymmetries that have been found between perception and imagery cannot be rejected on the basis of the simple consideration of a confounding between percept and physical object. Specifically, indeterminacy and possibility of reinterpreting appear more available for perception than for imagery according to many observations. Brandimonte and Gerbino show that representation is sometimes indeterminate. Chambers and Reisberg argue the opposite and suggest that an image must always be interpreted. Kaufmann, in his chapter, critiques other similar positions. For example, Shorter (1952) affirms that it is not possible to have the image without knowing what it is an image of. However, Brandimonte, Gerbino, and Kaufmann suggest that images can retain some ambiguity, even when they are interpreted. There is a sense in which their positions hark back to the problem of a definition of the levels of perceptual and imaginal experience.

With reference to the perceptual experience, we can find in the literature numerous suggestions as to the existence of different levels. Many authors (e.g., Treisman & Souther, 1985) have suggested that some aspects of the perceived

FIGURE 1.2. Matrices used by Giusberti et al. (1992, Experiment 3) for inclined and reversed conditions (see text for explanation).

object pop out in a primitive way before every intervention of attention. Only after a second viewing is the overall percept experienced. If imagery is a conscious, attention-demanding activity only this level of perceptual experience could be compared to the image level (Neisser, 1967). This is easily confirmed by a simple observation. If we look at the pattern in Figure 1.2, we immediately capture some emergent properties of the stimulus, like the inclined letter. The same letter when upside-down does not pop out in the same way. This effect has been related to the first phases of the formation of a percept and cannot be found in imagery.

In fact, if we generate the same patterns through verbal instructions, we will experience images but the two figures will have similar emergent properties, without any particular advantage for the inclined letter (Giusberti, Cornoldi, De Beni, & Massironi, 1992). However, there are suggestions that, for the imaginal representations, different levels of experience also could be considered. For example, in his early studies on the effects of imagery on memory, Paivio (1971) argued that very rapid imagery processes of which subjects were unaware could affect memory performance. This was evident, for example, in memory for high imagery words presented at rates of one or two per second. In a different way, Brandimonte raises the same problem concerning the distinction between different levels of mental representation—one level still ambiguous, the other one already interpreted. This issue is raised in a replication of Chambers and Reisberg's situation in which Brandimonte and Gerbino have shown that people can have the interpreted image, but also maintain the visual ambiguous information that can be used for a new interpretation. From the point of view of one of us, these data suggest the necessity of distinguishing between a visual memory trace and a visual mental image.

Visual Traces and Visual Images

In the psychological literature, visual memories and visual images have often been considered together. Also, short-term memory of a perceived object has been considered an image on the basis of the definition that states "a mental image is the representation of an object when it is not available to sensory experience." However, both common sense and the psychological literature implicitly seem to separate the case when people have a visual memory and the case when people generate a mental image. This distinction overlaps with the Brandimonte distinction between interpreted image and visual trace, only because the image also is a visual trace, but strengthens the need to distinguish between different levels of experience and representation.

A further consideration of the implications of Figure 1.2 can help the reader understand some of the problems that are involved. We already mentioned the fact that the image, generated through verbal instructions, is different from perception losing the perceptual properties and effects of the inclined letter. It is interesting to observe what happens with the visual trace. In fact, differently from a visual image, the visual trace of the inclined letter of Figure 1.2 still maintains some peculiar emergent properties, thus confirming that a visual trace is different from a mental image and shares more aspects with perception. But a further observation reveals also how perception can be considered at different levels. Suppose that a person is invited to draw and then to observe the pattern in Figure 1.2. In this case the observation follows a rather complex elaboration process that is in part mediated conceptually. With some surprise, we can see that the percept looks more like an image than as an immediate percept: The inclined letter is no more evident than the upside-down letter (Giusberti et al. 1992). The hypothesis of a raw visual trace that is distinct from an interpreted image can be introduced to explain the phenomenon of "release from verbal overshadowing" observed by Brandimonte and her co-workers. This phenomenon refers to the fact that subjects can retrieve from memory visual information that was not present in the interpreted image. A similar phenomenon was also found by Reisberg and Chambers when they invited their subjects to draw the image. The drawing included the additional information that was necessary for successful reconstrual. Obviously other only partially overlapping interpretations can be advanced—e.g., by suggesting that a single image may have parts that are differentially available. However, this hypothesis may appear more different from the visual trace–visual image distinction hypothesis than it is. In fact, if we argue that at a certain moment only some parts are available in the conscious image, we are forced to distinguish between different levels of representation.

Beyond this particular theoretical point, the problem remains open concerning the mechanisms that determine the differential fates of different components of the perceived object. A possibility is that elements included in the visual image and raw visual elements have a different interpretation directly primed by the stimulus properties. Another possibility is that all the elements access memory in the same way and then memory selects the ones that are most appropriate for the image. In this second case, it is necessary that memory also stores information concerning the rules for selecting information. These possible explanations are considered in the three chapters, although we are still seeking a clear answer to the problem.

Visuospatial Working Memory

A related problem concerns the psychological system involved in storing, maintaining, and elaborating visual and imaginal information. This system has been identified sometimes as a mental visual buffer (Kosslyn, 1980), sometimes as a visuospatial sketch pad—that is, the visuospatial component of the working memory system (Baddeley, 1986). As has been illustrated (Logie, 1995), the two systems share many features, both referring to a temporary memory system and both connected to visual perception and to long-term memory.

If we accept the suggestion that visual short-term memory may have both raw visual elements and an interpreted image, these two approaches can help us find how the system can handle the two aspects. From Kosslyn's point of view, a focusing operation could converge on some areas of the buffer. Notice that partly similar reflections are advanced by Reisberg, when he considers the possibility that the mind's eye has an angle unable to cover the entire image. However, the Brandimonte and Gerbino data seem to show that the conscious image selects information from all parts of the pattern.

From a visuospatial sketch pad point of view a storage function could be distinguished from an active processing function that also has an interest in generating and maintaining the image. Another possibility is that the raw visual information directly accesses long-term memory, as it seems to be the case for other raw sensory information, like olfactory information (Richardson & Zucco, 1989). In this respect it is interesting to examine data on the time interval within which a release from verbal overshadowing phenomenon can be observed. Only if this interval is short does it seem reasonable to hypothesize a critical role for visual short-term memory. Rather surprisingly, Brandimonte, suggests, in her chapter, that, at least for other contexts, raw visual information can be used after relatively long intervals.

If a role for the visuospatial sketch pad is not clear in maintaining raw visual information, its hypothesized role is clearer for maintaining the mental image and operating on it. In their chapters Brandimonte and Kaufmann mention processes like generation, regeneration, visual rehearsal, and transformation, which typically involve mental images and have important implications for understanding the reconstrual problem. Reisberg uses some ideas drawn from a more general overview that one of us recently elaborated with him (Reisberg & Logie, 1993). Specifically, Reisberg and Logie refer to two components of visuospatial working memory, an "inner eye" and an "inner scribe." The former retains the image in a passive, but interpreted form, while the latter implements operations and transformations on that image which may allow for reconstrual. Reisberg emphasizes that reinterpretation of the image requires some form of stimulus support, but it is possible that this support could be provided covertly with the inner scribe mentally redrawing the image, thereby providing the circumstances within which a new interpretation can emerge (see also Logie, 1995).

Imagery and Language

The Baddeley (1986) model of working memory assumes the existence of different slave systems involved in maintenance of visuospatial and of phonological-articulatory information, thus offering a general framework for considering some aspects of the interface between language and imagery. For example, the phonological-articulatory system includes an articulatory process that is involved in transforming visually presented, verbalizable information into a phonological format. When such a process is blocked through articulatory suppression, the transformation of visual information into a phonological format and its transfer into the verbal short-term memory system are prevented.

The working memory model is used as the basis for Brandimonte's assumption that image interpretation happens through language. This assumption justifies her experimental manipulation in which articulatory suppression is used to prevent verbalization. In Brandimonte's terms, verbalization is necessary to produce a name for the visually presented stimulus, and the argument follows that production of a name affects interpretation of the stimulus; ipso facto, articulatory suppression prevents naming and stimulus interpretation. However, it is this last feature of the argument that is crucial. In this sense, the involvement of the phonological-articulatory component of the working memory system may be seen as something of a red herring. Moreover, it raises the problem of justifying the use of articulatory suppression, other than by referring to the experimental outcome that articulatory suppression results in an increase in reinterpretations based on the image. The traditional use of articulatory suppression has been as a means to prevent the use of phonological and articulatory codes for temporary storage of a verbal sequence. There is very little evidence that articulatory suppression prevents access to the lexical or semantic system, or indeed the phonological system per se. For example, try reading these sentences while repeating an irrelevant word such as "the-the-the." The phenomenal experience is of "hearing" the phonology of the words in some form of inner ear. Baddeley and Lewis (1981) showed that under articulatory suppression it is possible to read and comprehend sentences solely on the basis of their phonology; for example, "Iff yew mentelly sowned owt thiss sentunss yew kan comprehenned it eefen iff yew arr repeeting ann irrellefant wurrd." There is also no strong evidence that access to the names of objects is prevented under articulatory suppression. For example, try mentally naming all of the objects in the room around you, while suppressing articulation.

All three chapters repeatedly show how difficult it is to tackle the relationship between language and imagery. As implied above, language, as well as imagery, can be considered at different levels, either in its surface phonological-articulatory properties (associated with the articulatory loop), or with reference to the mental lexicon(s), or even with reference to the subject's conceptual knowledge. Which is the level most relevant to the present context? More generally, which is the level possibly contributing to image representation and which its interface? For example, the classical dual-code theory (Paivio, 1971, 1986) assumes that, when a verbalizable figure is coded, all the language levels are involved. As argued above, Brandimonte seems to assume that the phonological-articulatory level and maybe the lexical level are involved, as is suggested by the effects of articulatory suppression.

This position is rather different from the classical positions concerning verbal interpretations (and distortions) of pictorial stimuli. The most famous experimental situation was presented by Carmichael, Hogan, and Walter (1932), who showed that a verbal label associated with a pictorial ambiguous stimulus determined the interpretation of the figure and how it was remembered subsequently.

Figure 1.3 presents some examples taken from the research of Carmichael and colleagues, such as the ambiguous stimulus that can be interpreted either as a letter "C" or as a crescent moon. If the subject was told that the stimulus was a crescent moon, not only was the interpretation affected by this label but also the successive graphic reproduction based on memory (Fig. 1.3, first column). If, on the contrary, the subject was told that it was the letter "C," interpretation and recall were completely different (Fig. 1.3, third column). The effect generalized to other cases of differently interpretable patterns. Figure 1.3 (row 5) presents the case of the two circles connected by a line, which could be interpreted either as eyeglasses or as a dumbbell.

The case of the Carmichael et al. (1932) research is interesting because it provoked debate that partially parallels the current debate. Those results showed that not only did the label affect perceptual interpretation but also that the resulting image was affected by the perceptual interpretation. A problem related to that situation and to the present one concerns the possibility that visual information, which was inconsistent with the perceptual interpretation, was not lost in memory but simply was made difficult to access. This hypothesis was tested by Prentice (1954), who proposed a recognition test showing that subjects also were able to recognize correctly the original stimuli. The Carmichael et al. paradigm raises another point related to the current discussion, namely that it demonstrates what Brandimonte and Gerbino are suggesting—i.e., that language affects interpretation of a visual stimulus. However, the similarity could be more apparent than real: In the classical studies the effect seems to have been produced by the verbal label, but it could easily be attributed to semantic coding induced by the verbal label. The same results that Carmichael et al. found by giving verbal labels could be found by giving appropriate contexts. The ambiguous stimuli discussed above are no more ambiguous when presented, as shown in Figure 1.4, but they are immediately interpreted even in the absence of verbal labels. The eyeglasses in the context of a face cannot be interpreted otherwise. The same is true for the segment of the circle in the context of a series of letters or of the sky.

In the case of these examples, articulation of language is not necessary for the interpretation of the stimulus, whereas this seems to be the case in the Brandimonte experiments. Thus, language appears critical as a cue inducing a context

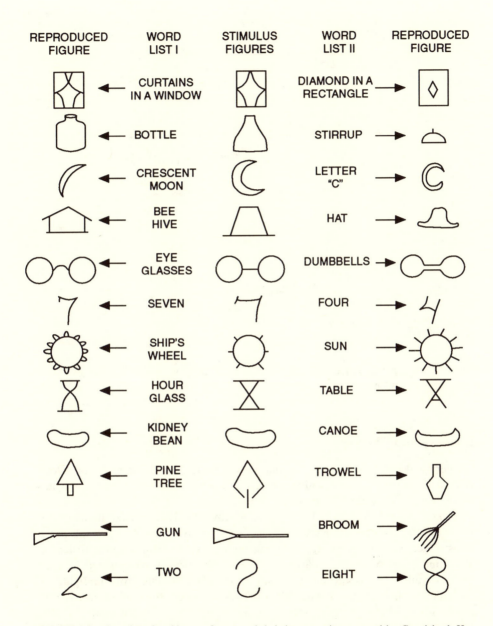

REPRODUCED FIGURE	WORD LIST I	STIMULUS FIGURES	WORD LIST II	REPRODUCED FIGURE
	← CURTAINS IN A WINDOW		DIAMOND IN A RECTANGLE →	
	← BOTTLE		STIRRUP →	
	← CRESCENT MOON		LETTER "C" →	
	← BEE HIVE		HAT →	
	← EYE GLASSES		DUMBBELLS →	
	← SEVEN		FOUR →	
	← SHIP'S WHEEL		SUN →	
	← HOUR GLASS		TABLE →	
	← KIDNEY BEAN		CANOE →	
	← PINE TREE		TROWEL →	
	← GUN		BROOM →	
	← TWO		EIGHT →	

FIGURE 1.3. Samples of ambiguous figures and their interpretation reported by Carmichael, Hogan, and Walter, 1932.

and the use of conceptual, not strictly articulatory-based, knowledge. These examples suggest that language and its relationships with visual memories and images can be considered at different levels, with different implications for the problem, largely raised by Kaufmann, as to how these systems communicate or collaborate.

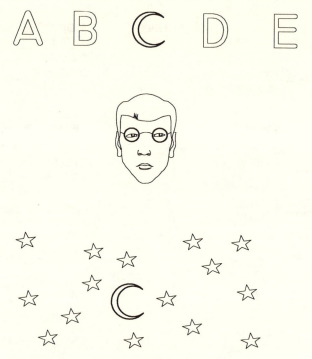

FIGURE 1.4. Immediate interpretation of ambiguous stimuli when in an appropriate context.

Imagery and Discovery

Imagery and imagination have always been considered as basic tools for discoveries and creative acts by which we arrive at new ideas, new views, and new relationships that were not obvious initially.

In *De vera religione* (10, 18) Saint Augustine clearly described the malleability of mental images: "Images originate from bodily things and through sensations: Once they are received, they can be very easily remembered, differentiated, multiplied, reduced, enlarged, ordered, transformed, reorganized in every way that thinking likes to do it." Many German philosophers of the eighteenth and nineteenth centuries distinguished between reproductive and productive imagery. Reproductive imagery was a passive system receiving information from the senses. Conversely, productive imagery was an active system capable of creative elaboration of information held by reproductive imagery, thus offering a tool to the creative arts. For example, Christian Wolff, in the work *Psychologia Empirica* (1732) described a "facultas fingendi" consisting of the "production of images never perceived by senses through the decomposition and the composition of images."

Traditionally, psychologists also have attributed to imagery a critical role in finding new solutions—e.g., in thinking and problem-solving (for a review, see

Denis, 1990) and in the arts (Arnheim, 1969). Thus, results denying a particular role for imagery in discovery may appear very provocative, going against a very long-standing tradition. The contemporary relevance of this debate is confirmed by the recent appearance of a book edited by Roskos-Ewoldsen, Intons-Peterson, and Anderson (1993) entitled *Imagery, Creativity, and Discovery,* which brings modern theories of cognition to bear on the intriguing characteristics of creative thought.

ISSUES OF THE EMPIRICAL DEBATE

Psychology, as an empirical science, continuously shifts in its discussion from the theoretical plane to the empirical one and vice versa. Theory needs to be supported by further empirical observations, and the empirical research is guided by the theoretical counterpoints. However, sometimes the counterpoints are more focused on the theoretical aspects, and sometimes they are more focused on the nature of the empirical methodologies and data.

As we mentioned at the beginning of this introduction, the authors of the three chapters present us with a robust debate on both the theoretical and the experimental planes. The differences on the empirical plane are relatively clear-cut, concrete, and quantifiable. It is true that a poor duck and a poor rabbit were the catalysts for the debate, but the theoretical implications of the debate are larger, raising many empirical issues, some of which we will review in this introductory chapter.

How We Look at a Figure

In the last section of their chapter, Brandimonte and Gerbino raise a delicate problem that emerges from the distinction between ordinary and pictorial vision. This distinction is roughly related to the distinction between different perceived objects—for example, between an object and a painting portraying it. Nevertheless, a better distinction interests the point of view of the spectator. In this respect pictorial vision can be identified with the "seeing as" experience, and there is pictorial vision any time the observer experiences the coexistence of a physical object and of a perceived object having a partially different meaning. This distinction is important because it extends the case of the vision of a painting to other possible cases. Further, it shows that the attitude during perception can change, consequently changing the perceptual experience. Following this argument we can explore whether the distinction between ordinary and pictorial vision is the only one possible or whether there are other distinct contrasts that are central to the debate. As we shall see, this point has important implications for the issues considered in this book.

If we return for a moment to the issue of subject strategy choice, let us consider a subject involved in an experiment on image reconstrual. Is the subject using pictorial vision? Probably not, because he or she knows that the figures, strictly speaking, are not pictures. However, we have doubts that ordinary vision is involved, and for many reasons. The stimulus is not an ordinary object, the context is unusual, and the instructions implicitly suggest that the subject is going to see something particular, which merits putting in some effort to please the experimenter. Also, it may offer the observer something surprising or unexpected.

When we look at the physical world, we usually know that we are looking at well-defined, unambiguous objects. In other words, we have two main certainties: (1) that there are no doubts about what we see, and (2) that what we see is only what we see and cannot be anything other than what we see. If we thought that we could be mistaken about what we see, it would significantly undermine our confidence when moving around in the world or attempting to interact with objects in the world. Nor should we think that the objects around us—the desk, the chair, the computer, etc.—are one thing, and are something else at the same time. It is common for experimental manipulations to throw doubt on many of these implicit assumptions about the constancy and predictability of our visual world. For this reason we would argue that there is a critical role for context, instructions, and metacognitive ideas developed by the subject about the nature of the experiment and of the psychological processes that might be implicated. These variables can affect the level of perceptual experience and/or the approach to the task and the use of cognitive strategies by the subject. Thus, we agree with Brandimonte and Gerbino that a distinction is necessary between different kinds of vision, but we suggest that the cases and kinds of vision may be multifarious. Further, we should like to argue for more informative descriptions of the procedures used in experimental research.

For example, experimental reports often include an account of the instructions given to the subject, but they do not describe how these instructions were expanded and clarified in response to requests from the experimental subjects. Rarely do researchers report subjects' descriptions of the strategies they adopted or what subjects believed was the aim of the experiment before, during, or after they had taken part (Della Sala, Logie, Marchetti, & Wynn, 1991; Logie, Della SalaLaiacona, Chalmers, & Wynn, in press). These factors appear particularly critical in the case of imagery experiments, which often involve some ambiguity (e.g. Yuille, 1983). For example, they offer the best explanation for the fact that, using the same procedure, Kerr's (1983) subjects were able to imagine concealed objects, whereas when using the same procedure the subjects in the Zimler and Keenan (1983) experiments could not.

These variables also can be critical during perceptual experience and could offer an explanation for divergent findings. For instance, Brandimonte and Gerbino's subjects, when required to perform simultaneous articulatory suppression, would receive the implicit message that the visual experience they are having is a little bit strange, bizarre, not ordinary. Subjects in a strict formal laboratory setting could think that they are involved in an engaging and difficult task, and so will be trying to see what they ordinarily do not see. Subjects more casually contacted could think that they must simply look at a picture and let the experimenter know what they remember as having been presented, perhaps by using whatever verbal label comes to mind. Therefore, these variables could have implications for the pattern of data obtained and for the conclusions reached about perception and memory.

Dan Reisberg's chapter offers some interesting reflections in this direction. In fact, he explicitly raises the possibility that the differences between his results and the results of other researchers could be explained in terms of the different experimental contexts used. In particular, his first experiments were carried out not in the traditional context of an experimental laboratory, but rather at coffee tables and in common rooms. The contrast between these two particular settings is reminiscent of the recent altercations between supporters of "laboratory-based research" and supporters of research based on "everyday life" (e.g., Banaji & Crowder, 1989; Conway, 1991, 1993; Crowder, 1993; Davies & Logie, 1993). In the present case, informal testing in the college setting represents one of the possible everyday life contexts; a more formal testing in a laboratory, along with the use of articulatory suppression (Brandimonte & Gerbino 1993), represents one of the possible laboratory settings.

In our view, here as in many other cases, the contrast between everyday and laboratory cognition does not capture the real essence of the problem. For example, the cognitive processing employed by Reisberg's subjects would be rather different from those of an artist examining the duck/rabbit picture, or a person asked to look at the picture in order to draw it, or a zoologist asked about its place in the taxonomy of fauna, and these differences would persist regardless of whether the tasks took place in a laboratory or in an everyday setting. We can argue that these different contexts and task demands should have some effect on perceptual processes and perceptual interpretation, but this raises the problem as to how exactly perceptual mechanisms might be involved and how they can be affected.

Mechanisms of Perceptual Interpretation

The chapters by Reisberg and by Brandimonte and Gerbino offer interesting suggestions as to the mechanisms underlying perceptual interpretation. They offer descriptions that can plausibly be used to understand not only how the percept is formed but also why in some cases the successive image can easily be reinterpreted, whereas in other cases reinterpretation is difficult and unlikely.

It is interesting to observe how the authors' main axioms are derived both from research on perception and from imagery research. For example, they examine critical perceptual mechanisms involved in parsing, centering, defining a reference frame, and focusing. Following a classic tradition in perception prevalent in Gestalt psychology (see Koffka, 1935), they start from anomalies and distortions in perception in order to glean information about perceptual functioning. It is interesting to observe that such a tradition characterized some well-known phenomena, which are relevant here, such as the perception of embedded figures (Gottschaldt, 1926; see Fig. 1.5a) and the possibility of reversing the interpretation of ambiguous figures either by changing the role of figure and ground (Kanizsa, 1980; Rubin, 1921; see Fig. 1.5c and 1.5d) or by attributing different roles to features of the perceptual pattern (Leeper, 1935; see Fig. 1.5b).

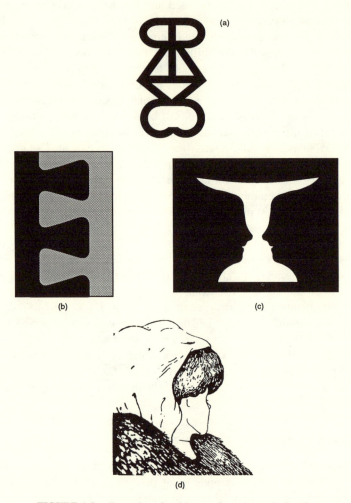

FIGURE 1.5.   Examples of ambiguous figure/ground stimuli.

The authors of the chapters review some major problems in this area and offer other examples. However, the reader will notice some differences in the perspective of the different chapters. For example, Gerbino's interest is focused on the stimulus properties that can induce different perceptual processes, whereas Reisberg is more focused on the nature of the underlying psychological processes.

Further, both chapters consider a major problem emergent from their data. If in memory there is more than what was interpreted, how is it possible that an image is simply the result of perceptual elaboration? Both Reisberg and Brandimonte try to solve the problem, but in different ways. Reisberg seems to suggest that the image is not the simple and direct by-product of perception, but is successively constructed from components. Memory should include visual information and, as a consequence of the perceptual interpretation, a series of "depictive priorities" prescribing the rules to be followed in generating the image. The main priority should be the representation "reference frame." Reisberg offers a nice example, which concerns the effects of rotating geographic maps of very well-known states or continents.

The rotated map of Africa or Texas is not easy to recognize. However, by simply rotating the map to its normal orientation we can immediately see what it represents. The same does not happen in imagery. People who have seen the rotated map and then imagine it continue to have difficulty in identifying the shape when they use imagery to rotate the shape to its correct position. Reisberg explains the phenomenon by suggesting that, in the perceptual condition, the rotation can induce a change in the reference frame thereby establishing the correct spatial coordinates for the figure. Conversely, this does not happen in imagery, where the original reference frame persists and the figure is interpreted as being a simple transformation of the unfamiliar shape that was presented. If we manipulate this variable in imagery, by inducing a change in the reference frame, then the correct interpretation becomes available.

This explanation still leaves several questions open. For example, the easy change of reference frame in perception that occurs in the case of the shape of Africa does not occur in all cases. If we rotate the figure of a vertical skyscraper by 90 degrees, thereby placing it horizontally, we do not change the reference frame and we still continue to see a skyscraper even if we had never seen a skyscraper in that orientation. In this case, our long-term knowledge, interacting with stimulus properties, results in a failure to change the reference frame. This simple example poses the question, also raised in the chapters of this book, on how much the stability of a reference frame is due to the nature of the cognitive and perceptual processes involved, and how much is due to the stimulus properties.

All three chapters seem to suggest that perception and imagery have different properties. However, the debate on this point is sometimes only implicit, and we cannot ascertain how variables like image size, resolution, density, detail, and vividness can be treated when exploring those differences and their implications. The authors seem to suggest that it may be an issue of capacity, and that a mental image is subject to strict capacity limitations, but they do not develop this point. However, they mention the related fact that the density of the representation may be low in imagery and, in particular, some parts of the image may have a better resolution than other parts. For example, if the ambiguous figure is interpreted like a duck, parts corresponding to the duck's face and eyes will enjoy better resolution than will other parts.

Geir Kaufmann develops a somewhat similar idea by distinguishing between an initial primary content and an alternative content of the image. The primary content is determined by the original intention (related to the interpretation). However, thanks to the perceptual content (evidently stored somewhere in memory) dormant potential interpretations co-exist, which were not included in the original intention and which can be discovered by inspecting the perceptual content. In this respect, Kaufmann comes close to Brandimonte's interpretation, with the difference that Kaufmann assumes that this perceptual content is not easily memorised, but it can be stored and maintained only by subjects with high visual ability. In conclusion, we can find three guiding ideas shared, but differently considered, by the authors of the three chapters: (1) The percept and especially the image are tied to the reference frame, (2) visual memory holds more than is included in the conscious image, and (3) the reference frame determines the selection of information included in the conscious image. These three ideas can explain why we often are not able to reinterpret an image, but they can also explain why sometimes the reinterpretation is possible. In fact, the reference frame construct can help us understand the cases in which imagery is able to discover new things on the basis of the suggestion that in those cases the reference frame has not to be changed.

For example, both Finke and Slayton (1988) and Anderson and Helstrup (1993) have found that we can construct an image by rotating the letter "D" by 90 degrees and locating it under the letter "J." If the reader tries to do the same there should not be any particular difficulty in concluding that the resulting image resembles a two-dimensional umbrella. Reisberg suggests that this discovery is easy because the reference frame is not changed. Is this explanation entirely convincing? This case seems in many respects different from other cases. For example, here no piece of visual information is lost because the visual stimuli were very simple and very well known, offering the possibility of regenerating them from long-term memory. Further, in this case a different reinterpretation problem seems involved requiring a shift between different semantic domains, rather than within the same domain. Probably the reference frame construct requires some integration with other psychological constructs.

The Role of Individual Differences

One of the main arguments used by Kaufmann both in his chapter and in his previous research with Tore Helstrup concerns the role of individual differences. In his view, the reinterpretation is made possible by high-ability subjects maintaining apparently irrelevant details of the figure that later become crucial for its reinterpretation.

Is this ability related to the capacity of a short-term visual memory store? If we look at the overall pattern of data described in the three chapters the answer seems to be no. In fact, nearly all subjects seem able to retrieve the necessary visual information when they are put in the appropriate conditions, either with adequate cues or with the possibility of drawing what they remember. Conversely, Kaufmann seems to refer to a particular ability only a few good visualizers should have, making it possible for them to reinterpret the image, even in the absence of any help. This particular ability seems to apply to the imagery operations rather than the raw visual information stored in memory. This point is not explicitly developed by Kaufmann but is implicit in the way he and Helstrup have operationally defined visual ability. In fact, they did not look for subjects expected to have good visual memory, but for subjects who often relied on imagery—that is, people who were "pronounced visualisers, and employed visualisation regularly in their work."

When attempting to explore the issue of individual differences, it is important to define the variable and the operations used for measuring it. The variable chosen by Kaufmann seems plausible because it assumes that differences can be found in the way imagery is used. Obviously he is not suggesting that subjects can be divided into those who use visualization and those who do not. All subjects use imagery when they try to perform the task. The problem is to see how expert they are at using imagery when carrying out a series of operations. Kaufmann only mentions the issue of image resolution, but following the same line it should be possible to examine other imagery operations as well. This happens in part in some more widely used or standardized tests of imagery that are used for examining individual differences, and these can be supplemented with more intuitive approaches, like that voiced by Kaufmann.

Thus, there are a range of individual differences that we can consider, such as visual memory capacity, image resolution, ability to carry out different operations on the image, etc. We also have different ways of measuring those abilities, like considering life choices and habits (Kaufmann & Helstrup, 1993), subjective experiences (Marks, 1973), or performance in mental imagery tests (Dean & Morris, 1991). There is evidence (Marschark & Cornoldi, 1990) that different imagery tests measure different aspects of ability. Scores on different tests do not always correlate highly, and are differentially predictive of different aspects of cognitive performance (Dean & Morris, 1991). Unfortunately, the psychological literature does not appear particularly interested in this issue. This is rather surprising if we think that it has a strict connection with the issue of discovery and creative abilities, which are based on individual differences, and with the study of people with particular talents. Therefore, Kaufmann offered a very interesting contribution when he tried to develop this issue, but his data are suggestive rather than conclusive, for they are derived from only a few cases and their generality to other forms of imaginal operation has yet to be tested. Nevertheless, these data can be contrasted with Reisberg's observations, which seem to suggest that individual differences are not influential in his case. Reisberg observes that even those of his subjects who had good visual ability were unable to reinterpret the image.

The Role of Articulatory Suppression

In psychology there are some experimental procedures and techniques that, although apparently very specific and of low relevance, have acquired great relevance and have been widely used because they offer tractable approaches to major issues. One such technique is articulatory suppression, which is intended to block articulation by asking people to articulate an irrelevant word or word sequence. Most readers who are familiar with recent cognitive research will have encountered experimental work that has employed articulatory suppression. In fact, the technique does not abolish articulation, but rather asks subjects to articulate in such a systematic way that no other information can be articulated. The technique has been especially used within the working memory literature in order to find specific effects related to the role of articulation in maintaining information in the phonological-articulatory component of working memory. Strictly speaking, suppression is thought to affect the articulatory and phonological properties of the stimulus rather than its deeper semantic properties. However, this point remains open because short-term verbal memory performance also appears to be affected by the semantic properties of the information it is required to retain (Hulme, Maughan, & Brown, 1991; Wetherick, 1975, 1976).

The recent use of articulatory suppression by Brandimonte and other researchers, (e.g., Brandimonte, Hitch, & Bishop, 1992) seems to attribute a more general function to the technique. In fact, it seems to suggest that the technique does not simply interrupt the stimulus verbalization and vocalization, but a wider range of nonvisual processes that could be carried out on the stimulus. In this way articulatory suppression should allow the representation of the stimulus to preserve its visual properties more faithfully, and to have the paradoxical effect that a disturbing activity enhances rather than impairs visual memory of a figure. This effect is so counterintuitive that it could raise doubts if we did not have such a convincing and extensive evidence as that reviewed by Brandimonte in her chapter.

Some insight into this issue may come from a close examination of the assumption underlying much of this research, namely that all subjects attempt to perform a given task in the same way given the same experimental conditions. As we have hinted, subjects may choose their strategy according to their interpretation of the task demands, and as such they may base their response on a visual image or they may choose to rely on conceptual knowledge. Thus, the effect of articulatory suppression may not be to prevent complete access to a verbal label and to conceptual knowledge, but to discourage use of that knowledge for this task. Thus, with a requirement to repeat an irrelevant word, a sufficient number of subjects in a given experiment may choose to adopt a strategy based on visual information, resulting in an overall increase in the number of reversals reported from the subject group as a whole. In the working-memory literature, evidence shows that different subjects adopt different strategies, and some subjects change strategies from one occasion to another. Moreover, their reported strategies are good predictors of the appearance or otherwise of phenomena such as the phonological similarity effect or the word-length effect in immediate serial recall (Della Sala et al., 1991; Logie et al., submitted). However, whether this fully accounts for the contrast between the sets of experimental results reported by Reisberg and by Brandimonte awaits further exploration.

In their chapters, Reisberg and Brandimonte do develop detailed and apparently contrasting analyses. Brandimonte's explanation of the effect makes things less counterintuitive, suggesting that articulatory suppression really reduces processing by eliminating extra verbal coding. This verbal coding may be an embellishment that could be useful in other circumstances, but in this particular case can overshadow specific visual features that are pivotal for image reconstrual. In other words, subjects who have used language do not remember less; rather, they remember too much and use the confounding verbal label as a critical focus for the image.

On the other hand, Reisberg seems to suggest that figure memorization includes both visual sensory information and rules for its organization. Among these organizational rules the reference frame is the most critical. Articulatory suppression would affect the organization rules, which should become weaker and less effective (there is passing reference to a similar explanation in the other chapters). This hypothesis seems to suggest that two distinct forms of representation are generated initially, and for reasons yet to be clarified, the perceptually based organizational rules are the most sensitive to an interfering event. Further, if this weakening is simply due to a general disturbance of elaboration, language should not be critical and other interfering events should have similar effects.

The chapter by Brandimonte offers detailed tentative explanations for the effects of verbal overshadowing and also extends its effects to a large range of cognitive situations. In fact, results by Brandimonte, Schooler, and others seem to suggest that overt verbalization can damage performance in many other cases. If this line of research is developed, as is promised, we can expect to find many other similar cases showing that language is a very risky tool for cognition, trying to make things clear and simple by shedding apparently excess baggage, when in fact the baggage being lost comprises information that is critical for task performance. This should give considerable food for thought to people who adopt a Vygotskian line and are wholly convinced that thinking and language are two critical synergic variables in cognition!

The Analogy Between Visual Imagery and Auditory Imagery

Auditory imagery represents a very strange case within the debate concerning the relationship between imagery and language. There is a sense in which it could be viewed as being at least partially based on language, and therefore reliant in part on the language system. On the other hand, it is an imaginal process that is similar to visual imagery in that it is derived in a large part from sensory input and should legitimately be considered as a component of the imagery system. Given its empirical and theoretical interest, it is surprising to find how auditory imagery has until recently generated little more than a marginal interest. A turning point is this trend was marked by a book on auditory imagery edited by Dan Reisberg (1992), and he himself has made a substantial contribution to the field (see, e.g., Reisberg, 1991; Reisberg, Smith, Baxter, & Sonenshine, 1989), developing and promoting an interesting line of research. Given his expertise, it was natural to expect that he should try to use it to examine the issues raised in this volume. His underlying assumption seems to be that visual and auditory imagery may function in a similar fashion, but that they involve separate systems and do not necessarily share the same cognitive mechanisms. Reisberg extends his argument that images cannot be reinterpreted by applying the same constraint to auditory images. To this end he presents some attractive evidence showing that auditory perceptual reversals occur only when the auditory stimulus is present or when it can be subvocalized, and they tend not to occur when the task is based on an auditory image of the stimulus. For example, when the word "life" is continuously repeated, subjects often report hearing the word "fly" instead, a reversal that relies on resegmenting the speech stream. Reisberg argues that this resegmentation requires some form of stimulus support and cannot be accomplished solely using the auditory image, which represents an unambiguous segmentation of the auditory input.

By subvocalizing the word the subject can reconsider its representation, presumably change its reference frame and reinterpret it. This effect is similar to the effect found when the subjects can draw the visual pattern and reinterpret it. Therefore, the data suggest a strong analogy between the visual image and the auditory image. The assumption of such an analogy is interesting both on empirical and on theoretical grounds. From an empirical point of view it can suggest fruitful lines of research extending the generality of the effects. From a theoretical point of view it raises the problem of why and how these analogies exist. It also raises a word of caution, in that while an exploration of the analogies between visual and auditory imagery may prove fruitful, we should be careful not to fall into the trap of concentrating on the similarities while missing the important differences, a criticism we have already voiced about the focus on analogies between visual perception and visual imagery.

One way of tackling this is to explore which characteristics of an imagery system might be emergent properties of any representational system that gleans information from sensory input and from prior experience. This can then be set in the context of the material and medium comprising the matter and function of cognitive systems that specifically support visual or auditory imagery.

For example, within a working-memory model, is the phonological-articulatory slave system involved in maintaining and processing auditory images? If yes, this should suggest that the systems for auditory and for visual images can function similarly, but are nevertheless distinct and separate. It is well known that a main assumption of the working-memory model (Baddeley, 1986) is the complete independence of the slave systems. Data along the same lines come from some imagery research. For example, Segal and Fusella (1970) found specific and completely separate effects of auditory imagery and of visual imagery, even when the auditory imagery involved natural sounds rather than speech. These data argued for a strict modality-specific approach to imagery (see Paivio, 1971).

A strict modality-specific approach can encounter difficulties. For instance, within the working-memory model, the phonological-articulatory system seems interested only in speech. Only unattended speech seems to disturb the phonological store. Where is the place for auditory, not speech-based, images? Can this view be included in a strict modality-specific approach? Some of these issues have been addressed in a paper by Baddeley and Logie (1992), who explored the possibility that the phonological storage component of working memory could be the seat of auditory imagery. Unattended speech may disrupt the contents of the phonological store because the subject's task is to retain a verbal sequence. In that paper, Baddeley and Logie presented some preliminary evidence that unattended nonspeech sounds may interfere with retention of nonspeech auditory images. Thus, either there are separate systems for auditory imagery and for phonological storage, or the same system can be used for storing both kinds of material. If the material from the unattended sensory input is acoustically distinct (e.g., music or environmental sounds) from the material in the store (e.g., words) then interference is minimal. However, when the store is retaining material that is acoustically similar to the unattended sounds, then interference is observed. This suggests, of course, that the filter for speech is based on the acoustic properties of the material and not its semantic content, a view that is entirely consistent with the operation of the phonological-articulatory system.

This still leaves the problem, well rehearsed in this volume, that images do not include only specific sensory information, but also their interpretation. The phonological-articulatory system as conceived does not truck well with semantics, although recent developments mentioned above have demonstrated how retention of verbal strings can be affected by their semantic as well as their phonological and articulatory properties (Hulme et al., 1991; Wetherick, 1975, 1976). These data provide hints that mental representations may incorporate information from more than one component of working memory to include, for example, the central executive as well as the phonological-articulatory system. But these are only hints, and the role of working memory in auditory imagery offers considerable scope for development.

As we can see, the consideration of auditory imagery can offer important phenomena and can raise relevant and intriguing questions. Therefore, the inclusion by Reisberg in his chapter of a section on auditory imagery offers a rare and important occasion to think about it.

Some Suggestions for the Reader

The new series "Counterpoints," which has given birth to the present volume, has the purpose of emphasizing different perspectives within contemporary psychology and of developing interaction and debate among them. The problems related to the nature of mental representation and of its relationship with perception have been presented in a fashion that is intended to invoke the spirit of "Counterpoints," not only because of their importance for theory, but also because of the strength of feeling frequently expressed by the supporters of different perspectives.

In this book, we have a case where different perspectives are related to different research traditions. Hence, the interest of the chapters stems not only from differences in the analysis and interpretation of individual discussion points, but also from diversities in background, terminology, approach, and focus. This variety can create some difficulty for people who seek homogeneity, but if we pander to that view we promote a psychology of subcommunities able only to develop a dialogue within the subcommunity, to read the papers produced within a group, and to preserve a narrow theoretical and empirical focus. If we think of psychology as a science, the debate must be spread across different countries and subcommunities, but at the same time it must be set in a coherent framework that has at least a common scientific vocabulary along with explicit acknowledgment of various underlying assumptions. Finally, we have tried in this opening chapter to make some of the various assumptions explicit, together with highlighting the issues considered and sometimes partially embedded in the three chapters that follow. In so doing, we hope to have set the scene, stimulated interest, and fostered a broader style of debate by orchestrating this diversity in a single volume.

REFERENCES

Anderson, J. R. (1978). Arguments concerning representations for mental imagery. *Psychological Review, 85,* 249–277.

Anderson, R., & Helstrup, T. (1993). Visual discovery in mind and on paper. *Memory & Cognition, 21,* 283–293.

Arnheim, R. (1969). *Visual thinking.* Berkeley-Los Angeles: University of California Press.

Augustine (1844/1866). *De vera religione.* In J. P. Migne (Ed.), *Patrologiae cursus completus.* Wien: Wiener Akademie.

Baddeley, A. (1986). *Working memory.* Oxford: Clarendon Press.

Baddeley, A. D., & Lewis, V. J. (1981). Inner active processes in reading: The inner voice, the inner ear and the inner eye. In A. M. Lesgold & C. A. Perfetti (Eds.), *Interactive processes in reading* (pp. 107–129). Hillsdale NJ: Erlbaum.

Baddeley, A. D., & Logie, R. H. (1992). Auditory imagery and working memory. In D. Reisberg (Ed.), *Auditory imagery* (pp. 179–197). Hillsdale, NJ: Erlbaum.

Banaji, H. R., & Crowder, R. G. (1989). The bankruptcy of everyday memory. *American Psychologist, 44,* 1185–1193.

Brandimonte, M. A., & Gerbino, W. (1993). Mental image reversal and verbal recoding: When ducks become rabbits. *Memory & Cognition, 21,* 23–33.

Brandimonte, M. A., Hitch, G. J., & Bishop, D.V.M. (1992). Verbal recoding of visual stimuli impairs mental image transformation. *Memory & Cognition, 20,* 449–455.

Carmichael, L., Hogan, H. P., & Walter, A. A. (1932). An experimental study of the effect of language on the reproduction of visually perceived forms. *Journal of Experimental Psychology, 15,* 73–86.

Chambers, D., & Reisberg, D. (1985). Can mental images be ambiguous? *Journal of Experimental Psychology: Human Perception and Performance, 3,* 317–328.

Clarke, E., & Dewhurst, K. (1972). *An illustrated history of brain function.* Oxford: Sanford.

Conway, M. (1991). In defense of everyday memory. *American Psychologist, 46,* 19–26.

Conway, M. (1993). Method and meaning in memory research. In G. M. Davies & R. H. Logie (Eds.), *Memory in Everyday Life* (pp. 499–524). Amsterdam: Elsevier.

Crowder, R. G. (1993). Faith and skepticism in memory research. In G. M. Davies & R. H. Logie (Eds.), *Memory in everyday life* (pp. 525–531). Amsterdam: Elsevier.

Davies, G. M., & Logie, R. H. (Eds.)(1993). *Memory in everyday life.* Amsterdam: Elsevier.

Dean, G., & Morris, P. E. (1991). Imagery and spatial ability: When introspective reports predict performance. In R. H. Logie & M. Denis (Eds.), *Mental images in human cognition* (pp. 331–347). Amsterdam: Elsevier.

Della Sala, S., Logie, R. H., Marchetti, C., & Wynn, V. (1991). Case studies in working memory: A case for single cases? *Cortex 27,* 169–191.

Denis, M. (1990). Imagery and thinking. In C. Cornoldi & M. McDaniel (Eds.), *Imagery and cognition* (pp. 103–131). New York: Springer.

Finke, R., & Slayton, K. (1988). Explorations of creative visual synthesis in mental imagery. *Memory & Cognition, 16,* 252–257.

Giusberti, F., Cornoldi, C., De Beni, R., & Massironi, M. (1992). Difference in vividness ratings of perceived and imagined patterns. *British Journal of Psychology, 83,* 533–547.

Gottschaldt, K. (1926). Uber den Einfluss der Erfahrung auf die Wahrnehmung von Figuren. *Psychologische Forschung, 8,* 261–317.

Hinton, G. (1979). Some demonstrations of the effects of structural descriptions in mental imagery. *Cognitive Science, 3,* 231–250.

Hulme, C., Maughan, S., & Brown, G.D.A. (1991). Memory for familiar and unfamiliar words: Evidence for a long-term memory contribution to short-term memory span. *Journal of Memory and Language, 30,* 685–701.

Intons-Peterson, M. J., & McDaniel, M. A. (1990). Symmetries and asymmetries between imagery and perception. In C. Cornoldi & M. McDaniel (Eds.), *Imagery and cognition* (pp. 47–76). New York: Springer.

Intons-Peterson, M. J., & Roskos-Ewoldsen, B. B. (1989). Sensory-perceptual qualities of images. *Journal of Experimental Psychology: Learning, Memory and Cognition, 15,* 188–199.

Kanizsa, G. (1980). *Grammatica del vedere.* Bologna: Il Mulino.

Kaufmann, G., & Helstrup, T. (1993). Mental imagery: Fixed or multiple meanings? In B. Roskos-Ewoldsen, M. J. Intons-Peterson, & R. E. Anderson (Eds.), *Imagery, discovery and creativity: A cognitive approach,* Amsterdam: Elsevier.

Kerr, N. H. (1983). The role of vision in visual imagery experiments: Evidence from the congenitally blind. *Journal of Experimental Psychology: General, 112,* 265–277.

Koffka, K. (1935). *Principles of gestalt psychology.* New York: Harcourt-Brace.

Kosslyn, S. M. (1980). *Image and mind.* Cambridge, MA: Harvard University Press.

Leeper, R. W. (1935). A study of neglected portion in the field of learning: The development of sensory organization. *Journal of Genetic Psychology, 46,* 41–75.

Logie, R. H. (1995). *Visuo-spatial working memory.* Hove/UK: Erlbaum Associates.

Logie, R. H., Della Sala, S., Laiacona, M., Chalmers, P., & Wynn, V. (in press). *Group aggregates and individual reliability: The case of verbal short-term memory. Memory and Cognition.*

Marks, D. (1973). Visual imagery differences in the recall of pictures. *British Journal of Psychology, 64,* 17–24.

Marschark, M., & Cornoldi, C. (1990). Imagery and verbal memory. In C. Cornoldi & M. McDaniel (Eds.), *Imagery and Cognition* (pp. 133–182). New York: Springer.

Mecacci, L. (1993, September). *The classical heritage.* Paper presented at the workshop "Memory and Mental Representations," Rome, Italy.

Neisser, U. (1967). *Cognitive psychology.* Englewood Cliffs, NJ: Prentice-Hall.

Paivio, A. (1971). *Imagery and verbal processes.* New York: Holt, Rinehart & Winston.

Paivio, A. (1986). *Mental representations: A dual coding approach.* Oxford: Oxford University Press.

Piaget, J., & Inhelder, B. (1966). *L'image mentale chez l'enfant.* Paris: Presses Universitaires de France.

Prentice, W.C.H. (1954). Visual recognition of verbally labeled figures. *American Journal of Psychology, 67,* 315–320.

Reed, S. K. (1974). Structural descriptions and the limitations of visual images. *Memory & Cognition, 2,* 329–336.

Reisberg, D. (1991). Auditory imagery. In R. H. Logie & M. Denis (Eds.), *Mental images in human cognition.* Amsterdam: Elsevier Science Publishers.

Reisberg, D. (Ed.). (1992). *Auditory imagery.* Hillsdale, NJ: Erlbaum.

Reisberg, D., & Logie, R. (1993). The in's and out's of working memory: Escaping the boundaries on imagery function. In B. Roskos-Ewoldsen, M. Intons-Peterson, & R. Anderson (Eds.), *Imagery, creativity and discovery: A cognitive approach.* Amsterdam: Elsevier.

Reisberg, D., Smith, J. D., Baxter, D. A., & Sonenshine, M. (1989). "Enacted" auditory images are ambiguous; "Pure" auditory images are not. *Quarterly Journal of Experimental Psychology, 41A,* 619–641.

Richardson, J., & Zucco, G. (1989). Cognition and olfaction: A review. *Psychological Bulletin, 94,* 352–360.

Roskos-Ewoldsen, B., Intons-Peterson, M., & Anderson, R. (1993). *Imagery, creativity and discovery: A cognitive approach.* Amsterdam: Elsevier.

Rubin, E. (1921). *Visuell wahrgenommene Figuren.* Copenhagen: Gyldendal.

Segal, S. J., & Fusella, V. (1970). Influence of imaged pictures and sounds on detection of visual and auditory signals. *Journal of Experimental Psychology, 83,* 458–464.

Shorter, J. M. (1952). Imagination. *Mind, 61,* 527–542.

Treisman, A., & Souther, J. (1985). Search asymmetry: A diagnostic for preattentive processing of separable features. *Journal of Experimental Psychology: General, 114,* 285–310.

Wetherick, N. E. (1975). The role of semantic information in short-term memory. *Journal of Verbal Learning and Verbal Behavior, 14,* 471–480.

Wetherick, N. E. (1976). Semantic information in short-term memory: Effects of presenting recall instructions after the list. *Bulletin of the Psychonomic Society, 8,* 79–81.

Wolff, C. (1732). *Psychologia empirica.* Frankfurt-Leipzig.

Yuille, J. C. (1983). The crisis in theories of mental imagery. In J. C. Yuille (Ed.), *Imagery, memory, and cognition. Essays in honour of Alan Paivio,* (pp. 263–284). Hillsdale, NJ: Erlbaum.

Zimler, J., & Keenan, J. M. (1983). Imagery in the congenitally blind: How visual are visual images? *Journal of Experimental Psychology: Learning, Memory and Cognition, 9,* 269–282.

CHAPTER 2

When Imagery Fails: Effects of Verbal Recoding on Accessibility of Visual Memories

Maria A. Brandimonte and Walter Gerbino

In the last two decades, the relationship between imagery and memory has varied from being an essential element of imagery theories to being incidental and of little importance. Much of the research and theory developed in the 1970s viewed imagery as a mediator of memory performance. Such research has usually focused on the usefulness of imagery as a mnemonic technique (Bower, 1972; Paivio, 1971, 1975) and on the effects of imagery quality (e.g., vividness) on memory performance (Marks, 1972).

Theoretical and empirical developments in imagery research came from the work of Kosslyn (1980). Kosslyn provided answers to fundamental questions concerning the nature of visual images and the structure of the imagery representation system. Yet the relationship between imagery and memory is not crucial to the early formulation of his theory (Kosslyn, 1980, p. 479; but see Kosslyn, Flynn, Amsterdam, & Wang, 1989).

A different approach emphasizes the role of the format of memory representation in influencing imagery performance, the main focus being on how people's ability to manipulate and transform their images is affected by the nature of the memory code used at the time of learning. Following this approach, for the past five years we have been engaged in the study of the role of the visual and verbal components of working memory in affecting long-term memory (LTM) and therefore performance in visual imagery tasks (Brandimonte & Gerbino, 1993; Brandimonte, Hitch, & Bishop, 1992a, 1992b).

In this chapter, various lines of evidence are examined to try to shed light on the relationship between memory codes and visual image processing. In particular, we shall discuss some implications of the verbal recoding hypothesis. According to this hypothesis, when learning visual material, people tend spontaneously to recode it into a verbal form. Under particular conditions, verbal processing of visual stimuli turns out to be beneficial (see, e.g., Paivio & Csapo, 1973). However, when the task requires visual analysis, verbal processing of visual stimuli may impair subsequent visual image processing.

We also address the more basic question of the "accessibility" of visual memories. The accessibility question runs parallel to the question of verbal overshadowing. The term "verbal overshadowing" has been recently used by Schooler and Engstler-Schooler (1990) to describe a kind of LTM recoding interference that does not eradicate the original visual memories, but makes them temporarily inaccessible. As studied by Schooler and Engstler-Schooler (1990), the verbal overshadowing effect refers to LTM tasks in which overt verbalization subsequent to encoding interferes with the recollection of the original visual memories. More recently, we have shown that verbal overshadowing can also occur as a consequence of covert verbal recoding of the visual input at the time of learning (Brandimonte & Gerbino, 1993), i.e., while information is undergoing transfer from short-term memory (STM) to LTM. Most important for the accessibility question, it has been shown that, once it has occurred, verbal overshadowing may be removed so as to allow access to the original visual memories. This effect, termed "release from verbal overshadowing," demonstrates that visual information which has undergone verbal recoding at the time of input is simply "inaccessible," not definitively "lost" (Brandimonte, Schooler, & Gabbino, 1995b).

We believe that there are some fascinating puzzles connected with verbal recoding of visual stimuli and that a deeper analysis of the mechanisms of the interaction between visual and verbal forms of encoding both in LTM and in STM would increase our understanding of the imagery process.

The present chapter will address the following questions: (1) interaction between visual and verbal codes; (2) the role of working memory in visual imagery; (3) the relationship between verbal recoding and verbal overshadowing; (4) availability versus accessibility of visual information; (5) figures' ambiguity, memory codes, and the reinterpretability of mental images; and (6) the relationship among images, pictures, and verbal processes.

VISUAL AND VERBAL CODES: FACILITATION OR INTERFERENCE?

Perhaps the most useful theoretical distinction in the field of memory has been the distinction proposed by Paivio (1971) between two modes of representation, or coding systems: nonverbal and verbal. Given its explanatory value, Paivio's dual-coding theory has remained substantially unchanged up to the present time (Paivio, 1975, 1986, 1991).

The theory assumes that cognitive behavior is mediated by two independent but interconnected systems, which are specialized for encoding, organizing, storing, transforming, and retrieving information. The verbal system is regarded as a more abstract, logical mode of representation, while the imagery system is assumed to be a more concrete, analogical mode. The most important assumptions of the theory concern the independence and interconnectedness of the two systems. "Independence" means that either system may work or be influenced in isolation of the other; "interconnectedness" means that information can be transferred from one system to the other. An important corollary of the independence assumption is that the two codes may be additive in their effects (Paivio, 1975, 1986, 1991). The prediction that dual coding facilitates performance applies, for instance, to the effect of recoding versus repetition in learning pictures and words. Imaginal coding of words and verbal coding of pictures should have an additive effect on subsequent recall, whereas repeated presentations of a stimulus in the same modality (picture-picture, word-word) should not. Evidence for such effects emerged in the context of recall of pictures and words (Paivio & Csapo, 1973). Results supported the additivity hypothesis: Stochastic independence was observed, and subjects recalled twice as much when they imaged printed words than when they just pronounced the words.

Stated in its simplest form, the additivity hypothesis means that two codes are better than one (Paivio, 1991). That is, when both codes (visual and verbal) are readily available, one should expect facilitation rather than interference. Indeed, the concept of interference has typically been defined in terms of disruption of the memory trace by other traces, with the degree of interference depending on the *similarity* of the two mentally interfering memory traces (Baddeley, 1990). The classical studies by Brooks (1967, 1968) and by Segal and Fusella (1970) clearly demonstrated that use of imagery in a given modality affects performance in a perceptual task involving the same sensory modality. For instance, if subjects are requested to form and hold visual images while detecting visual signals, their sensitivity to the signal drops dramatically. On the other hand, the detection of the visual signal is much less affected when the concurrent imaginal activity is in the auditory modality (Segal & Fusella, 1970). This kind of effect, which has been termed "modality-specific interference" (see also Murray & Newman, 1973), seems to suggest that interference mainly occurs for tasks involving the same system. In the same vein, results on the positive effect of verbal rehearsal (see, e.g., Bartlett, Till, & Levy, 1980; Darley & Glass, 1975; Rundus, 1971) and verbal elaboration of visual stimuli (Craik & Tulving, 1975; Daniel & Ellis, 1972; Kerr & Winograd, 1982; Klatzky, Martin, & Kane, 1982; Rafnel & Klatzky, 1978; Wiseman, MacLeod, & Lootsteen, 1985) support the view that information from multiple sources independently and additively favors memory.

In the field of memory for complex visual material, a substantial body of literature emphasizes the beneficial consequences of verbal processing of visual stimuli. For example, Wiseman et al. (1985) had subjects study photographs presented alone or followed by a descriptive sentence. Subsequent yes-no recognition tests for the pictures demonstrated better memory for those pictures that had been followed by descriptive sentences.

A number of studies in the domain of memory for faces showed improved face recognition when additional verbal information is provided. Klatzky et al. (1982) presented subjects with pictures of faces coupled with information concerning the occupation of the people depicted in the pictures. Kerr and Winograd (1982) showed subjects pictures of faces with or without simultaneous verbal information. Results from both studies showed clear improvement in face recognition.

However, a more detailed analysis of these studies reveals that the facilitation due to verbal processing of visual stimuli is restricted to situations in which the verbal information is of some value because it simplifies or integrates visual information. For instance, Klatzky et al. (1982) observed that verbal information improved recognition only when the target and the distractor resembled different occupational types. Similarly, in the study by Bartlett et al. (1980) visual recognition of pictures was facilitated only when the verbal description allowed subjects to better discriminate between the target and the distractors, whereas in the experiments reported by Wiseman et al. (1985) the descriptive sentences following the photographs provided additional information not available in the original pictures. A straightforward conclusion from these studies is that verbal processing of pictorial information has a beneficial effect only when it provides more data or makes existing data more salient or distinctive. To the contrary, we will argue that when the task depends on modality-specific analysis of visual stimuli, and verbal processing is a "translation" of selected aspects of sensory information rather than an "addition" to it, verbal processing of visual stimuli may disrupt rather than facilitate performance.

Intermodal Interference

One of the earliest and most famous demonstrations that verbal processing may interact with visual memory comes from the well-known study by Carmichael, Hogan, and Walter (1932), who demonstrated that labeling ambiguous patterns at the time of input influenced the manner in which subjects later drew the shapes. Subjects tended to distort their drawings in the direction of the appropriate label (but see Kurtz & Hovland, 1953; Prentice, 1954). Similar distortions due to verbalization were discussed by Koffka (1935, p. 501), who analyzed such memory effects as "pointing" (the exaggeration of peculiarities in the reproduction of visual material), which are typically accompanied by spontaneous verbal recoding.

More recently, a few studies have shown that concurrent verbal processing can interfere with subjects' ability to distinguish a target from verbally similar distractors (Bahrick & Boucher, 1968; Nelson & Brooks, 1973; Nelson, Brooks, & Borden, 1973; Pezdek, Maki, Valencia-Laver, Whetstone, Stoeckert, & Dougherty, 1988). For instance, in the study by Bahrick and Boucher (1968) subjects were shown drawings of common objects (e.g., a coffee cup) and later given verbal recall tests for the objects' names, followed by visual recognition tests. In the recognition test, each object had to be selected from an array of objects (e.g., eight cups) all bearing the same name but differing in subtle visual ways. Verbal recall and shape recognition were uncorrelated, suggesting that they are based on two independent types of information. In addition, verbalization during training impaired subjects' ability to distinguish between different objects with the same name.

In a pair-associate learning task, Nelson and Brooks (1973) observed that phonological similarity among pairs impaired performance not only when the stimuli were words but also when they were pictures that had to be overtly named. No interference was found when the stimuli were pictures that did not have to be articulated. However, it should be noticed that in a subsequent study, Nelson, Brooks, and Borden (1973) reported that when sequential memory for pictures is required, visual stimuli are implicitly labeled even though subjects are not requested to name the pictures overtly (see also Brandimonte et al., 1992a, 1992b).

The above review suggests that verbally recoding pictorial stimuli is detrimental when the task requires the maintenance of "literal" visual information. Words are often not sufficient for characterizing visual memories. In all these cases, concurrent verbal processing may interfere with the utilization of nonverbal memories.

Compelling evidence that verbalizing under conditions when verbal codes are difficult to generate can result in interference comes from recent research by Schooler and his associates. For example, Schooler and Engstler-Schooler (1990) explored the effect of verbalization on face recognition. Memory for a face is a type of visual memory that is particularly difficult to put into words. Schooler and Engstler-Schooler (1990) observed that when subjects were requested to describe a previously seen face, their ability to recognize the face was significantly reduced compared to control subjects who did not describe the face. This pattern of results extended to other nonverbalizable stimuli (color), but not to spoken statements. In another study, Wilson and Schooler (1991) examined the effect of verbalization in the domain of affective judgments. Subjects were asked to evaluate different brands of strawberry jams. Subjects in the verbalization group were asked to analyze the reasons why they felt as they did, while the control subjects tasted the jams and then rated them. Subjects' preferences were then compared with experts' ratings of the jams. Control subjects agreed well with experts, whereas verbalization subjects' choices corresponded less to experts' judgments.

Most recently, the verbalization effect was examined in the domain of reasoning and problem solving (Schooler, Ohlsson, & Brooks, in press). The suggestion that verbalization can disrupt nonverbal processes led these authors to the hypothesis that verbalization may interfere with insight. Indeed, insight problem solving was thought of as being susceptible to verbal processing as it clearly involves nonreportable information-processing components such as perception and spreading activation (Schooler et al., 1993). Results from four experiments confirmed this hypothesis and generalized the view that verbalization can result in the neglect of nonreportable processes that are critical to a number of cognitive tasks.

This being said, let us return to the specific interaction between visual and verbal codes. The interfering effect of verbal processes on visual memories has been indirectly demonstrated in recent research by Brandimonte et al. (1992a,

1992b), who found that the ability to manipulate visual mental images generated from LTM is markedly affected by the kind of STM code used at the time of input. When viewing novel visual stimuli, subjects have a strong tendency toward verbal recoding; this influences encoding in LTM in such a way as to impair mental image operations.

At least two important general questions arise from the bulk of results discussed in this section. First, how can one reconcile the observation of intermodal (visual/verbal) interference with the additivity assumption of the dual-coding theory? Interference clearly implies nonadditivity. In contrast to the dual-coding theory, the use of both codes does not lead to better performance than the use of either type of code alone. Rather, in particular situations, dual coding turns out to be detrimental. Two explanations (not necessarily mutually exclusive, as we shall discuss later) have been proposed to accommodate the negative effects of verbal processing on memory performance. On the one hand, it has been suggested that verbal processing dramatically reduces visual encoding (Bahrick & Boucher, 1968). Verbal encoding would occur at expense of visual learning, possibly because the involvement of the verbal system has reduced the time and cognitive resources available for coding pictorial information (Nelson & Brooks, 1973). An alternative explanation has been proposed by Schooler and Engstler-Schooler (1990). According to this hypothesis, verbal processing of visual stimuli does not reduce the time and the amount of encoded visual information. Rather, it overshadows visual memories, thereby disrupting performance when the task requires visual rather than verbal analysis (p. 39). As we shall see, the latter interpretation raises the question of the availability versus accessibility of visual memories for further processing.

The second question concerns the STM/LTM distinction. Indeed, although a number of studies investigated the relation between the two modes of representation, visual and verbal, within each memory system, much less is known about the role of visual and verbal STM codes in influencing LTM encoding. Brandimonte et al. (1992a, 1992b) suggested that when novel visual stimuli have to be learned, the type of STM code used will affect LTM encoding and subsequent image processing. The general hypothesis about the importance of STM codes for subsequent image generation and processing is derived from the working memory model (Baddeley, 1986; Baddeley & Hitch, 1974). Working memory has been shown to play a fundamental role in reading, mental arithmetic, reasoning, and language comprehension (Baddeley, 1986). Not surprisingly, it also appears to play a crucial role in mental imagery.

WORKING MEMORY SUBSYSTEMS

The notion of working memory refers to a hierarchical system involved in temporary storage and processing of information (Baddeley, 1986; Baddeley & Hitch, 1974). This consists of a supervisory attentional system, the Central Executive (CE), responsible for decision making, reasoning, and coordination of a set of slave systems. Although it is conceivable that a number of slave systems exist which are coordinated by the CE, the two most extensively studied are the Articulatory or Phonological Loop (AL) and the Visual-Spatial Sketch Pad (VSSP). The first is responsible for maintaining and manipulating speech-based information. Most importantly for our aims, it is also involved in the translation of visually presented material into a verbal form (Logie & Baddeley, 1990). The second is thought to be involved in maintaining and manipulating visuo-spatial information. In the next two sections we shall briefly analyze the structure and the functions of these two slave systems.

The Articulatory Loop

A considerable body of literature explored the characteristics of the AL system. As a result, a number of robust findings and sophisticated techniques are today available for its investigation.

Four major phenomena have been isolated that clearly support the AL model. They are: the phonological similarity effect, the irrelevant speech effect, the word-length effect, and the effect of articulatory suppression (see Baddeley, 1992, for a discussion).

The *phonological similarity effect* refers to poorer immediate serial recall of items (letters or words) that are similar in sound (Baddeley, 1966; Conrad, 1964). This effect has been interpreted as indicating that a store exists that relies purely on a phonological code and is accessed directly by speech. Similar items will have similar codes; they will be harder to distinguish, hence leading to poorer recall.

Impaired immediate serial recall is also observed when visually presented items are coupled with concurrent *irrelevant speech* (Salamé & Baddeley, 1982). It was assumed that irrelevant speech obligatorily accesses the phonological store, hence corrupting the memory trace and leading to a lower level of recall.

The *word-length effect* refers to the difficulty in recalling long words than short words (Baddeley, Thomson, & Buchanan, 1975). This effect seems to be inversely related to spoken duration. Longer words take longer to rehearse, hence allowing the memory trace of earlier words to fade. The presence of the word-length effect implies some form of subvocal rehearsal that has the function of maintaining items in the phonological store by refreshing their traces. Therefore, the faster the rehearsal the longer the memory span (Baddeley, 1990).

Finally, *articulatory suppression* is a dual-task technique used to prevent subvocal rehearsal (Murray, 1967). When subjects are induced to suppress rehearsal by uttering an irrelevant sound, immediate memory span is dramatically reduced. Importantly, the effects of irrelevant speech and phonological similarity are removed when the material to be recalled is presented visually and articulatory suppression is used (Baddeley, 1992; Baddeley, Lewis, & Vallar, 1984). An even stronger effect of articulatory suppression has been observed on the word-length effect, which is removed regardless of whether presentation is auditory or visual (Baddeley et al., 1984).

On the basis of these findings, the AL is thought to comprise two components: (a) a phonological memory store that can hold traces of speech-based material and is responsible for phonological similarity and (b) an articulatory rehearsal process responsible for the word-length effect and, most importantly for our aims, for translating visually presented material into a verbal form.

Many auditory tasks require a "partnership" between the active rehearsal process (inner voice) and the passive phonological store (inner ear), with subjects literally talking to themselves, and then listening to hear what they have covertly pronounced (see also Reisberg & Logie, 1993, for a discussion). According to this conception of working memory, the activity of speech provides the efferent channel (the inner voice), the rules of language provide the coding scheme, and the inner ear provides the relevant afferent channel (Reisberg & Logie, 1993).

Articulatory suppression removes the word-length effect because it prevents rehearsal; it also removes the phonological similarity effect with visual presentation because it prevents translation from a visual to a speech-based code (Baddeley, 1986).

The articulatory suppression technique has been typically used to *disrupt* performance in tasks that involve the phonological component of working memory. However, the converse may occur with visual tasks if one hypothesizes that people tend to recode visually presented stimuli spontaneously whenever this is possible (that is, when the stimuli are easily translatable into a verbal form). When the task is visual, and the stimuli are readily verbalizable, articulatory suppression may *improve* performance by eliminating interference from the speech code. Indeed, this is the case with image transformation tasks, which almost by definition require visual analysis to be correctly performed (Brandimonte & Gerbino, 1993; Brandimonte et al., 1992a, 1992b; Hagendorf, 1992).

Articulatory suppression may be seen as a means for preventing intermodal interference. The positive effect of suppression does not depend on the additivity of positive effects whatsoever, but on the prevention of verbal overshadowing of visual information held in working memory. The working memory subsystem that is involved in such tasks performs a function similar to that performed by the AL, but for visuo-spatial material.

The Visual-Spatial Sketch Pad

The second slave system of working memory is the Visual Spatial Sketch Pad (VSSP; Baddeley, 1986), which is thought to be responsible for setting up and manipulating visual-spatial images. The VSSP has received less attention than the AL, mainly because of difficulties in devising suitable techniques for its investigation (Logie, 1986, 1989). Perceptual-motor tracking of a moving target (Baddeley & Lieberman, 1980), concurrent arm movements (Quinn & Ralston, 1986), and irrelevant visual information (Logie, 1986) have been used as techniques for the study of the VSSP. Concurrent spatial tracking has been shown to disrupt recall of spatially coded material (Baddeley & Lieberman, 1980). Similarly, recall of the Brooks spatial material was disrupted by concurrent passive arm movements (Quinn & Ralston, 1986). The use of a secondary visual task involving the matching of successively presented random matrix patterns was shown to selectively interfere with use of a peg-word mnemonic (Logie, 1986).

Tracking and passive arm movements might be regarded as two kinds of "spatial suppression" techniques that impair functioning of a hypothetical spatial component in the working memory system, whereas unattended visual information might be viewed as a form of "visual suppression" technique whose disruptive effect suggests that the visual short-term memory system is accessed directly by visual input.

On the basis of these findings it has been suggested that, as with the AL, the VSSP may comprise a passive visual store and an active visual rehearsal process (Logie, 1989). Whereas tracking would act to disrupt some kind of active visual rehearsal process, the effect of irrelevant visual input suggests the idea of a passive store that is directly accessed by visually presented material and that retains information in an unparsed and uncategorized form (see also Frick, 1990).

These results provide a coherent package as to the main characteristics of the VSSP. However, they leave at least two important questions open: (1) Whether the VSSP should be regarded as a unitary subsystem, having both visual and spatial components, or whether different working-memory subsystems are involved in visual and spatial tasks (see, e.g., Baddeley, 1992; Baddeley & Lieberman, 1980; Humphreys & Bruce, 1989; Logie, 1986; Logie & Baddeley, 1990; Farah, Hammond, Levine, & Calvanio, 1988; Phillips, 1983); (2) what visual rehearsal means in the context of the working-memory (WM) model. The first issue raises the question of the existence of other WM rehearsal loops, while the second stimulates a deeper analysis of the notion of a VSSP as comparable to the "visual buffer" postulated by the imagery theory.

Reisberg and Logie (1993) have recently argued that there is nothing unique about the link between the inner voice and the inner ear, and that other links between other rehearsal loops may exist. They suggest that visual images might be enacted via some sort of efferent "inner scribe," analogous to the inner voice (Reisberg & Logie, 1993). According to this view, there is more than one species of "visual imagery"; one species is more properly considered "spatial/motoric imagery," but not visual. This motoric imagery can produce a covert stimulus that then "feeds into" the channels of vision (the inner eye). In this sense, a "partnership" in visual imagery may exist between an inner scribe and inner eye, similarly to what happens for the inner voice and the inner ear.

The inner scribe might be equated to some sort of "cognitive map generator," which provides the organism with virtual environments to be visited, restructured, and filled in using all three dimensions of conventional Euclidean space (Neisser, 1976; Shepard, 1984). Probably, in everyday life, this is the most extensively used working-memory function, as it supports action in a physical environment, survival skills, and exploratory planning.

Visual Rehearsal

Another question concerns the rehearsal processes in the VSSP. Whereas the process of articulatory subvocal rehearsal has proved to be susceptible of investigation, the nature of the rehearsal in the visuo-spatial system is at present far from clear and results are controversial (Baddeley, 1992). Indeed, what is not clear is whether covert rehearsal can take forms (such as pictorial or visual) other than the well-known verbal one. Watkins, Peynircioglu, and Brems (1984) suggest that distinct pictorial and verbal modes of rehearsal exist that serve not only to maintain information in conscious mind, but also to build up memory proper (p. 553).

Theories of visual imagery (Farah, p 84; Kosslyn, 1980) and the relationship between visual STM and visual imagery seem immediately relevant to this question. Kosslyn's (1980) theory of visual imagery postulates that mental images are "functional" pictures existing in a medium that functions as a coordinate space. The imagery medium, called the "visual buffer," is shared with perception. Information is represented by activating local regions of the space. The visual buffer has a limited extent and a specific shape (roughly circular). For this reason it can support representations that depict a limited visual arc (Kosslyn, 1980, 1981). Imaged objects are represented in an image as having specific spatial and geometrical features. They actually lack the above spatial characteristics, but nonetheless function as *if* they had those features. Images can be generated from LTM or loaded from the eyes. Three main processes operate on images in the visual buffer: generation, inspection, and transformation. A set of processing modules act to produce, maintain, and elaborate images. For example, once an image is constructed by means of generation procedures, a part begins to fade and work is necessary to refresh and maintain it. A processing module, called REGENERATE, reactivates those parts of the surface image that were to fade.

At first glance, the notion of a "visual buffer" seems to fit well with the notion of a VSSP (see, e.g., Humphreys & Bruce, 1989; Logie, 1989; Logie, Zucco, & Baddeley, 1990). Similarly to the VSSP, the visual buffer has in fact a limited capacity; its content is subject to decay over time unless some process of visual rehearsal is put into action, and it is sensitive to interference from any new material that accesses the visual buffer. However, at present, the similarity between the two concepts may not stand close scrutiny. In fact, there is a body of literature on the VSSP and a large body of literature on the visual buffer. What is missing, however, is a literature that examines the links between them (but see Logie, 1990).

For example, the analogy between the structure of the AL and the VSSP of the WM system implies that the VSSP also consists of a passive store and an active rehearsal process. The visual buffer postulated by the Kosslyn theory is simply a passive medium, a screen that supports visual representations generated from LTM or loaded through visual perception processes. Moreover, no mention is made in the theory as to whether the buffer represents the whole STM system or it is just a part of it. Hence, a straightforward conclusion is that either the visual buffer can only be equated to the passive store of the VSSP (and therefore it *does not* fit well with the notion of a VSSP) or the analogy with the AL does not work. Furthermore, the rehearsal process in the VSSP, often postulated but never clarified in detail, makes the link even more difficult. Whereas in the Kosslyn theory visual rehearsal occurs by means of the REGENERATE module, which is activated by a permanent controlling procedure that "calls" the appropriate modules at the appropriate occasions, it is not clear what "visual rehearsal" means in the context of the WM model. What is clear is that further research is needed to clarify this point.

VERBAL RECODING AND VERBAL OVERSHADOWING

The Verbal-Recoding Process

As stated in the introduction, visual stimuli are readily translated into a verbal form, whenever this is possible. This process has been typically termed "verbal recoding."

The negative effect of verbal recoding is not a new one. Early studies by Carmichael et al. (1932) addressed this question and showed that naming a form immediately before it is visually presented changes the manner in which it will be reproduced. More recently, investigators of perceptual memory have contended that verbal encoding of visual stimuli governs memory performance. For example, Glanzer and Clark (1964; see also Scott, 1967) proposed the "verbal loop hypothesis" which states that subjects translate visual patterns into a series of words, and that such a "verbalization" controls subsequent memory performance. This hypothesis holds that the encoding of visual information is typically verbal, and that retrieval of visual information is subject to recall of the verbalized information at the time of testing. Direct reference to *spontaneous* verbal recoding is also made in the work by Bahrick and Boucher (1968). These authors suggested that in order to facilitate storage and retrieval nonverbal information may be encoded verbally, and that this kind of verbal recoding occurs almost automatically at the time of the input. In a similar vein, Nelson, Brooks, and Borden (1973) reported some findings that are consistent with the view that the verbal system is involved in coding pictorial information. However, they specified that pictures are implicitly labeled only when the task requires acquisition of their relative order; when the task does not require sequential memory for the pictures, spontaneous verbal recoding does not occur (Nelson & Brooks, 1973). These results are consistent with the assumption of independence/interconnectedness of the two systems advanced by the dual coding theory (Paivio, 1971).

A further step toward a more sophisticated explanation of the verbal recoding process has been made by research attempting to manipulate the encoding modality of visual information. For instance, B. Tversky (1969, 1973) presented evidence that not only can pictorial material be verbally encoded (and vice versa), but that whether and how the material is recoded depends on subjects' anticipation of what they are to do with the material. She showed that picture-word stimuli are differentially encoded in anticipation of a recognition test than in anticipation of a free-recall test. Subjects performed better on the retention test of which they had been forewarned (Tversky, 1973). In the same vein, Frost (1972) examined memory for visually and semantically categorized pictures. Free recall of pictures' names and recognition were performed by subjects who expected either recall or recognition tests. However, she reported that those subjects expecting recognition recalled by combining visual and semantic categories and were able to perform the visual recognition task, while those subjects expecting recall used semantic encoding only and were able to perform only name recognition. She concluded that pictures are encoded differently according to expectations. Parallel access to visual and semantic memory codes occurs, but when recognition is expected a visual cue provides faster access, whereas when recall is expected verbal access is more efficient.

The major prediction of the dual-coding theory is that verbalization contributes to picture memory (Paivio, 1971, 1975, 1986, 1991). However, an alternative view exists that relegates verbal coding to the status of an ancillary component of pictorial representation (Intraub, 1979; Potter, 1976; Potter & Faulconer, 1975). According to this view, pictorial representations have both imagelike and abstract components, and the well-known picture superiority effect—that is, the higher accuracy observed in recall when common nouns are pictured rather than merely labeled (Paivio, 1971)—is not due to the beneficial effect of additional verbal encoding, but to the visual and conceptual distinctiveness of pictures as compared to words. For instance, Intraub (1979) failed to find significant correlations between naming latency and memory for pictures even at slow presentation time and concluded that, contrary to the dual-coding theory, implicit naming was not responsible for the improvement in picture memory at slower rates as reported by Paivio and Csapo (1973). Although Paivio (1991) recently criticized Intraub's interpretation as being incomplete, he nonetheless admitted that these negative findings remain embarrassing for the dual-coding model (p. 360).

Recently, in reconsidering the assumption of modality-specific memory codes Marschark and Cornoldi (1990) concluded that, while modality-specific representations are involved at the level of "on-line" processing, they are not involved at the level of long-term storage. According to this view, modality-specific processing systems (working memory) interact with a long-term memory system whose information is "amodal" rather than analogical with STM representations (but see Hitch, Brandimonte, & Walker, 1995).

Another controversial issue concerning the verbal-recoding hypothesis refers to the level of subject's control over recoding of pictorial stimuli. A number of studies suggested that verbal recoding of pictures does not occur automatically (Babbit, 1982; Nelson & Brooks, 1973; Nelson & Reed, 1976). For example, Babbit (1982) used a color-naming interference task to assess the amount of verbal coding occurring in response to picture and word stimuli. Subjects were asked to name the color of ink in which words were printed following either word or picture stimuli. The dependent measure was the latency of color naming. If verbal labeling of the input occurs, then latency should increase when the input item and the color naming word are related. Results showed that verbal activation occurred when the items were words, even when a recognition test was used.

On the other hand, with pictures, the presence of verbal activation was a function of task demands: Apparently, when a recognition test was expected verbal recoding was not activated, whereas when a recall test was expected the level of verbal activation was the same as that found when items were words. These results are in accordance with the position by Nelson and Brooks (1973) and Nelson and Reed (1976), who suggested that verbal labeling of pictures is not an automatic process, and these results are also consistent with Intraub's findings that indicated no relationship between verbal labeling and picture memory. However, such a straightforward conclusion is difficult to generalize and, indeed, it has been recently challenged by studies demonstrating that the tendency to rely on some form of verbal coding is hard to control voluntarily (Brandimonte et al., 1992a; see also Chambers & Reisberg, 1985; Peterson, Kihlstrom, Rose, & Glisky, 1992).

Brandimonte et al. (1992a) found that, although subjects were forewarned about the nature of the imagery task they would be asked to do (and therefore they had precise expectations about the task), when easily nameable pictures were used performance was as poor as when subjects were not forewarned, suggesting that verbal recoding of visual stimuli occurs almost automatically when pictures are easily nameable. People seem not to rely predominantly on a visual form of encoding, but on verbal recoding of pictorial stimuli. It remains to be established whether both kinds of information (visual and verbal) are stored after recoding, or some loss in visual information occurs. We shall discuss later in the chapter the question of accessibility versus availability of visual information in memory.

Before analyzing in detail the notion of "verbal overshadowing" and its relationship to verbal recoding, some terminological clarifications are in order.

Thus far we have been using the terms "verbal recoding" and "verbal labeling" as synonyms, mainly because this has been the prevailing tendency in the literature (see, e.g., Babbit, 1982; Ellis, 1973). However, beyond their common link to more general verbal processes, an important distinction is that whereas the term "verbal recoding" directly refers to a process, the term "verbal labeling" is somewhat more confusing, in that it may refer either to a process such as covert labeling, or to a technique such as verbal pretraining or stimulus predifferentiation (cf. Ellis, 1973) aimed at inducing verbal coding.

Most importantly, it should be noticed that the concept of verbal recoding is not a unitary one, since it may refer to a number of different kinds of processes. For example, it may refer to covert/overt articulation of a verbal label, or to verbal-semantic processes, or to verbal-phonological coding. Except for their common reference to the verbal aspects of the process and for the fact that they always refer to a process (rather than, for example, a technique), these kinds of recodings probably involve different mechanisms that, if analyzed in detail, might account for the different patterns of results often reported in the literature. It seems worth noticing that such a distinction has been widely underestimated, and that the term "verbal recoding" has been mainly used in its general meaning, with no specification of the level of processing.

The Verbal Overshadowing Effect

Generally speaking, the term "overshadowing" refers to situations in which multiple sources of information result in the domination of a source over another. As applied in the memory domain (Schooler & Engstler-Schooler, 1990), it indicates the interaction of internal memory traces and shows its effect at the time of recollection. The verbal overshadowing effect is thought to stem from the interaction of two processes: (a) the influence of retrieval cues present at the time of recollection; and (b) the consequences of inaccurate recollection (Schooler & Engstler-Schooler, 1990). Indeed, while the relative activation of verbal and visual memory codes depends on the specific retrieval cues (Tulving & Thomson, 1973; Paivio, 1986), with the degree of activation depending on the specificity of the cue (i.e., verbal cues tend to activate the verbal code and visual cues tend to activate the visual code), the consequences of inaccurate recollection are thought to result in the generation of multiple memory representations corresponding to the same stimulus. The combination of these two processes predicts verbal overshadowing.

An interesting result, reported in Schooler and Engstler-Schooler (1990, Experiment 6), showed that limiting the time subjects were given to recognize target faces alleviated the impairment. An important assumption necessary to test the effect of time limitation was that picture recognition involves serial access of the two codes. Subjects first access an accurate visual code followed by a verbally biased code; therefore, limiting the time given for recognition was expected to reduce the impairment. As we shall see later in the chapter, this phenomenon, termed "release from verbal overshadowing," has been recently observed during imagery tasks using different paradigms and procedures. Such an effect strongly favors the hypothesis of the coexistence in memory of the original visual information and a new conceptual representation that overshadows the original visual memories (see also Bartlett et al., 1980; Schooler, Ryan, & Reder, 1990) as compared to a memory distortion hypothesis (see Bahrick & Boucher, 1968; Carmichael et al., 1932; E. F. Loftus, 1991; Nelson & Brooks, 1973).

It seems worthwhile noticing that verbal overshadowing may be experimentally induced after an accurate visual encoding, as showed by Schooler and Engstler-Schooler (1990). However, it can also be seen as a by-product of spontaneous verbal recoding during initial learning (see Brandimonte & Gerbino, 1993). That is, verbal overshadowing may be regarded as the direct *effect* of a *process* of verbal recoding that may occur during learning (at the time of input) or after learning (subsequent to encoding).

Verbal Recoding and Memory Distortions

Another relevant question concerns the existence of memory distortions attributable to verbal recoding. For instance, Tulving (1983) defined as "recoding" the class of processes that take place after an event has been encoded and that produce changes in the "engrams" associated with that event. More recent studies on the "misinformation effect" using implicit tests of memory have suggested that the ability to remember the details of an event can be altered by the introduction of misleading post-event information (E. F. Loftus, 1991). The important conclusion advanced in these studies is that recoding and reorganization due to addition of new elements alter the original memories. This is consistent with a

Gestalt view of memory in which individual traces depend upon the system of traces (Koffka, 1935, Chapter 11). This position clearly conflicts with that of other authors who suggest that verbal recoding does not alter the original information, but rather generates new information that coexists with the original one, and may eventually overshadow it if the trace corresponding to the new code is stronger than the trace corresponding to the original code (Schooler & Engstler-Schooler, 1990). In a study on eyewitness testimony, Bekerian and Bowers (1983) showed that the effect of misleading information can be removed if subjects are given critical cues at the time of retrieval that were present during original encoding.

On a more general ground, the distinction between the distortion and the co-existence hypotheses reflects that between *changed-trace* and *multiple-trace* hypotheses (see, e.g., Chandler, 1991). Both the changed-trace and the multiple-trace accounts hold that additional information can impair memory for preceding events, but, while the former hypothesis assumes the existence of memory distortions, the latter assumes coexistence and competition among the traces.

According to the first hypothesis, the interpolated event displaces the original trace permanently: There is no way to recover the information; it is lost forever. Loftus (1981, 1991) has argued that when subjects receive misleading verbal information after visual information, the new information is integrated into the visual scene in such a way as to "update" the previously formed memory. Most recently, Intraub, Bender, and Mangels (1992, see also Intraub & Richardson, 1989) have described in detail a phenomenon of memory distortion, called "boundary extension" (subjects tend to remember close-up photographs as having had extended boundaries), which occurs spontaneously, without the experimenter providing any misleading information. The authors conclude that memory for pictures includes a distortion that is the rule rather than the exception, and that this phenomenon provides another example of the dynamic nature of mental representation (p. 191).

Evidence against the distortion hypothesis have been presented by several researchers who offered alternative interpretations. For example, Christiaansen and Ochalek (1983) argued that the original and the post-event information coexist, but that the latter is more accessible. A revised version of the traditional multiple-trace hypothesis has been proposed by Chandler (1991) to account for both the decrease in retroactive interference (RI) across a 48-hour retention interval and the absence of proactive interference (PI) either after 15 minute or after 48 hours. Lindsay and Johnson (1989) reported findings inconsistent with the idea of "updating" proposed by E. F. Loftus (1981). They obtained a misinformation effect when the misleading information preceded rather than followed the visual scene. According to the authors, these results are compatible with an integration hypothesis that holds that memories of verbal and pictorial presentations somehow "blended" together irrespective of source. That is, the misinformation effect may reflect a failure to identify the sources of memories during remembering. However, whereas such an interpretation clearly challenges the updating hypothesis, it leaves open the question of whether the phenomenon of memory blends can be attributed to changes in the original trace or to confusion between multiple traces.

Moreover, as Schooler and Tanaka (1991) have recently pointed out, the term "memory blends" is itself problematic, as it may refer to the subject's memory performance (recollection blends) or to the underlying memory trace (representation blends; see Metcalfe, 1990). The link between these two kinds of recollections and the underlying representations is, at present, far from clear, and the evidence for the notion of "blend representations" remains somewhat equivocal (but see Metcalfe & Bjork, 1991).

At this point, let us return to the effect of verbal recoding. One possibility is that verbal recoding during learning, but not verbal recoding after learning, causes memory alterations (cf. Bahrick & Boucher, 1968; Carmichael et al., 1932). However, earlier studies on verbal recoding cannot speak to this question. At present, virtually nothing is known as to whether a coexistence hypothesis holds even for verbal recoding during learning. That is, the coexistence and the memory alteration hypotheses might not be mutually exclusive: When recoding visual stimuli during initial learning, part of visual information may be distorted, but another part may be preserved (given the assumption of direct access of visual inputs to the VSSP) and simply overshadowed by the verbal code.

Accessibility Versus Availability

The above debate fully justifies the resurgence of interest in the question of availability versus accessibility of information in memory, with specific consideration for visual information.

In their classical study on memory for words, Tulving and Pearlstone (1966) explored the hypothesis that "a substantial part of nonrecall of familiar words under typical experimental conditions is attributable to inaccessibility of otherwise intact memory traces" (p. 382). That is, memory traces would be available, but if they are not accessible their availability cannot be proved. Of course, accessibility of the information depends on its availability, but, according to Tulving and Pearlstone (1966), it also depends on retrieval cues. In their study, immediate recall was tested either in presence or in absence of category names as retrieval cues. Cued recall was higher than noncued recall, indicating that sufficiently intact memory traces of nonrecalled words were actually available. Since then, a body of research has shown that items are not simply either remembered or forgotten. Apparently unrecallable items can be easily recalled at a subsequent point in relation to modification in the environmental context (Smith, Glenberg, & Bjork, 1978) and in the nature of the task (Lupker, Harbluk, & Patrick, 1991). Furthermore, people are able to predict (in terms of feeling of knowing ratings) which items will be recalled (Lupker et al., 1991).

In the domain of visual memories, the accessibility/availability question has received less attention. Earlier studies that demonstrated functional independence of visual and verbal codes of the same stimuli (Bahrick & Boucher, 1968; Nelson & Brooks, 1973) attempted to accommodate the negative effects of verbal processing on visual memory by suggesting that verbal processing reduces the amount of visual information that is encoded; that is, the original visual information would no longer be available. The "verbal interference" hypothesis (see Schooler & Engstler-Schooler, 1990), on the other hand, can be regarded as supporting the accessibility side of this twofold question. The release from verbal overshadowing effect clearly speaks to this question.

Indirect support for the hypothesis of accessibility comes from research on the phenomenon of "savings" for pictures (MacLeod, 1988). It has been known for a long time that *relearning* is faster and easier than original learning (Ebbinghaus, 1885). This relearning advantage has been called "savings," and it has been recently shown to represent a useful tool for studying inaccessible memories, both for verbal and visual materials. MacLeod (1988) examined savings for words, simple pictures (line drawings), and complex photographic pictures. He found that, when savings were tested by recall following relearning, for those items that were neither recalled nor recognized, the identical item was relearned better than an unrelated control item. This advantage held for all three classes of materials. It seems that even when a picture cannot be recalled, information relevant to that item persists in memory. However, it should be noticed that a recognition test following relearning failed to find the same advantage. One might argue that such a finding challenges the view that information relevant to nonverbal material persists in memory. Indeed, people may well have learned the verbal counterpart of the pictures (that is, they verbally recoded the pictures and accessed their verbal labels on retrieval). If so, it is not surprising that savings were observed in the recall test but not in the recognition test following relearning, and this finding would say nothing as to whether visual information was simply "forgotten" or completely "gone."

On the other hand, this important concern is alleviated by results from experiments using complex naturalistic scenes that should be difficult to recode verbally (in the sense of giving them a single label). In this case, too, recall following relearning was better than recognition, suggesting that the dissociation was not due to verbal codability of the items and might be attributed to different retrieval information associated with recall and recognition; that is, recall and recognition may rely on different aspects of retrieval and this is the reason why savings are not evident on a recognition test (MacLeod, 1988, p. 209).

Stronger support for the accessibility hypothesis comes from recent studies by Chambers and Reisberg (1992) on the reinterpretability of visual mental images. In these studies, subjects were biased to view the duck/rabbit figure as a duck or as a rabbit; they were asked to create an image of the figure and then they were given a recognition test that included the figure originally shown and one that departed slightly from the original figure (modified either on the duck's bill or on the rabbit's nose). Subjects who constructed their image as a duck were able to correctly detect this modification if the test pair included the figure modified on the duck's bill, but failed if the test pair included the figure modified on the rabbit's nose. The opposite was true for those subjects who constructed the image as a rabbit.

In another experiment, after creating an image under one of the two construals, subjects were informed that the image that they had imaged resembled another figure and were asked if their image reminded them of this other form. If subjects could "see" the new construal, they were given a recognition test. The interesting result, which is relevant to the question under discussion here, is that subjects who changed their construal of the image from a duck to a rabbit were better able to recognize the figure modified on the rabbit's nose, but their performance was at chance with the duck-modified pair, and vice versa for those subjects who changed their interpretation from the rabbit to the duck (Chambers & Reisberg, 1992, Experiment 4). The authors interpret this finding as indicating that the specific meaning given to the image determines which aspects of the image will be maintained and which will be lost. However, these results can equally be taken as speaking directly to the availability/accessibility question.

Indeed, an "access" interpretation seems to be favored by these findings, because to explain the changes in the interpretation and the subsequent recognition data one has to assume that the "image files" in LTM contain both the pictorial features of the duck's bill and of the rabbit's nose, and that it is the *access* to the whole information rather than its availability that is influenced by the semantic bias (cf. Brandimonte & Gerbino, 1993). It should be noticed that when speaking about accessibility or availability of information, one may refer either to the surface image content or to the image file content. In Chambers and Reisberg's terms, the information in the image file is complete but not accessible, while in the surface image part of the information that is necessary for reversal is simply lost, and therefore unavailable. We shall return to the question of the reinterpretability of visual mental images later in the chapter.

"Available but not Accessible": The Release from Verbal Overshadowing Effect

Initial support for the hypothesis that the verbal overshadowing effect can be removed, once it has occurred, comes from the study by Schooler and Engstler-Schooler (1990, Experiment 6; see also Bekerian & Bowers, 1983, for some support to the accessibility hypothesis). However, no systematic attempt has been made thus far to investigate this issue.

Recent research by Brandimonte, Schooler, and Gabbino (1995b) has explored whether spontaneous and/or induced verbal overshadowing can be eliminated by using a visual retrieval cue (e.g., color) that was encoded at the time of initial learning (Tulving & Pearlstone, 1966). Two experiments were carried out in which subjects learned either easy or difficult-to-name pictures that were drawn on colored cards. They were then asked to rotate each picture mentally to discover two joined capital letters (see Brandimonte et al., 1992b; Fig. 2.1 in this chapter). In each condition, half the subjects were shown the color of the background on which each picture was drawn just before performing the mental rotation task, while the other half were directly required to perform the task. In the first experiment, easy and difficult-to-name pictures were used. Previous studies had shown that easily nameable pictures tend to be spontaneously recoded into a

Easy Nameability   Difficult Nameability

FIGURE 2.1. Example of stimuli used in Brandimonte, Hitch, and Bishop (1992b).

verbal format (Brandimonte et al., 1992a, 1992b). However, if the original visual information is simply overshadowed by the verbal one, the re-presentation of the color in which each picture was initially learned could make it accessible, hence improving performance in the imagery task. No such effect was expected in the difficult-to-name picture condition, which should be as good with as without color representation. Results confirmed these predictions in showing an interaction between nameability and presence of the cue: Color cues at retrieval were effective only for easily nameable pictures, which were supposed to produce verbal overshadowing, but not for difficult-to-name pictures for which no verbal overshadowing effect was expected to occur.

In another experiment, verbal overshadowing was experimentally induced by supplying verbal labels to the difficult-to-name pictures. The retrieval cue had the effect of improving performance in the imagery task only in presence of labels (which were supposed to induce verbal overshadowing). Without labels, performance was as good with as without color re-presentation.

The release from verbal overshadowing effect clearly demonstrates that visual information which has undergone verbal recoding at the time of input is simply "inaccessible," not definitively "lost." This holds true both when verbal overshadowing occurs as a consequence of spontaneous recoding of easily nameable pictures and when it is a result of recoding induced by labeling difficult-to-name pictures.

IMPROVING IMAGERY PERFORMANCE THROUGH VERBAL CODING INHIBITION

Given the assumption of a trade-off between visual and verbal memory codes, a straightforward hypothesis follows: Whenever a task that requires visual analysis is to be performed, preventing people from verbally recoding the stimuli should work as a means for eliminating the interference and hence improve performance. Several recent investigations have examined the effects of verbal coding during learning on the ability to retrieve and manipulate mental images of the stimuli (Brandimonte & Gerbino, 1993; Brandimonte et al., 1992a, 1992b; Intons-Peterson, 1992; Hagendorf, 1992; Hitch et al., 1995).

FIGURE 2.2.   An example of stimuli used in the subtraction task (from Brandimonte, Hitch, and Bishop, 1992a).

In one series of experiments, Brandimonte, Hitch, and Bishop (1992a) used an image transformation task, called *Subtraction,* consisting of mentally taking away part of an image in order to discover, in the remainder, a familiar object (see Fig. 2.2). Subjects first learned a set of visual stimuli, and then performed the subtraction task on images retrieved from LTM. For nameable stimuli, performance in the imagery task was significantly enhanced if verbal recoding was prevented by requiring articulatory suppression during learning. However, for unnameable stimuli, performance was unaffected by articulatory suppression.

Recently we reported results on image reversal of the duck/rabbit configuration that are consistent with the finding that articulatory suppression facilitates imagery performance if the original figure is easy to name (Brandimonte & Gerbino, 1993). In accordance with previous results in the literature (Brandimonte et al., 1992a, 1992b; Hagendorf, 1992; Hitch et al., 1995), performance was greatly improved if the initial inspection of the duck/rabbit figure was accompanied by articulatory suppression (Brandimonte & Gerbino, 1993). The duck/rabbit configuration supports two easy-to-name interpretations. Whatever the one instantiated during initial inspection was, articulatory suppression had the direct effect of preventing verbal recoding and the indirect effect of facilitating mental discovery of the alternative interpretation.

In another series of studies, Brandimonte et al. (1992b) used an imagery task involving mental rotation. When rotated 90 degrees counterclockwise, each stimulus revealed a new pattern consisting of two conjoined capital letters (see Fig. 2.1). Subjects first memorized one of two series of pictures that were either easy or difficult to name, and then attempted to rotate a mental image of each pattern and to segment it in such a way as to allow the two letters to be identified. Half the subjects were required to articulate the syllable "la" during the learning of the stimuli and half were asked to remain silent. Articulatory suppression during learning enhanced performance on the imagery task for stimuli that were easy to name, but had no effect for stimuli that were difficult to name.

A second experiment looked at the effect of supplying verbal labels during initial learning. It was assumed that making a plausible verbal label available to subjects in the difficult-nameability condition would encourage them to use verbal recoding when memorizing the series. Hence, supplying a name to an otherwise meaningless stimulus was expected to hinder performance in the imagery rotation task. On the other hand, no effect of labeling was expected for easily nameable stimuli as it was assumed that subjects would rely on verbal coding even in the absence of labels. As predicted, performance was severely disrupted by labeling when the stimuli were difficult to name, but had no effect when items were easy to name.

Most recent studies replicated and extended the results concerning the beneficial effect of articulatory suppression on imagery performance (Intons-Peterson, 1992; Hagendorf, 1992). In one of these studies (Hagendorf, 1992), a reconstruction of dot-in-matrix patterns task was used. Subjects inspected each pattern for 2 seconds and then were asked to reconstruct the just-presented pattern on a response sheet. In one condition, they were required to count backwards by threes. Counting was assumed to prevent verbal recoding and rehearsal. Children, adults, and experts were tested in this experiment. Results showed that young adults and experts reproduced more correct positions with, than without, suppression. No positive effect of suppression was found for the children's group (see Brandimonte & Gerbino, 1993, for similar results with children).

Taken together, these results demonstrate a consistent pattern of effects across different kinds of imagery task and different ways of varying the use of verbal codes. They establish the robustness and generality of the disruptive effects of verbal recoding on the utilization of visual information. In turn, these results raise a number of further questions, part of which are currently under study. One question regards the possibility that verbal recoding affects the representation of visual information. The other concerns the kinds of visual information that is represented in memory. This latter question will be discussed in the next section.

Visual Information in STM and LTM

Research on visual imagery has suggested that images of objects typically possess features such as size, shape, color, orientation, and location (e.g., Finke & Schmidt, 1977; Kosslyn, 1980). According to these models of visual imagery, such features are represented in the short-term visual buffer. Visual representations of this sort can be contrasted with more abstract representations that have been assumed to underlie object recognition, such as pictogens (Warren & Morton, 1982) or the structural descriptions proposed by Marr (1982). These more abstract representations are necessary for object recognition processes to take account of changes in the appearance of an object under viewing conditions that differ in parameters such as illumination, distance, and orientation. An intuitively appealing hypothesis is that visual LTM involves more abstract representations like those that are thought to underlie object recognition, while visual STM is concerned with surface appearances. Analogous coding differences are commonly assumed in the domain of verbal memory, where the short-term store is typically thought to be concerned with preserving the surface characteristics of sentences, while long-term memory stores deeper representations (Clark & Clark, 1977). However, one challenge to such an account of visual memory is how to explain the detailed nature of visual images generated from LTM. This could be taken as suggesting that long-term visual memory stores appearance-specific information, just like short-term visual memory. So far, however, no systematic evidence has been found for fundamental differences between the nature of representations in visual STM and visual LTM.

To investigate this issue, Hitch et al. (1995) recently explored the effects of stimulus contrast on the ability to manipulate an image of the stimulus. More specifically, subjects were required to combine mentally an image of a line drawing (derived from either short-term or long-term visual memory) with an image of a second figure. Successful combination revealed a new form, which subjects had to identify. In a first experiment, it was investigated whether information about stimulus contrast is represented in visual STM and visual LTM. This was achieved by manipulating the contrast of the two line drawings that subjects had to combine using mental imagery. In the "congruent contrast" condition, one stimulus was shown in normal contrast (black lines on a white background) and the other in reversed contrast (white lines on a black background). In the "incongruent contrast" condition, both stimuli were shown in the same contrast (either both normal or both reversed). If visual memory preserves information about stimulus contrast, performance in the imagery task should be impaired when the contrasts of the two stimuli are incompatible. However, a differential effect of stimulus contrast should be observed according to whether visual STM and visual LTM contain different kinds of information (surface appearance vs abstract descriptions). Results from this experiment showed an adverse effect of presenting stimuli in incongruent contrasts under STM conditions, but a small nonsignificant impairment associated with contrast incongruency under LTM conditions.

At first glance, these results are consistent with the hypothesis that images generated from LTM are based on more abstract visual descriptions that do not preserve surface details like stimulus contrast. However, there are good grounds for being cautious before accepting this interpretation. Indeed, the stimuli were ones that subjects tend to label spontaneously (see Brandimonte et al., 1992a). Therefore, it is difficult to establish whether the difference in the way contrast affected performance in the imagery task is a general property of images generated from visual LTM, or whether it is specific to stimuli that have undergone verbal recoding.

This hypothesis was tested in a second experiment, in which the opportunity for subjects to engage in verbal recoding was manipulated by using articulatory suppression. Results showed that suppression during encoding rendered imagery based on LTM sensitive to congruency of stimulus contrast in just the same way as imagery based on STM (see Table 2.1). This suggests that visual LTM, like visual STM, maintains representations that preserve surface characteristics of the stimuli. As far as these data are concerned, there seems to be no support for the hypothesis that visual LTM relies exclusively on abstract representations; rather, it seems that, when interference from the presence of verbal descriptions is removed, surface characteristics are present in visual LTM (Hitch et al., 1995). Most recent studies on size-congruity effects in STM and LTM extended and clarified this interpretation (Brandimonte et al., 1995a).

An important assumption concerns the interconnectivity of visual and verbal

TABLE 2.1. Mean number of correct responses on the image combination task in Experiment 2 (max = 6)

| | Contrast agreement | |
Memory condition	Congruent	Incongruent
Control (No suppression)		
STM	3.81	2.62
LTM	2.62	2.68
Articulatory suppression		
STM	3.81	2.31
LTM	4.06	2.68

components of LTM. The interconnectivity explains why verbal-coding manipulations such as articulatory suppression, nameability, and labeling can produce or remove the verbal overshadowing effect. This assumption allows verbal descriptions to influence either the accessibility or the availability of visual information. Thus, a verbal description might block access to a visual representation or might distort it in some way. That is, verbal recoding might reduce the accessibility of visual representations (cf. Schooler & Engstler-Schooler, 1990) or might impair them—for example, by reducing their accuracy (cf. Bahrick & Boucher, 1968). Unfortunately, no direct evidence for one or the other interpretation can be drawn from these results (but see Brandimonte & Gerbino, 1993; and Brandimonte et al., 1995b). A possible implication of these findings is that the phenomenon of verbal overshadowing extends to verbal processing during learning (recall that as studied by Schooler & Engstler-Schooler [1990] verbal overshadowing involved overt verbalization subsequent to stimulus encoding). The data from the release from verbal overshadowing study discussed above in the chapter directly speak to this question: Even when verbal overshadowing is induced during learning (e.g., by using verbal labels), it can be removed and the original visual information accessed again (Brandimonte et al., 1995b).

More generally, the results discussed in this section are in accordance with the existence of a dual form of encoding for visual stimuli (Paivio, 1971, 1991). However, in showing a detrimental effect of having verbal and visual codes available, these results do not support the additivity assumption of the dual-coding theory. A possible explanation is that, unlike Paivio's work, in all of the above studies the verbal information was of little (if any) value in performing the task. Indeed, Paivio was essentially interested in memory for the names of stimuli shown in the pictures rather than memory for the details of a picture. Such an explanation is related to the question of the appropriateness of encoding for the task to be performed. Interestingly, for certain kinds of imagery tasks the use of verbal coding does not prevent people from successfully reinterpreting their mental images (see, e.g., Finke, Pinker, & Farah, 1989).

An interesting and important further question concerns the possible effect of semantic encoding on subsequent image manipulation. It has been suggested that verbal recoding *during learning* (in STM) may prompt the establishment of some form of verbal/semantic encoding in LTM that, in turn, is detrimental when the task to be performed requires the recovery of visual memories (Brandimonte et al., 1992a, 1992b). However, it might be useful to distinguish between naming and describing visual stimuli. These two kinds of verbalization may prompt different levels of semantic encoding, and may be differentially affected by articulatory suppression. For instance, naming a picture *after* having visually encoded it may be just the same as attaching a number or a signal to a visual representation that will be picked up by means of that signal. This process of verbal recoding would not be expected to induce verbal overshadowing, as the label given to the visual representation might have lost its verbal/semantic function. In contrast, naming a picture *during* visual encoding is more likely to produce a verbal overshadowing effect because the construction of the visual representation itself would be affected by the recoding process. On the other hand, we know that describing a picture or a face *after* visual encoding has a disrupting effect because it forces subjects to put into words nonverbal information (Schooler & Engstler-Schooler, 1990). It would be interesting to explore whether describing a picture *during* encoding has a similar effect.

A related issue concerns the mechanisms underlying the effect of articulatory suppression and its relationship to semantic encoding. An often-raised question concerns the phenomenological experience that people have of being able to covertly "name" a simple line drawing while articulating irrelevant sounds. It seems plausible to hypothesize that articulatory suppression does not impede naming in the sense of object identification through lexical categorization. When viewing a picture, identification will probably precede any further semantic analysis. Thus, naming can be seen as a more primitive, almost automatic process that especially takes place in presence of easily nameable pictures. What articulatory suppression may disrupt is a deeper semantic analysis such as the inner description of the labeled object. With respect to simple identification, deeper semantic descriptions may involve a larger amount of verbalization that, in turn, may have the effect of fixing the meaning. As already noticed, the term "verbal recoding" may refer to a number of processes. If one accepts that it may refer to some sort of verbal/semantic analysis of the stimulus, it is conceivable that articulatory suppression blocks such a kind of recoding process.

Although we are aware of the speculative nature of this discussion, we believe that it may open interesting avenues for future research.

CAN AN IMAGE BE "UNBIASED"?

A core question about the nature of imagery and its relation to other forms of representation (e.g., percepts) refers to the *reinterpretability* of visual mental images. Nowadays, debates on this issue are still developing, and research is producing a growing body of interesting results.

The question of whether mental images can be ambiguous was originally raised by Chambers and Reisberg (1985), who asked subjects to form a mental image of the duck/rabbit by Jastrow (1900) when only one interpretation was experienced during perception. Despite training to reverse other bi-stable figures in perception, and despite prompting, no subject reversed the mental image of that figure. Chambers and Reisberg (1985) concluded that mental images are inherently unambiguous, and that, as such, they cannot be reinterpreted. Unlike the stimulus, which requires an interpretation, the image embodies a specific interpretation. That is, an image is created to represent a particular object, and hence its "meaning" is in place at the outset. Further, they argued that shape representations are accessed by means of semantic representations, and that the two cannot be separated.

In seeming contrast, several other studies have recently provided compelling evidence that people can "discover" unanticipated forms in their images. Importantly, successful discoveries were obtained both when images represented familiar objects and geometrical shapes (Brandimonte et al., 1992a, 1992b, 1992c; Finke et al., 1989; Finke, 1990) and when they represented bi-stable configurations such as the duck/rabbit figure (Brandimonte & Gerbino, 1993; Hyman & Neisser, 1991; Kaufmann & Helstrup, 1993; Peterson et al., 1992). However, whereas the former group of studies cannot be taken as challenging the conclusions by Chambers and Reisberg (1985), the latter raises the important question of the degree of generality that can reasonably be attributed to the Chambers and Reisberg (1985) results.

For instance, Hyman and Neisser (1991) showed that subjects can mentally reverse bi-stable configurations, such as the duck/rabbit figure, if they are given the "right kind" of instructions. Hyman and Neisser (1991) gave their subjects both orientation and category information (full information condition) about the alternative interpretation of the figure. Namely, they told subjects to consider the back of the head they already saw as the front of the head of a different animal. Under this condition, 11 out of 20 subjects reversed the figure in mental imagery. Hyman and Neisser's findings emphasize the role of instructions in prompting the reversal. Similarly, Peterson et al. (1992) found that this kind of figure can be reversed in imagery when subjects are prompted by either explicit suggestions (e.g., hints to change their reference frame) or implicit suggestions (e.g., more appropriate demonstration figures). In addition, they showed that the rate of reversal can be increased by manipulating the quality of the image components (good parts vs. poor parts of the image).

While these findings are in marked contrast with Chambers and Reisberg's (1985) early position, they do not conflict with the enlarged proposal of Reisberg and Chambers (1991) and Chambers and Reisberg (1992). In fact, their most recent suggestion is that subjects can nonetheless learn from their images by changing some aspects of the interpretation. According to the authors, images are obligatorily accompanied by an understanding that "shapes" the image in an important way. What will be included in an image depends on how subjects interpret the form. As a consequence, if subjects change their understanding of the figure, many are able to find target shapes in their images. The main conclusion is that what subjects can discover in a mental image is bounded by how the subjects understand the image (Chambers & Reisberg, 1992; Reisberg & Chambers, 1991). Such a claim implies that if subjects have understood the image in a certain way (for example, as a duck) and they are given no instructions about the strategy to use for reversal, no image reversal should be observed.

However, in marked contrast, recent studies reported results that clearly support the view that image reversal is not only possible but highly probable even in the absence of instructions, and despite a specific understanding of the figure (Brandimonte & Gerbino, 1993; Kaufmann & Helstrup, in press). For instance, Kaufmann and Helstrup (1993) replicated the Chambers and Reisberg (1985) experiment, with the modification that a group of art students who were supposed to be better visualizers than ordinary university students was tested on image reversal. The suggestion was that "uncued" reconstrual may require superior visualization abilities. Results showed that, using a strict reversal criterion, 4 subjects out of 26 were able to discover the alternative interpretation of the duck/ rabbit figure. Given that zero was the expected frequency, this result has been interpreted as a demonstration that uncued reconstrual is at least possible.

A straightforward conclusion from these results is that the higher the visualization abilities the more likely is image reversal. But, if this was the case, why did Chambers and Reisberg's (1985) subjects fail to report a single reversal despite the inclusion in the sample of several high vividness imagers? A tentative explanation of these seemingly contrasting results is that imagery vividness differs in an important way from the ability to use imagery strategies. Whereas vividness refers to a static property of images, the ability to exploit one's own visual resources is, by definition, a dynamic property of the imagery system (see, e.g., Paivio & Clark, 1990). Having vivid images does not ensure successful image manipulation. On the other hand, successful image manipulation may be taken as demonstrating sufficiently vivid underlying visual representations. Therefore, both Chambers and Reisberg's (1985) and Kaufmann and Helstrup's (1993) subjects may have constructed a vivid image of the duck/rabbit figure, with the fundamental difference that the latter subjects were eventually better able to use appropriate strategies for retrieving/accessing it.

While such an interpretation may be plausible, the question remains open as to the role of understanding in image reversal. Recall that despite their being experts in using visual memory strategies, only 4 subjects out of 26 were able to discover the alternative interpretation in their images (the difference between the expected and the observed frequencies was near to significance). Therefore, being good visualizers (in the sense of vivid imagers) seems not to be sufficient for image reversal to occur. On the other hand, even among skilled visualizers very few people make spontaneous use of appropriate imagery strategies. In this respect, these results, rather than contrasting the "understanding" hypothesis, make it even stronger, as they show that good visualizers such as art students perform worse than instructed normal people. Therefore, it seems plausible to hypothesize that an interpretive bias is active even in the case of good visualizers.

A stronger test for the understanding hypothesis is to investigate whether, given a specific understanding of the figure (either as a duck or as a rabbit), the same (high) level of performance that has been obtained in image reversal under conditions of presence of instructions can be obtained when no information on the strategy to use for image reversal is given. The heart of the problem here is to explore whether a more primitive mechanism than understanding may be responsible for the failure in image reversal.

As we have recently argued (Brandimonte & Gerbino, 1993), an alternative explanation for the poor performance observed in most of the above-mentioned studies is that this interpretive bias may be caused by a verbal recoding process of the stimulus that overshadows its visual representation. If subjects spontaneously recode the picture in a verbal form when loading the image, it seems likely that the image content will differ accordingly with the kind of encoding processes. Therefore, any manipulation aimed at emphasizing visual encoding should facilitate image reversal of the duck/rabbit figure. One such manipulation is to prevent subjects from verbally recoding the picture at the time of presentation.

In a series of four experiments, we showed that when subjects were prevented from verbally recoding visual stimuli during initial learning, they fared systematically better in mentally reversing their images, even when they received no instructions to change the way in which the image was understood. The first experiment tested the hypothesis that adults tend to spontaneously rely on a verbal form of encoding when loading an image into the visual buffer. In an attempt to replicate and extend Hyman and Neisser's (1991) results, Experiment 2 examined the effects of stimulus exposure time and articulatory suppression, comparing 2-second vs. 5-second presentations. Experiment 3 analyzed the effect of articulatory suppression when full (category and orientation), partial, or no information is given. Finally, Experiment 4 was an attempt to establish whether verbal recoding occurs during loading the image into the visual buffer, during image manipulation, or during both stages. On this basis, we suggested a model of image reversal that takes into consideration the interaction between memory codes and that provides a new perspective on the relationship between visual imagery and memory.

The model is based on the following assumptions: interaction between visual and verbal codes; automatic verbal recoding of the visual input in STM; possible prevention of verbal recoding by articulatory suppression; influence of presentation time on the quality of the visual representation; existence of verbal overshadowing; possible removal of verbal overshadowing by postpresentation information. The main assumption of the model holds that verbal recoding occurs spontaneously, almost immediately at the time of input (see also Bahrick & Boucher, 1968). Another assumption is that the duration of the inspection phase influences the quality of the visual representation. If subjects are shown the picture for a short time (e.g., 2 seconds), part of visual information is lost as a consequence of verbal recoding. Another consequence is that, after verbal recoding, the remaining part of visual information is overshadowed by the verbal code.

If subjects are shown the picture for a longer time (e.g., 5 seconds), they learn more visual details by virtue of a double shifting in the use of STM codes (visual-verbal-visual). That is, a 5-second presentation may prompt a process in which the visual input automatically loaded into the visual buffer is readily (e.g., within the first 2 seconds) recoded in a verbal form. However, because the stimulus is easily recognizable and nameable, one could use the time left available after recoding to keep visually analyzing the figure. As stated earlier, when both codes are present, the verbal information tends to overshadow the visual information. In the case of a longer inspection time, though, the visual representation overshadowed by the verbal code is more detailed.

Our tentative model also takes into account the possible removal of verbal overshadowing by manipulating instructions. Providing appropriate suggestions about the alternative interpretation may facilitate removal of verbal overshadowing by inducing the most effective strategy to use for exploiting the encoded visual information. Therefore, performance in image reversal tasks should reflect both the amount and the accessibility of the visual information originally encoded during loading.

However, it should be noted that more or less effective strategies may be prompted by different kinds of suggestions. Implicit suggestions (such as the use of demonstration figures whose reversals entail a change in the reference frame that is similar to the change necessary to reverse the test figure) were found to be more helpful in prompting reversals than were explicit hints (Peterson et al., 1992). Indeed, explicit hints such as information about either the orientation or the category of the second interpretation of the image showed no beneficial effect on reversals, unless they were combined (Hyman & Neisser, 1991; Peterson et al., 1992). One way of explaining these findings is that implicit hints intervene prior to picture presentation, hence affecting the way in which the picture is initially encoded in STM. That is, implicit hints may act similarly to articulatory suppression: They simply prevent people from verbally recoding the picture in STM. On the other hand, explicit hints are active after encoding. Hence, their effect may be due to the removal of verbal overshadowing.

This model, although partially speculative, explains a large body of results. It accounts not only for the lack of reversal reported by Chambers and Reisberg (1985), Hyman and Neisser (1991), and Peterson et al. (1992), but also for the positive results reported by Hyman and Neisser (1991), Peterson et al. (1992), and, most recently, by Reisberg and Chambers (1991), Chambers and Reisberg (1992), and Kaufmann & Helstrup (1993).

In general, our results are in accordance with Chambers and Reisberg's suggestion that image reversal is constrained by an interpretive bias that limits its occurrence. However, this interpretive bias can be *prevented* by using manipulations which are effective before inspection (implicit hints) or during inspection (articulatory suppression); alternatively, it can be *removed* by providing instructions that act on people's understanding of their images (explicit hints). The first case would reflect prevention of STM verbal recoding, whereas the second case would reflect release from verbal overshadowing (Brandimonte & Gerbino, 1993; see also Brandimonte et al., 1995b).

Yet, the notion of an "interpretive bias" remains somewhat vague if it is not related to the issue of the relationship between ambiguity and interpretability/ reinterpretability of visual mental images. To try to shed some light on the question asked in this section, it seems worthwhile to analyze in more detail the notion of "ambiguity" of a mental image.

In their 1985 paper, Chambers and Reisberg claimed that images cannot be ambiguous and *therefore* they cannot be reinterpreted. That is, the concepts of ambiguity and interpretability were treated as synonyms. If an image was ambiguous, it would be interpretable and therefore reinterpretable. But, according to their view, an image is not ambiguous because it is already interpreted and, as such, it is not reinterpretable. No reconstrual can exist because a construal process does not exist.

In most recent studies, Chambers and Reisberg's position has gradually shifted toward a more articulated explanation of the relation between ambiguity and interpretability of mental images. Reisberg and Chambers (1991) and Chambers and Reisberg (1992) have suggested that, although unambiguous, images can be open to reinterpretation. That is, an image is always interpreted (and, therefore, unambiguous) in the sense that it is obligatory, understood within a reference frame that specifies orientation, figure-ground organization, parsing, and a center. Nonetheless, it can be given a different interpretation, provided understanding of it is changed.

Thus far we treated the relation between ambiguity of an image and its interpretation as a symmetrical relation. More specifically, the claim was that what is interpreted is by definition unambiguous and, vice versa, what is unambiguous has been necessarily interpreted. However, at this point we would like to break the symmetry and suggest that at least a possibility exists that an image that has been interpreted is, nonetheless, ambiguous. The claim here is that the concept of "ambiguity" may refer to the existence in the surface image of elements that are not functional to the current interpretation. Stated in other words, such a claim means that under particular conditions an active image in working memory may exist that contains both interpreted parts and elements in a not-yet-analyzed state. These latter elements make the image "ambiguous" in the traditional sense of not being interpreted. However, the same image is also an interpreted one. In normal conditions (without articulatory suppression), the construction of an image from the image file implies that only the understood aspects shape the surface image and that reinterpreting that image simply means that another surface image is constructed that reflects the new understanding (see Chambers & Reisberg, 1992). Neither the first nor the second surface image can be regarded as ambiguous.

To the contrary, in our view the important effect of articulatory suppression is that it makes more difficult the verbal/semantic analysis and forces a kind of construction process that takes from the image file more information for the interpretation than is needed. Such a "surplus" will be interpreted only later, and therefore until then part of the image will remain ambiguous. It is important to bear in mind that, once it has occurred, verbal overshadowing cannot be removed by using articulatory suppression, although it can be alleviated by using explicit hints or retrieval cues (release from verbal overshadowing). On the other hand, if articulatory suppression is used during learning, verbal overshadowing *does not* occur.

One often-raised question concerning the effect of articulatory suppression is that it may simply reflect distraction, rather than specific interference with verbal encoding. That is, subjects would be focused away from carrying on other mental operations including verbal recoding. If so, any other task similar to articulatory suppression, but not specific to the verbal modality, should produce the same effect. To test this hypothesis, in a recent study on the duck/rabbit reversal, we replaced articulatory suppression with tapping as a secondary task. Results showed no facilitation in the imagery task (only 2 subjects out of 20 reversed the image), hence supporting the view that the effect of articulatory suppression reflects specific interference with the verbal/semantic modality rather than general distraction.

As is clear from this discussion, there seems to be no disagreement between Chambers and Reisberg's position and ours. What we suggest is that the mechanisms underlying the image-construction process will differ according to the presence of articulatory suppression. In our view, the most important implication is that without articulatory suppression, given that the image lacks important information for image reversal, it is necessary to go back to the image file and retrieve the raw material needed for the construction of a new image. When articulatory suppression is added during learning, the image contains all information needed for reinterpretation, and no need of going back to the image file is assumed. Such a mechanism would explain why, under articulatory suppression, instructions about the strategy to use for reversal have no effect, whereas in normal conditions they yield remarkable results. It is conceivable that the specific role of instructions and retrieval cues is that of suggesting to subjects the correct way to go back to the image file and take the correct information for the new interpretation. In this way, the image is never ambiguous, although it can be said that the original representation has been reinterpreted.

If one analyzes the mental representations stemming from these two different mechanisms in terms of *depictive potentiality,* a further distinction arises, in that images formed under conditions in which articulatory suppression is not present are fully interpreted, and therefore they have virtually zero depictive potentiality, whereas images formed under articulatory suppression embody not-yet-actual interpretations, and therefore they can be seen as having a high depictive potentiality.

To turn to the question asked in this section, that is, whether an image can be unbiased, the points made above imply a yes answer. Let us illustrate why such an answer descends from the above discussions.

Ambiguity and Centering

Consider Mach's square/diamond demonstration shown in Figure 2.3 (see Mach, 1885), which is probably the most famous and straightforward effect of orientation on perceived shape. In the Mach effect, the same geometrical form looks "different" depending on orientation, and is spontaneously described by using different words. When sides are vertical/horizontal the pattern is usually called "a square"; when sides are oblique the pattern is usually called "a diamond." It is commonly assumed that these words reflect distinct perceptual organizations,

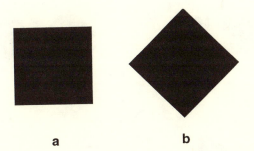

a   **b**

FIGURE 2.3. The Mach square/diamond.

evoking an impression of stability in the first case and of instability in the second.

As recently noted by Leyton (1992, p. 349), the meaning of this phenomenon is not always fully appreciated. In the attempt to understand it better, we shall use a neutral term—"tetragon"—to denote the abstract stimulus pattern, namely the regular polygon with four equal sides and angles, regardless of its orientation. The Mach effect clearly reveals that the tetragon is potentially ambiguous, given that the same stimulus can support two different percepts.

There are no obvious reasons why perception of the tetragon should be influenced by orientation. One could argue that in such simple conditions orientation constancy should prevail. "Orientation constancy" is defined as the invariance of the perceptual representation despite changes of the projected image (due to rotation of the object or the observer in the image plane) and constitutes the rule in most natural conditions of observation (Rock, 1975).

The Mach effect can be regarded as a failure of orientation constancy. As such it suggests that observers cannot perceive all properties of the tetragon simultaneously. Only part of its structure is perceptually represented, depending on orientation. But what is the reason for such a failure of orientation constancy, despite the simplicity of the tetragon as a stimulus configuration?

It is unlikely that the reason is stimulus complexity or limitation of representational resources. Rather, a possible reason is the dominance of dynamics over geometry in perception. Let us discuss two alternative ways in which dynamic aspects could be embodied in form perception, and see how both predict the Mach effect.

Dynamic aspects could be embodied in the "visual gravity" assumption. Many phenomena suggest that forms, even when displayed in isolation, are perceptually referred to the top-bottom direction of visual space. The visual gravity assumption implies different roles for bottom versus top parts of the figure. When tetragon sides are vertical/horizontal, the lower one becomes the perceptual *base,* which phenomenally supports the whole form. Hence, the square conveys a sense of stability. When tetragon sides are oblique, diagonals are captured by the vertical/horizontal frame of reference and the form appears unstable.

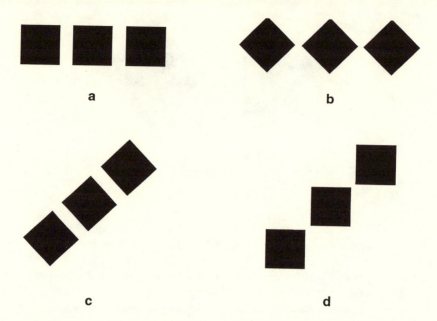

FIGURE 2.4. An example of multiple dynamic descriptions compatible with the same pattern.

An alternative way in which dynamic aspects could be embodied in form perception refers to the "generative procedure" assumption. Two procedures are available for the creation of the tetragon, both sufficient and compact, both simple and elegant. The square procedure is a symmetrical growth corresponding to a centrifugal displacement of sides; the diamond procedure is a symmetrical growth corresponding to a centrifugal displacement of vertices. These procedures are different, as shown by the fact that perturbations of the first would generate rectangles, and perturbations of the second would generate nonrectangular quadrilaterals.

Failure of orientation constancy of the tetragon is the deceptively simple demonstration that geometrical identity may be misleading, if used as the only foundation of form perception. Pattern perception must take into account dynamic factors, embodied as either visual field forces or generation constraints (for a recent formulation consider Leyton, 1992).

From a dynamic point of view, the geometrical fact that the tetragon has a fourfold symmetry is unfortunate, given that perception seems to be organized around only a pair of axes, the vertical and the horizontal. When two dynamic descriptions are compatible with the same pattern, only one will be instantiated in perception, the choice being dependent upon the main directions of the empty visual space (Figure 2.4) or of the including configuration (Figure 2.5).

The type of ambiguity illustrated by the Mach effect is easily captured by the notion of *centering*. According to Metzger (1963, Chapter 5), the same configu-

FIGURE 2.5. The drop/flame figure (adapted from Metzger, 1963, p. 25).

ration, under the same figure/ground and unification/segregation organization, can nevertheless support two (or more) interpretations corresponding to different centerings. This notion is intended to capture the phenomenal hierarchy of parts within a given whole. Certain parts are perceived as primary and necessary, others as secondary, derived, and accessory. The primary part can be a point, like the center of star structures, that is clearly perceived as the origin of the pattern, or a line, like the axis of a bilateral structure (e.g., a leaf).

Sometimes the same shape supports centering in two different origins, alternatively. This is the case with the drop/flame figure (Fig. 2.5, adapted from Metzger, 1963, Fig. 2.5). When the point of origin is on the top the pattern is perceived as a drop, with a downward directionality. When the point of origin is on the bottom the pattern is perceived as a flame, with an upward directionality.

Let us now discuss the Mach effect according to the centering notion. When the diamond is perceived (Fig. 2.3), parallelism of sides appears as a derived or secondary property, which goes unnoticed unless special attention is given to it. Parallelism of sides, if noticed, is perceived as something following from the symmetry of vertices. The opposite is true when the square is perceived. Orthogonality of the diagonals connecting the vertices appears as a secondary property, derived from the symmetrical pairings of equal sides.

Having clarified that two different generation procedures are equally effective, we have still left unanswered the basic question: Why are observers unable to hold a percept in which these two interpretations coexist? To grasp the meaning of this question, one has to use imagination and think of how a tetragon would appear if its square and diamond structures were simultaneously and equally present in awareness. The reason why this is not the case could simply be economy: Why should the system activate two descriptions if one is enough?

Note that this requirement does not hold for centering only. It regards other types of ambiguity as well—for instance, those dependent upon alternative parsings of the same pattern or upon relating the pattern to different reference frames.

Parsing

Study the two patterns in Figure 2.6. Then suppose you are asked to discover, using mental imagery, if the left or the right pattern contains a square. The dis-

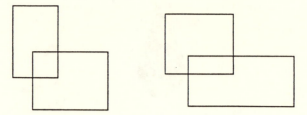

FIGURE 2.6.   An example of parsing-type reorganization.

covery requires a parsing-type reorganization. To support the alternative interpretation (two L-shaped surfaces surrounding a rectangular hole or juxtaposed to a rectangular surface) the line patterns must be analyzed in a way different from the most obvious one (i.e., two interlaced rectangles). As shown by Gottschaldt (1926; for a discussion see also Koffka, 1935, pp. 152–159), finding the embedded figure can be virtually impossible when the new parsing required by the task involves the breakage of strong natural bonds between parts, like the segmentation of portions of the same continuous line. Results obtained by Reed (1974) point in the same direction. The perception of embedded shapes is disrupted by the utilization of contour lines for an alternative construal.

Reference Frames

The typical ambiguity connected with the shifting between two alternative viewpoint-pattern relationships is represented by the Necker cube (Fig. 2.7). This phenomenon makes especially clear that what is ambiguous is not the graphical pattern, nor the percept. The graphical pattern simply is what it is: a distribution of pigments on a surface. As regards perception, one must say that two unambiguous percepts follow each other in close succession. The ambiguity pertains to the observer–object relationship. It is a relational property of the interpretation. This point must be kept in mind so as to maintain the appropriate critical position toward statements like "mental images can (or cannot) be ambiguous."

This being said, let us now return to the improvement in reversing the image of the duck/rabbit configuration observed under articulatory suppression conditions. One suggestion might be that articulatory suppression, by discouraging subjects from focusing on the duck or the rabbit conceptualization, diminishes the degree to which the image is *centered* on either the duck's bill or the rabbit's nose. If so, it is more likely that the image is clear enough on both contours to support both interpretations, and therefore reinterpretation. That is, being discouraged from thinking of a specific interpretation might push subjects into a more "neutral stance" and leave them with an unbiased image that is uniformly clear and detailed. Apparently, then, one can find a visual center in the image that favors neither the duck nor the rabbit. If the subjects are induced to imagine the form with this specific center, then they will have a mental representation that is compatible with both construals (Daniel Reisberg, personal communication).

The centering idea implies that the representation is "sympathetic" to more

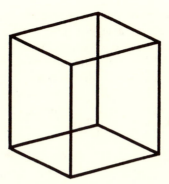

FIGURE 2.7. The Necker cube.

than one form, and therefore that it is multiply interpretable. According to Reisberg, the image is always unambiguous although it can be centered in a fashion that allows reinterpretation. Although this proposal is fascinating, we would like to endorse a more general interpretation that, nonetheless, incorporates the "centering" idea. In our view, the duck/rabbit image can be unbiased not just because it has been centered in a way that makes both construals possible (this is a special case of a more general process) but because the constraints posited by the reference frame have been weakened, in the experiments discussed here, by articulatory suppression. In a sense, one might argue that articulatory suppression emphasizes ambiguity, and whenever ambiguity is preserved, images can be reorganized by virtue of their depictive potentiality. Such a view embodies the "centering" idea. However, it also relates ambiguity and centering under a more general principle.

IMAGES AND PICTURES

The imagery debate—i.e., the attempt of answering questions about the pictorial versus propositional nature of mental images—has involved the evaluation of a huge number of theoretical arguments and empirical data (Tye, 1991). Apart from its complexity, which mainly depends upon the amount of relevant information accumulated during the last two decades, another aspect of the debate may generate some perplexity.

Several arguments utilize the comparison between imagery and perception as a source of clarification. Because imagery appears more mysterious and obscure than perception, or at least fuzzier, arguments by analogy or contrast use the second as the known term, to elucidate features of the first. The assumption, which in most cases is accepted without even a short word of caution, is that we know enough about perceptual facts and mechanisms to use this domain as a safe reference for our "as well as" or "differently from" arguments (a notable exception is the position represented by Reisberg & Chambers, 1991).

The recent debate on the possibility of mental images being ambiguous has shown that very often the analogy between imagery and perception subtends a naive theory of perception. An adequate analogy presupposes a sophisticated theory of perception, based on a few basic dogmas: pictures as physical bodies and pictures as perceived objects are different entities; percepts always are partially indeterminate; pictorial vision is different from ordinary vision.

The definition of mental images as "pictures in the head" is so appealing that a clarification of what counts as a picture is necessary.

Pictures

Generally speaking, a picture P of an object O is another object, different from O itself, but capable of "standing for" it, because of some intrinsic similarity.

This definition tries to capture four important requirements of pictures, relative to neighbouring concepts.

1. A picture is a linguistic notion in the sense that it involves reference to an object. Note, by contrast, that not all paintings are pictures. If an abstract painting is evaluated as such, and no depicting function is attributed to it, then it is an object, not a picture.

2. Normally, a picture is distinguishable from the depicted object. We can tell them apart and judge which is which, if they happen to be side by side. Therefore, pictorial self-reference (a picture which represent only itself) should be considered as a degenerate case.

3. Reference, as defined by requirement 1 above, is supported by an intrinsic relationship between P and O. This requirement characterizes pictures as elements of iconic language, as opposed to verbal language. If the relationship between sign S and object O is arbitrary, then S is not a picture. This is not the case, however, for all elements of natural verbal languages.

4. An intrinsic relationship between P and O supports phenomenal similarity between the percept induced by picture P and the percept induced by object O. This phenomenal homology is critical to the overall symmetry of picture/object recognition: We can recognize our house in a photograph, or find a house in a novel district thanks to knowledge acquired through inspecting its photograph. Of course, failures of recognition can occur in both cases and for different reasons, but they do not invalidate the claim that recognition eventually depends on the similarity of the two experiences.

Given this definition, the term "picture," if it is used in its literal sense, should be restricted to denote a two-dimensional depiction only, which refers to the painting technology. It is almost trivial to observe that, in the context of the imagery debate, limiting ourselves to this literal meaning would be misleading. The essential aspect of pictures is that they are means for displaying information (to use a Gibsonian formula). They provide information supporting pictorial perception, which is different from claiming that they are objects of pictorial perception. This last capability is crucial to the issue of mental imagery.

Three further points need some clarification before considering the relationship between pictures and images.

Origin of pictures: Artifactual vs. natural

Most people know how to produce simple pictures of objects, although difficult cases exist and sometimes a special training is required. Furthermore, as a result of technological development, we know several artifactual procedures for picture making. However, these achievements should not obscure the fact that pictures can occur in nature—for instance, as by-products of complex or quasi-chaotic phenomena (clouds, flames, rock formations, coast profiles). The origin of the picture is irrelevant, if we are primarily interested in the phenomenology of pictorial representations. Therefore, suppose that the mind produces pictures as the fire produces recognizable flame patterns. In both cases we can concentrate on the interpretation of these peculiar materials, disregarding their origin.

Stability vs. instability over time

Pictures can be very stable, as the cave paintings of our ancestors, or transient as the majestic physiognomies that come and go in the sky, when winds play with clouds. Duration as such is irrelevant to the basic definition of pictures as symbols. In the case of imagery, if the transformation of a given mental content is consistent with a single imaginal event, then the observer will experience continuity, otherwise he or she will experience substitution of an imaginal scenario with another.

Pictorial vs ordinary vision

One can define pictorial vision in two ways: with reference to the stimulus or with reference to the observer. If the stimulus is considered, any time we look at pictures, and only when we look at pictures, the pictorial vision modality is activated. This is true very often, but not always. However, pictorial vision can also be identified with the "seeing as" experience. Whenever the observer experiences a separation between the meaning of the object that is being experienced and the object per se then the pictorial modality is activated. In this sense, pictorial vision is our "metaphorical modality" that allows humans (the most inventive of them) to see the face of a monkey in the front of a car, for instance. The notion of *seeing as* is discussed at length by Hanson (1972, Chapter 1).

Images as Pictures

Given these premises, we can now address the question: Are mental images pictures-in-the-head? Certainly they are not, if one correctly thinks of pictures as two-dimensional, or even three-dimensional, uninterpreted physical objects. But they are, if one fails to distinguish between pictures and the results of looking at pictures. In this second sense, images are like pictures because they are experienced as objects of pictorial perception.

Phenomenologically speaking, experiencing mental imagery is like pictorial perception in one important respect. Let us make explicit this connection. In the absence of the object of reference, which can be absent because it is too far, too close, too large, too small, or—fatal defect—inexistent, a public or private simulacrum can be generated. A convenient name for the first is *picture* and for the second *image,* although in everyday language the term "image" is commonly used to denote also public pictures, making indispensable to qualify the second as "mental." These two ways of evoking what is absent are unified by the awareness that the object of reference is not really there, in front of us, and yet we are not just imposing an interpretation to raw stimulus or memory material. This is probably the meaning of Wittgenstein's remark: *"seeing as . . . is not part of perception. And for that reason it is like seeing and again not like"* (Wittgenstein, 1953, p. 196).

Representational Indeterminacy

Public and private pictures have their own distinct advantages and drawbacks. Public pictures are mailable, hangable, or locatable in the middle of a square for the enjoyment and benefit of future generations. Furthermore, being an external means for displaying information, once generated they support exploration and discovery without overloading the observer's cognitive resources. However, what is saved on the perception side is spent on the production side. To allow communication between different agents, the production of public pictures must take into account receivers' limitations. Not trivial instances of picture production (like those involved in naturalistic painting, film making, sculpturing, mimic acting, and dancing) require a great deal of know-how, well beyond the explicit capabilities of many people. Only part of this knowledge has to do with the control of the medium, in a low-level sense. The real, difficult problems regard the ability to anticipate the effects that the information so displayed will induce in a new observer who, in principle, should apprehend features of the displayed object only through the supporting power of the picture.

The situation with mental images, our private pictures, is different. They need to satisfy ourselves and therefore allow us to be more sketchy about aspects that, at a given time, are not critical to the current goal (see Kolers & Smythe, 1984, on personal symbols). Playing with indeterminacy is central in both public and private picture making, but in the case of private pictures the risks of leaving important aspects out of the representations are minimal. Whatever the current goals directing imagery are—support of action, satisfaction of desire, reduction of anxiety—they will guarantee a high degree of correspondence between relevant and generated aspects. Failures to generate the relevant image support this claim. Suppose you are struggling with the following visualization problem: "Find the solid which perfectly fits three holes: circle, square, and isosceles triangle (such that circle's diameter, square's side, basis, and height of the triangle are all the same)." The inability to generate the relevant image is immediately detected and a new generation routine is started.

One goal in the generation of private pictures has to do with exploration and discovery. Suppose you need to reach a distant place, which is out of view, and the conventional route is blocked. If you know the environment, the achievement of this goal is facilitated by inspection of a mental map in which alternative routes can be planned and possible difficulties can be evaluated. These possibilities depend upon a basic feature of all pictures, which is characteristic also of mental images: their capability of supporting simulation.

MAKING THE CONNECTIONS: IMAGES, PICTURES, AND VERBAL PROCESSES

When considering the important role of imagery in discovery and exploration, the debate about the hypothesized "rigidity" of mental images (their being tied to a specific interpretation, when the original picture is ambiguous) may appear paradoxical. Often, imagery and creativity are treated as synonymous, so that images might be considered as the best medium for mental discoveries. Our work on verbal recoding represents one attempt at distinguishing between the intrinsic richness of images (their depictive potentiality) and some constraints on their utilization. Such constraints are somewhat "extrinsic" in that they do not belong to the image itself, but to the processes through which images can be utilized. Images are neither rigid nor flexible. However, they do have picture-like properties. For example, the phenomena of centering and parsing discussed earlier emphasize the possibility for images to embody multiple organizations. Such a "possibility of" reflects their being potentially depictive in more than one way and, therefore, ambiguous. However, the necessary condition for such a possibility to become real is that those external constraints (such as verbal recoding), which would fix the meaning of an image and focus the subject away from alternative interpretations, be unbound. Indeed, the difference in the rate of reversals commonly observed during imagery and perceptual conditions might reflect the need for maintainance processes, in the imagery conditions, which, being based on verbal recoding, posit important constraints to subsequent image manipulation. This view strictly relates to the more general question of the distinction between articulated and nonarticulated thought.

The relationship between language and thought is not always a symbiotic one: Imagery, as well as other forms of thoughts (such as insight processes, see Schooler et al., 1993), may not be mediated by language. As a consequence, trying to articulate images may result in interference.

To conclude, we believe that the best answer to the question of why mental images are so effective (for instance, as mnemonic tools) is still "Because, for a *good observer*, inspection and manipulation of mental images (our private pictures) is like inspection and manipulation of a public picture."

Mental discoveries involve making explicit what is implicit in a given set of data and not represented in the current interpretation (see our definition of ambiguity). In this sense, a good observer is one who is able to exploit the depictive potentiality of mental images. The more the observer will rely on nonarticulated thought, the more he or she will succeed in mental discoveries. Some of the results discussed in this chapter demonstrated that, under appropriate conditions, anyone can behave as a *good observer*, provided verbal recoding is blocked and the use of nonarticulated thought facilitated.

CONCLUSIONS

An explanation of how memory influences imagery is central to our understanding of both the imagery process and the organization and functioning of memory systems. In this chapter we have argued for a view emphasizing the importance of verbal recoding processes in affecting the accessibility of visual memories. Memory for a visual stimulus is susceptible to verbal overshadowing, and this affects people's ability to manipulate their mental images. These negative effects of verbal recoding may, nonetheless, be either prevented to occur or removed once they have occurred. The latter case can be taken as a demonstration that the visual memories necessary for successful image transformations are simply "inaccessible," not definitively "lost." Finally, our work suggests important differences between articulated and nonarticulated thought.

Some ideas and findings reported in this chapter are somewhat preliminary. Nonetheless, they were presented in the hope that they draw attention to the issue and perhaps stimulate further discussion.

ACKNOWLEDGMENTS

The research reported in this chapter was supported by grants from the NATO (CRG 9111031) to Walter Gerbino, Graham Hitch, and Peter Walker, and from the National Research Council of Italy (90.03517.CT08) to Walter Gerbino. We wish to thank Cesare Cornoldi, Bob Logie, and Marc Marschark for helpful discussions and suggestions on an earlier version of this work.

REFERENCES

Babbit, B. C. (1982). Effect of task demands on dual coding of pictorial stimuli. *Journal of Experimental Psychology: Learning, Memory & Cognition, 8,* 73–80.

Baddeley, A. D. (1966). Short-term memory for word sequences as a function of acoustic, semantic, and formal similarity. *Quarterly Journal of Experimental Psychology, 18,* 362–365.

Baddeley, A. D. (1986). *Working memory.* Oxford: Clarendon Press.

Baddeley, A. D. (1990). *Human memory: Theory and practice.* London, LEA.

Baddeley, A. D. (1992). Is working memory working? The fifteenth Bartlett lecture. *Quarterly Journal of Experimental Psychology, 44,* 1–31.

Baddeley, A. D., & Hitch, J. G. (1974). Working memory. In G. H. Bower (Ed.), *The psychology of learning and motivation.* (Vol. 8, pp. 47–90). New York: Academic Press.

Baddeley, A. D., Lewis, V. J., & Vallar, G. (1984). Exploring the articulatory loop. *Quarterly Journal of Experimental Psychology, 36,* 233–252.

Baddeley, A. D., & Lieberman, K. (1980). Spatial working memory. In R. S. Nickerson (Ed.), *Attention and performance* (Vol. 8, pp. 521–539). Hillsdale, NJ: Laurence Erlbaum.

Baddeley, A. D., Thomson, N., & Buchanan, M. (1975). Word length and the structure of short-term memory. *Journal of Verbal Learning and Verbal Behavior, 14,* 575–589.

Bahrick, H. P., & Boucher, P. (1968). Retention of visual and verbal codes of the same stimuli. *Journal of Experimental Psychology, 78,* 417–422.

Bartlett, J. C., Till, R. E., & Levy, J. C. (1980). Retrieval characteristics of complex pictures: Effects of verbal encoding. *Journal of Verbal Learning and Verbal Behavior, 19,* 430–449.

Bekerian, D. A., & Bowers, J. M. (1983). Eyewitness testimony: Were we misled? *Journal of Experimental Psychology: Learning, Memory & Cognition, 9,* 139–145.

Bower, G. H. (1972). A selective review of organizational factors in memory. In E. Tulving & W. Donaldson (Eds.), *Organization of memory* (pp. 93–137). New York: Academic Press.

Brandimonte, M. A., & Gerbino, W. (1993). Mental image reversal and verbal recoding: When ducks become rabbits. *Memory & Cognition, 21,* 23–33.

Brandimonte, M. A., Hitch, G. J., & Bishop, D. V. M. (1992a). Influence of short-term memory codes on visual image processing: Evidence from image transformation tasks. *Journal of Experimental Psychology: Learning, Memory & Cognition, 18,* 157–165.

Brandimonte, M. A., Hitch, G. J., & Bishop, D. V. M. (1992b). Verbal recoding of visual stimuli impairs mental image transformations. *Memory & Cognition, 20,* 449–455.

Brandimonte, M. A., Hitch, G. J., & Bishop, D. V. M. (1992c). Manipulation of visual mental images in children and adults. *Journal of Experimental Child Psychology, 53,* 300–312.

Brandimonte, M. A., Hitch, G. J., Walker, P., & Del Bello, R. (1995a). *Size-congruency effects in short-term memory and long-term memory.* Unpublished manuscript.

Brandimonte, M. A., Schooler, J. W., & Gabbino, P. (1995b). Attenuating verbal overshadowing through visual retrieval ones. Unpublished manuscript.

Brooks, L. R. (1967) The suppression of visualization by reading. *Quarterly Journal of Experimental Psychology, 19,* 289–299.

Brooks, L. R. (1968). Spatial and verbal components of the act of recall. *Canadian Journal of Psychology, 22,* 349–368.

Carmichael, L., Hogan, H. P., & Walter, A. A. (1932). An experimental study of the effect of language on the reproduction of visually perceived forms. *Journal of Experimental Psychology, 15,* 73–86.

Chambers, D., & Reisberg D. (1985). Can mental images be ambiguous? *Journal of Experimental Psychology: Human Perception and Performance, 3,* 317–328.

Chambers, D., & Reisberg, D. (1992). What an image depicts depends on what an image means. *Cognitive Psychology, 24,* 145–157.

Chandler, C. C. (1991). How memory for an event is influenced by related events/Interference in modified recognition tests. *Journal of Experimental Psychology: Learning, Memory & Cognition, 17,* 115–125.

Christiaansen, R. E., & Ochalek, K. (1983). Editing misleading information from memory: Evidence for the coexistence of original post-event information. *Memory & Cognition, 11,* 467–475.

Clark, H. H., & Clark E. V. (1977). *Psychology and Language,* New York: Harcourt.

Conrad, R. (1964). Acoustic confusion in immediate memory. *British Journal of Psychology, 55,* 75–84.

Craik, F. M. I., & Tulving, E. (1975). Depth of processing and the retention of words in episodic memory. *Journal of Experimental Psychology: General, 104,* 268–294.

Daniel, T. C., & Ellis, H. C. (1972). Simulus codability and long-term recognition memory for visual form. *Journal of Experimental Psychology, 93,* 83–89.

Darley, C. F., & Glass, A. L. (1975). Effect of rehearsal and serial list position on recall. *Journal of Experimental Psychology: Human Learning and Memory, 104,* 453–458.

Ebbinghaus, H. (1885). *Über das gedächtnis.* Leipzig: Dunker.

Ellis, H. C. (1973). Stimulus encoding processes in human learning and memory. In G. H. Bower (Ed.), *The psychology of learning and motivation* (Vol. 7, pp. 123–182). New York: Academic Press.

Farah, M. J. (1984). The neurological basis of mental imagery: A componential analysis. *Cognition, 18,* 245–272.

Farah, M. J., Hammond, K. M., Levine, D. N., Calvanio, R. (1988). Visual and spatial mental imagery: Dissociable systems of representation. *Cognitive Psychology, 20,* 439–462.

Finke, R. A. (1989). *Principles of mental imagery.* Cambridge, MA, and London: MIT Press.

Finke, R. A. (1990). *Creative imagery.* Hillsdale, NJ: Erlbaum.

Finke, R. A., & Schmidt, M. J. (1977). Orientation-specific color aftereffects following imagination. *Journal of Experimental Psychology: Human Perception and Performance, 3,* 599–606.

Finke, R. A., Pinker, S., & Farah, M. (1989). Reinterpreting visual patterns in mental imagery. *Cognitive Science, 13,* 51–78.

Frick, R. W. (1990). The visual suffix effect in tests of the visual short-term store. *Bullettin of the Psychonomic Society, 28*(2), 101–104.

Frost, N. (1972). Encoding and retrieval in visual memory tasks. *Journal of Experimental Psychology, 95,* 317–326.

Glanzer, M., & Clark, W. H. (1964). The verbal loop hypothesis: Conventional figures. *American Journal of Psychology, 77,* 621–627.

Gottschaldt, K. (1926). Über den einfluss der erfahrung auf die wahrnemung von Figuren. I. *Psychologische Forschung, 8,* 261–317.

Graefe, T. M., & Watkins, M. J. (1980). Picture rehearsal: An effect of selectively attending to pictures no longer in view. *Journal of Experimental Psychology: Learning, Memory, and Cognition, 6,* 156–162.

Hagendorf, H. (1992, September). *Effects of verbal tasks on visual working memory.* Paper presented at the *5th Conference of the European Society for Cognitive Psychology,* Paris.

Hanson N. R. (1972). *Patterns of discovery.* Cambridge: Cambridge University Press.

Hitch, G. J., Brandimonte, M. A., & Walker, P. (1995). Two types of representation in visual memory: Evidence from the effects of stimulus contrast on image combination. *Memory & Cognition, 23,* 147–156.

Hitch, G. J., Woodin, M. E., & Baker, S. (1989). Visual and phonological components of working memory in children. *Memory & Cognition, 17,* 175–185.

Humphreys, G., & Bruce, V. (1989). *Visual cognition: Computational, experimental, and neuropsychological perspectives.* Hillsdale, NJ: Erlbaum.

Hyman, I. E., & Neisser, U. (1991, April). Reconstruing mental images: Problems of Method. *Emory Cognition Project Report 19.* Atlanta, GA: Emory University.

Intons-Peterson, M. J. (1992, December). *The role of verbal and visual factors on short-term memory and on a mental subtraction task.* Paper presented at the 5th European Workshop on Imagery and Cognition (FEWIC), Tenerife. Canary Islands.

Intraub, H. (1979). The role of implicit naming in pictorial encoding. *Journal of Experimental Psychology: Human Learning and Memory, 5,* 78–87.

Intraub, H., Bender, R. S., & Mangels, J. A. (1992). Looking at pictures but remembering scenes. *Journal of Experimental Psychology: Learning Memory & Cognition, 18,* 180–191.

Intraub, H., & Richardson, M. (1989). Wide-angle memories of close-up scenes. *Journal of Experimental Psychology: Learning, Memory & Cognition, 15,* 179–187.

Jastrow, J. (1900). *Fact and fable in psychology.* Boston: Houghton Mifflin.

Kaufmann, G., & Helstrup, T. (1993). Mental imagery: Fixed or multiple meanings? In B. Roskos-Ewoldsen, M. J. Intons-Peterson, & R. E. Anderson (Eds.), *Imagery, discovery and creativity: A cognitive approach.* Amsterdam: Elsevier.

Kerr, N. H., & Winograd, E. (1982). Effects of contextual elaboration on face recognition. *Memory & Cognition, 10,* 603–609.

Klatzky, R. L., Martin, G. L., & Kane, R. A. (1982). Semantic interpretation effects on memory for faces. *Memory & Cognition, 10,* 195–206.

Koffka K. (1935). *Principles of gestalt psychology.* New York: Harcourt, Brace & World.

Kolers, P. A., & Smythe, W. E. (1984). Images, symbols, and skills. *Canadian Journal of Psychology, 33,* 158–184.

Kosslyn, S. M. (1980). *Image and mind.* Cambridge, MA: Harvard University Press.

Kosslyn, S. M. (1981). The medium and the message in mental imagery: A theory. *Psychological Review, 1,* 46–66.

Kosslyn, S. M., Brunn, J., Cave, K. R., & Wallach, R. W. (1984). Individual differences in mental imagery ability: A computational analysis. *Cognition, 18,* 195–243.

Kosslyn, S. M., Holtzman, J. D., Farah, M. J., & Gazzaniga, M. S. (1985). A computational analysis of mental image generation: Evidence from functional dissociations in split-brain patients. *Journal of Experimental Psychology: General, 114(3),* 311–341.

Kosslyn, S. M., Flynn, R. A., Amsterdam, J. B., & Wang, G. (1990) Components of high-level vision: A cognitive neuroscience analysis and accounts of neurological syndromes. *Cognition, 34,* 203–277.

Kurtz, K. H., & Hovland, C. I. (1953). The effect of verbalization during observation of stimulus objects upon accuracy of recognition and recall. *Journal of Experimental Psychology, 45,* 157–164.

Leyton M. (1992). *Symmetry, causality, mind.* Cambridge, MA: MIT Press, Bradford Book.

Lindsay, S. D., & Johnson, M. K. (1989). The reversed eyewitness suggestibility effect. *Bulletin of the Psychonomic Society, 27,* 111–113.

Loftus, E. F. (1981). Mentalmorphosis: Alterations in memory produced by the mental bonding of new information to old. In J. Long & A. Baddeley (Eds.), *Attention and Performance* (Vol. 9). Hillsdale, NJ: LEA.

Loftus, E. F. (1991). Made in memory: Distortions in recollection after misleading information. In G. H. Bower (Ed.), *The psychology of learning and motivation* (Vol. 27, pp. 187–215). New York: Academic Press.

Logie, R. H. (1986). Visual-spatial processing in working memory. *Quarterly Journal of Experimental Psychology, 38A,* 229–247.

Logie, R. H. (1989). Characteristics of visual short-term memory. *European Journal of Cognitive Psychology, 1,* 275–284.

Logie, R. H. (1990). Visuo-spatial long-term memory: Visual working memory or visual buffer? In C. Cornoldi & M. McDaniel (Eds.), *Imagery and Cognition.* New York: Springer-Verlag.

Logie, R. H., & Baddeley, A. D. (1990). Imagery and working memory. In P. J. Hampson, D. F. Marks, & J. T. E. Richardson, *Imagery: Current developments* (pp. 103–128). London: Routledge.

Logie, R. H., Zucco, G. M., & Baddeley, A. D. (1990). Interference with the visual short-term memory. *Acta Psychologica, 75,* 55–74.

Lupker, S. J., Harbluk, J. L., & Patrick, A. S. (1991). Memory for things forgotten. *Journal of Experimental Psychology: Learning, Memory & Cognition, 17,* 897–907.

Mach, E. (1885). *Die analyse der empfindungen* The analysis of sensations. New York: Dover.

Maki, R. H., & Schuler, J. (1980). Effects of rehearsal duration and levels of processing on memory for words. *Journal of Verbal Learning and Verbal Behavior, 19,* 36–45.

Marks, D. (1972). Individual differences in the vividness of visual imagery and their effect on function. In P. Sheenan (Ed.), *The function and nature of imagery.* New York: Academic Press.

Marr, D. (1982). *Vision.* San Francisco: W. H. Freeman.

Marschark, M., & Cornoldi, C. (1990). Imagery and verbal memory. In C. Cornoldi & M. McDaniel (Eds.), *Imagery and cognition.* New York: Springer-Verlag.

Massironi, M. (in press). *Il fisico e il fenomenico nelle immagini mentali.* In Marucci F. (Ed.), *Le immagini mentali. Firenze: NIS.*

MacLeod, C. M. (1988). Forgotten but not gone: Savings for pictures and words in long-term memory. *Journal of Experimental Psychology: Learning, Memory & Cognition, 14,* 195–212.

Metcalfe, J. (1990). Composite holographic associative recall model (CHARM) and blended memories in eyewitness testimony. *Journal of Experimental Psychology: General, 119.* 145–160.

Metcalfe, J., & Bjork, R. A. (1991). Composite models never (well, hardly ever) compromise: Reply to Schooler and Tanaka (1991). *Journal of Experimental Psychology: General, 120,* 203–210.

Metzger, W. (1963). *Psychologie.* Darmstadt: Steinkopff.

Murray, D. J. (1967). The role of speech responses in short-term memory. *Canadian Journal of Psychology, 21,* 263–276.

Murray, D. J., & Newman, F. M. (1973). Visual and verbal coding in short-term memory. *Journal of Experimental Psychology, 100,* 58–62.

Neisser, U. (1976). *Cognition and Reality.* San Francisco: Freeman.

Nelson, D. L., & Brooks, D. H. (1973). Functional independence of pictures and their verbal memory codes. *Journal of Experimental Psychology, 98,* 44–46.

Nelson, D. L., Brooks, D. H., & Borden, R. C. (1973). Sequential memory for pictures and the role of the verbal system. *Journal of Experimental Psychology, 101,* 242–245.

Nelson, D. L., & Reed, V. S. (1976). On the nature of pictorial encoding: A level of processing analysis. *Journal of Experimental Psychology: Human Learning and Memory, 2,* 95–102.

Paivio, A. (1971). *Imagery and verbal processes.* New York: Holt, Rinehart and Winston.

Paivio, A. (1975). Imagery and long-term memory. In A. Kennedy & A. Wilkes (Eds.), *Studies in long-term memory* (pp. 57–85). New York: John Wiley.

Paivio, A. (1986). *Mental representations: A dual-coding approach.* New York: Oxford University Press.

Paivio, A. (1991). *Images in mind: The evolution of a theory.* New York: Harvester Wheatsheaf.

Paivio, A., & Clark, J. M. (1990). Static versus dynamic imagery. In C. Cornoldi & M. McDaniel (Eds.), *Imagery and Cognition.* New York: Springer-Verlag.

Paivio, A., & Csapo, K. (1973). Picture superiority in free recall: Imagery or dual coding? *Cognitive Psychology, 5,* 176–206.

Peterson, M. A., Kihlstrom, J. F., Rose, P. M., & Glisky, M. L. (1992). Mental images can be ambiguous: Reconstruals and reference-frame reversals. *Memory & Cognition, 20,* 107–123.

Pezdek, K., Maki, R., Valencia-Laver, D., Whetstone, T., Stoeckert, J., & Dougherty, T. (1988). Picture memory: Recognizing added and deleted details. *Journal of Experimental Psychology: Learning, Memory & Cognition, 14,* 468–476.

Phillips, W. A. (1983). Short-term visual memory. *Philosophical Transactions of the Royal Society of London, B302,* 295–309.

Potter, M. C. (1976). Short-term conceptual memory for pictures. *Journal of Experimental Psychology: Human Learning and Memory, 2,* 509–522.

Potter, M. C., & Faulconer, B. A. (1975). Time to understand pictures and words. *Nature, 253,* 437–438.

Prentice, W. C. H. (1954). Visual recognition of verbally labeled figures. *American Journal of Psychology, 67,* 315–320.

Quinn, J. G., & Ralston, G. E. (1986). Movement and attention in visual working memory. *Quarterly Journal of Experimental Psychology, 38A,* 689–703.

Rafnel, K. J., & Klatzky, R. L. (1978). Meaningful interpretation effects on codes of nonsense pictures. *Journal of Experimental Psychology: Human Learning and Memory, 4,* 631–646.

Reed, S. K. (1974). Structural descriptions and the limitations of visual images. *Memory & Cognition, 2,* 329–336.

Reisberg, D., & Logie, R. H. (1993). The ins and outs of working memory: Overcoming the limits on learning from imagery. In B. Roskos-Ewoldsen, M. J. Intons-Peterson, & R. E. Anderson (Eds.), *Imagery, discovery and creativity: A cognitive approach.* (pp. 39–76), Amsterdam: Elsevier.

Reisberg, D., & Chambers, D. (1991). Neither pictures nor propositions: What can we learn from a mental image? *Canadian Journal of Psychology, 45,* 336–352.

Reisberg, D., Smith, D. J., Baxter, D. A., & Sonenshine, M. (1989). "Enacted" auditory images are ambiguous; "pure" auditory images are not. *Quarterly Journal of Experimental Psychology, 3,* 619–641.

Richardson, J. T. E. (1980). *Mental imagery and human memory.* London: Macmillan.

Rock, I. (1975). *An introduction to perception.* New York: Macmillan.

Rundus, D. (1971). Analysis of rehearsal processes in free recall. *Journal of Experimental Psychology, 89,* 63–77.

Salamé, P., & Baddeley, A. D. (1982). Disruption of short-term memory by unattended speech: Implications for the structure of working memory. *Journal of Verbal Learning and Verbal Behavior, 21,* 150–164.

Schooler, J. W., & Engstler-Schooler, T. Y. (1990). Verbal overshadowing of visual memories: Some things are better left unsaid. *Cognitive Psychology, 22,* 36–71.

Schooler, J. W., Ohlsson, S., & Brooks, K. (1993). Thoughts beyond words: When language overshadows insight. *Journal of Experimental Psychology: General, 122,* 166–183.

Schooler, J. W., Ryan, R., & Reder, L. M. (1990, July). *Better the second time around: Representation reverses verbalization's impairment of face recognition.* Paper presented at the Conference on Memory, Lancaster, UK.

Schooler, J. W., & Tanaka, J. W. (1991). Composites, compromises, and CHARM: What is the evidence for blend memory representation? *Journal of Experimental Psychology: General, 120,* 96–100.

Scott, K. G. (1967) Clustering with perceptual and symbolic stimuli in free recall. *Journal of Verbal learning and Verbal Behavior, 6,* 864–866.

Segal, S. J., & Fusella, V. (1970). Influences of imaged pictures and sounds on detection of visual and auditory signals. *Journal of Experimental Psychology, 83,* 458–464.

Shepard, R. N. (1984). Ecological constraints on internal representation: Resonant kinematics of perceiving, imagining, thinking, and dreaming, *Psychological Review, 91* (4), 417–447.

Smith, S. M., Glenberg, A. M., & Bjork, R. A. (1978). Environmental context and human memory. *Memory & Cognition, 6,* 342–353.

Tulving, E. (1983). *Elements of episodic memory.* Oxford: Oxford University Press.

Tulving, E., & Pearlstone, Z. (1966). Availability versus accessibility of information in memory for words. *Journal of Verbal Learning and Verbal Behavior, 5,* 381–391.

Tulving, E., & Thomson, D. M. (1973). Encoding specificity and retrieval processes in episodic memory. *Psychological Review, 80,* 352–373.

Tversky, B. (1969). Pictorial and verbal encoding in a short-term memory task. *Perception and Psychophysics, 6,* 225–233.

Tversky, B. (1973). Encoding processes in recognition and recall. *Cognitive Psychology, 5,* 275–287.

Tye, M. (1991). *The imagery debate.* Cambridge, MA: MIT Press, Bradford Book.

Warren, C. E. G., & Morton, J. (1982). The effects of priming on picture recognition. *British Journal of Psychology, 73,* 117–130.

Watkins, M. J., Peynircioglu, Z. F., & Brems, D. J. (1984). Pictorial rehearsal. *Memory & Cognition, 12,* 553–557.

Wilson, T. D., & Schooler, J. W. (1991). Thinking too much: Introspection can reduce the quality of preferences and decisions? *Journal of Personality and Social Psychology, 60,* 181–192.

Wiseman, S., MacLeod, C. M., & Lootsteen, P. J. (1985). Picture recognition improves with subsequent verbal information. *Journal of Experimental Psychology: Learning, Memory & Cognition, 11,* 588–595.

Wittgenstein, L. (1953). *Philosophical Investigations.* New York: Macmillan.

CHAPTER 3

The Many Faces of Mental Imagery

Geir Kaufmann

A particularly recalcitrant problem in the philosophy and science of mind has been the clarification of the nature and function of imagery. The debate has been particularly long-standing and heated both in psychology and philosophy. This may seem strange since mental imagery seems to be a fairly minor, and even remote, corner of the mind. Some people (e.g., John B. Watson) even claimed that they did not have any mental imagery, and that they did well without it! Galton (1883) argued that imagery was a primitive form of cognition, prevalent in children and housewives. Yet an overwhelming amount of empirical evidence seems to show that imagery is a remarkably effective mediator of cognitive performance, ranging from short-term memory to creativity.

The general issue of the number, nature, and function of mental codes is, of course, important. Besides, the proper placement of imagery in the structural and functional context of the issue over mental representations clearly belongs to this debate.

There may, moreover, be deeper reasons why the imagery debate has taken such prominence in psychological and philosophical discussions. Apart from the specific interest of questions pertaining to the nature and functional properties of mental imagery, there are more far-reaching questions intimately related to these issues that speak directly to the validity of basic premises of general theories of mind.

In the context of philosophy, Alistair Hannay (1971) has suggested that the conceptual problems relating to the nature of imagery may lay the groundwork for an *experimentum crucis* on the validity of different philosophical theories of mind. According to Hannay, a clarification of such concepts as "mental image," "picturing," "seeing in the mind's eye," etc., is a particularly strategic way of getting to the basic premises of different general philosophical theories of mind. The psychological study of imagery has been driven by the same spirit and aimed at scrutinizing the basic premises of different theories of the nature of mental representations.

More specifically, the answers to the basic questions about the nature and functions of mental imagery may have critical implications for the validity of the mainstream computational theory of mind. Several prominent authors in the field have made explicit claims along these lines. Thus, the cognitive science philosopher Ned Block put forward the following argument:

> The relevance of the pictorial/descriptional controversy to the viability of the computer metaphors in cognitive science should be becoming visible. The computer metaphor goes naturally with descriptional representations, but it is not at all clear how it can work when the representations are nondescriptional. (Block, 1983, p. 535)

In a similar vein, the cognitive science critics Hubert and Stuart Dreyfus assess the importance of the issue in the following way:

> Computers, programmed as logic machines, cannot use images or any picture-like representations without transforming them into descriptions. (Dreyfus & Dreyfus, 1986, p. 90)

As will be argued later in some detail, these critical arguments seem to apply to current computational models of imagery processes, even to Kosslyn's analogy of a bit-mapped display (Kosslyn, 1980), which is probably the one that is worked out in most detail.

The importance of the imagery reconstrual debate lies precisely in the possibility of finding an empirically based answer to this question, which has languished in perennial, barren armchair speculations that seem largely to be premised on dubious a priori conceptions of the nature of mind (cf. Hannay, 1971), but can only be resolved by appeal to empirical evidence obtained by way of controlled experimentation.

In view of the multiplicity of theoretical models in the field of imagery (e.g., Hampson & Morris, 1978b, 1990; Kieras, 1978; Kosslyn, 1980, 1983; Marks, 1977, 1983; Marschark, 1987; Morris & Hampson, 1983; Neisser, 1976; Paivio, 1971b, 1975b, 1986, 1991), it may seem improper to put forward still another candidate. Yet, although all of the existing theories focus on important aspects of imagery, it seems clear that none of them are entirely logically coherent, and none are fully equipped to deal with the empirical evidence available.

The major aim of the present chapter, then, is to develop an alternative view of the conceptual status of imagery as a symbolic system, which I will argue is logically coherent. I will then use this conceptual platform to develop a theory of the nature of imagery and its functional role in cognitive performance. Although particular emphasis is placed on the role of mental imagery in the more complex mental activities involved in problem solving and creativity, the theory aspires to the status of a general model of imagery effects in cognitive performance.

Reaching for this goal I will proceed along the following path: To get to the roots of the assumptions behind the main theories currently in circulation, I will trace their historical-philosophical origins. It is hoped that this will provide a firm and comprehensive basis for a critical evaluation of the core ideas of the theories in their present form. The conclusions drawn will form the point of departure for working out an alternative theoretical position.

The theoretical territory covered in this chapter is occupied by three major groups of imagery models:

1. *The Pictorialist theory.* In this theory, images are seen as analog representations of perceptual information. The image representation is held to correspond rather directly to concrete objects and situations, and to symbolize by way of resemblance to the object it "stands for." The conscious image is given a functional role in cognition by virtue of its quasi-perceptual properties, and the perceptual analog is thus seen to cover both the structural and functional properties of image and imaging (Kosslyn, 1980, 1983; Paivio, 1971b, 1975b, 1986, 1991; Shepard, 1978a).

2. *The Descriptionalist theory.* Both verbal and nonverbal information is held to be represented in a common, more abstract format. This underlying "deep structure" code is seen as "amodal," consisting of language-like, propositional representations. The real (or most important) cognitive work is seen to take place at this abstract and conceptual level of representation. Images are either regarded as epiphenomenal or assigned a secondary, supportive function in cognition (Anderson & Bower, 1973; Chase & Clark, 1972; Pylyshyn, 1973, 1981).

3. *The Process theory.* With reference to the traditional act-content distinction (e.g., Humphrey, 1959), the *process* aspect of imagery is emphasized, and the static, content aspect is either totally dismissed or considerably scaled down in importance.

THE PICTORIALIST THEORY

Pictorial Representations and the Imagist Theory of Classical Empiricism

The Pictorialist theory has firm roots in the Imagist theory of classical empiricism (cf. Price, 1969, and Tye, 1991, for comprehensive philosophical expositions, and Kaufmann, 1980, 1986, for implications for psychological theory). Because many of the basic conceptual ideas have been carried over into contemporary variants of the theory, it may be worthwhile to recapitulate its main features, as well as the arguments that have been brought against it.

In the Imagist theory, the mental image is given an epistemological key role. Its central thesis is that mental images, and especially *visual* images, constitute the very bedrock of cognition. The most clear-cut and systematically developed version of the theory was formulated by Berkeley (1710). In Berkeley's theoretical system, a distinction is drawn between *primary* and *secondary* symbolic systems. Mental images are the primary symbols, whereas all other symbols are secondary and derived. Among the secondary symbolic systems, language is the most important. Words get their meaning indirectly through their relation to images. Words, then, are *substitutes* for images. As substitutes, words may have an important function in cognition, since they can be manipulated more easily and quickly than can images. The theory does *not* entail, then, that thinking necessarily is done in images, as it is often erroneously interpreted (e.g., Horowitz, 1970). To the contrary, Berkeley claims that thinking occurs mainly in the medium of words, but that thinking is only *meaningful* when the words are *convertible,* either directly or indirectly, into the relevant images.

The Imagist conception of thinking was transferred in a wholesale fashion to the Structuralist psychology organized by Wundt and Titchener: Images form the basic substrate of thinking, whereas language is seen as a secondary symbolic system that is expedient to employ as a substitute for images (e.g., Titchener, 1910, 1914).

Why such primacy to images? As pointed out by the philosopher Price (1969), the thesis follows as a logical consequence of the Empiricist standpoint: Thinking must be related to reality. As thinking is mainly cognition *in absence* of direct contact with the objects in reality, images have the clear advantage over words in being nearer to the objects and situations they represent. Images serve, then, as the *fundamental link* between thinking and reality, and they thus constitute the basic meaning substrate of language.

However, this line of reasoning invites a number of serious problems. The basic assumption is that we have an immediate access to an independently given reality, directly accessible without intervening cognitive interpretations. The foundation for objective knowledge is, then, provided by way of the immediate sensations being represented in images in pure, undistorted form.

According to the classical image theory, then, concept formation is regarded as a matter of abstracting recurrent features directly given in sense experience. But, as many philosophers have convincingly argued (e.g., Geach, 1971; Rorty, 1980; Wittgenstein, 1953), there is nothing unambiguously given in sense experience. The content of our sense experience may always be interpreted in different ways, and the meaning is constructively conferred *upon* it, rather than directly given *in* it. Taking this argument one step further to imagery, it is instructive to consider some of the purely conceptual problems involved in the image theory of meaning. If a word elicits an image, it will always contain many features that are irrelevant to its meaning function. Let us say that the word "five" evokes an image of a hand with five fingers. We know that the form, color, and spatial arrangements of the fingers do not matter as far as the meaning is concerned. But this means that *the image itself has to be interpreted.* This implies that meaning *conceptually* precedes image. The conclusion seems to be that the image cannot fulfill any basic meaning function, and we have only pushed the problem of meaning one step further away.

Moreover, it can be shown that the grammar of "understanding the meaning" and "having images" is totally different (see, e.g., Baker & Hacker, 1980). A person's avowal concerning his or her images is authoritative. One's avowal concerning understanding may well be contested on the basis of his or her subsequent performance. Furthermore, while it is possible to keep an image in mind for two and a half minutes (see McKellar, 1957), it does not make similar sense to talk of keeping an understanding in mind for two and a half minutes. The conclusion must be that the meaning of a word cannot be equated with imagining its denotation.

In addition to the problems related to the semantic dimension of imagery, difficulties also accrue to the *conceptual* component of the image. How is it possible for images to function as *general* symbols, representing classes of objects and events?

The problem here is twofold: The image resembles one thing too closely, and at the same time resembles too many things (an image of a dog may resemble, say, an Alsatian—at the same time it also resembles wolves, foxes, animals, organisms, etc.). Thus, the image seems to be both too *specific* and too *ambiguous* to function as a general, conceptual representation. The problem is a serious threat to the Imagist theory. Verbal symbols easily meet the requirements for conceptual representation by way of their general token significance, yet they are regarded as secondary and derived from images. A convincing account of the way an image can function as a general symbol somehow must be provided by the Imagist theory.

A solution to the specificity problem is suggested by making a distinction between "occurrent images" and "dispositional (potential) images" (see Price, 1969). If, for instance, we attempt to think about dogs in general and form an image of a black dog, we are not misled into believing that all dogs are black, since other images are queued up (say, of a white dog) that may supplement and generalize the original image. But now we must ask what guides the supply of relevant images. The answer seems inescapable that we must somehow possess the abstract concept in the first place.

Where the ambiguity of images is concerned, it is suggested that the less vivid and detailed, and the more "general" and "schematic" the image is, the more easily it can fulfill its conceptual representational function. But how is such a "schematic" image formed? The world contains no schematic dogs! Thus, we seem to be faced with a paradox. It seems true that we can think about something quite general and abstract when imaging, although the precise test of this proposition ultimately hinges on controlled, experimental observation. At the same time, it seems clear that the image does not have a source of its own from its pure perceptual content to provide the conceptual content of our thoughts.

In view of the serious shortcomings of the Imagist theory, it is amazing how many of its intellectual genes have been active in shaping the form of our generation's imagery theories. Some of the more influential ones will now be reviewed.

With the primary aim of accounting for cognitive development, Bruner (1964; Bruner, Olver, & Greenfield, 1966) has treated imagery within a general theory of symbolic representation in cognition. Although Bruner clearly goes beyond the general empiricist theory of knowledge (e.g., his treatment of language as a cognitive instrument), his concept of iconic representation has many features in common with the orthodox Imagist theory.

First, images are seen to symbolize by way of *resemblance* to the objects they represent. Consequently, images are held to be closely linked to the *surface attributes* of things and are *concrete* and *static*. Second, imagery is seen as developmentally prior to language, and Bruner thus seems to think that imagery has a sort of bedrock function in providing a necessary substrate of knowledge for language to be founded upon. Imagery representations, then, function literally before language enters into the picture. No underlying representational code of a more abstract nature is specified, which could control the imagery function. To Bruner, then, images seem to be mental *pictures,* and here he seems to come close to one of the fatal ideas of the Imagist theory, which is the notion that an image can "stand on its own feet" in cognition. According to Bruner's theory, there is a long period in the child's life where thinking mainly occurs in pictures, before language gets internalized and makes it possible to mount to higher and more advanced levels of thought. However, as already suggested above, this is a very questionable idea.

The problem may be illustrated by way of an example presented by Fodor (1976). How could a sentence like "John is fat" be represented in a picture? A picture of John with a bulging tummy? If so, the picture representation does not distinguish the thought that "John is tall" or that "John is sitting, standing, or lying" for that matter. The conclusion must be that a picture cannot "speak for itself," and that images, consequently, are always *images under description.* In general, then, a typical mental image does not seem to be a mental entity that can "stand alone" as something that is "self-understanding" purely on the basis of its pictorial layout.

The major stimulus for the renewed interest in the nature of imagery and its functional role in cognition undoubtedly came from the monumental research contribution of Allan Paivio (1971b, 1976b, 1991). In Paivio's conceptual scheme, both imagery and verbal processes are given the status of theoretical constructs within the framework of a neobehaviorist mediational model. Paivio postulates a fundamental distinction between two symbolic codes—a verbal and a nonverbal imagery system, where *visual* imagery constitutes the main component. Although fundamentally independent, the two systems are assumed to be interconnected by way of implicit associations (a word may elicit an image and vice versa). Paivio's theory has, no doubt, served as a fruitful working model, and it has the merit of explaining a large number of interesting imagery effects in cognition. Nevertheless, his theoretical scheme seems to suffer from several weaknesses that limits its predictive and explanatory power (cf. Brandimonte, this volume). Here we will concentrate on some of the more important *conceptual* difficulties inherent in the model (see Kaufmann, 1980, 1986) for a more comprehensive critical discussion of Paivio's theory). The conceptual platform of Paivio's initial model seems to a large extent based on the premises of the orthodox Imagist theory. The image is seen to correspond rather directly to the thing it represents, and it symbolizes by way of resemblance to the thing it "stands for." The image is conceived, then, to be directly derived from perceptual experience, and the external events are held to be efficient causes of the resulting representation. As Yuille and Catchpole (1977) observe, no further mechanisms are required on the initial Paivio model for the acquisition of knowledge.

A corollary of this position is to regard the image as a *dominant component of meaning* (see also Bugelski, 1977, 1982). This position is, however, highly problematic. As argued above, the image cannot in general serve any basic meaning function, since the image itself has to be interpreted. Consequently, there must be something basically wrong with this kind of theory.

It is true that Paivio has argued against such criticism by claiming that it is directed against a straw man (Paivio, 1976b). As percepts are organized, selected, and interpreted, why should it be so difficult to accept that analog representations in imagery are interpreted as well? However, this line of reasoning merely seems to push the problem one step further and leave us with the question of how percepts are interpreted.

The dual-code theory has been defended by Anderson (1978) against such charges of internal inconsistencies. According to Anderson, images may be interpreted by being linked to words. Taken on its own, this argument has substance to it, yet now we must answer the question of how words gain meaning and are interpretable. Here Paivio would have to point to the image as the basic meaning substrate. However, we seem to be caught in a conceptual Catch-22 situation, leading into a vicious circle where it is impossible to escape. Certainly, one cannot explain the meaning of an image by reference to a word, and then interpret the meaning of the word by way of the image.

The conclusion seems inevitable, then, that there are serious shortcomings in Paivio's theoretical scheme. Problems also crop up when it comes to the *conceptual* dimension of the image. Paivio (1971b, 1986) asserts that images may be schematic and abstract. In fact, he criticizes Bruner for not acknowledging this possibility. It is certainly true that when we have an image, it may mean something highly abstract to us. Since it seems that Paivio endorses the classical distinction between images and words in the sense of imagery being a primary symbolic system, and language being secondary and derived, an answer somehow must be given to this question.

Because Paivio claims that the two symbolic systems are fundamentally *distinct,* we may conclude our discussion by asking how it is possible to think in a fundamentally nondiscursive pictorial medium at all. As any picture is indeterminate in its semantic and conceptual content, how are we to avoid getting utterly confused when thinking in a pictorial representational medium?

Recently, Paivio (1986; see also Paivio & Begg, 1981) has made an attempt to handle these problems by way of postulating a distinction between an *imagery system* and the *conscious imagery* itself.

The imagery system is characterized as a system "which somehow retrieves or generates conscious images as well as other external manifestations and the conscious imagery itself. The system can function without necessarily producing conscious imagery, although such images can occur if necessary" (Paivio & Begg, 1981, p. 114). This maneuver seems to us to be unsatisfactory for several reasons:

1. It is unacceptably vague, and no specification is given as to the nature of the postulated imagery system beyond the point that it is somehow responsible for the generation of images.

2. It invites the slippery concept of unconscious imagery. One of the disturbing things here is that in operating with such an extended concept of imagery, a protective belt may be laid around the theory and, thus, immunize it against criticism based on conceptual considerations as well as on empirical findings. The problem relating to the existence of abstract and conceptual images may be "solved" by reference to the ill-defined and elusive "imagery-system." Negative empirical findings may be "explained" by postulating unconscious imagery processes.

3. Moreover, if it is true that images are constructed under intentional descriptions and can stand for abstract ideas, as Paivio and Begg (1981, p. 114) admit, it must mean that the imagery system is fundamentally a *propositional* representational system. This is, perhaps, a possible solution, but it is not an attractive one, and it also leaves unsolved the problem of how to *translate* between the different representational systems.

The other major theory of the analog variant is the one developed by Kosslyn (Kosslyn, Pinker, Smith, & Schwartz, 1979; Kosslyn, 1980, 1983; Pinker & Kosslyn, 1983). According to Kosslyn, visual images are most properly conceived as temporary spatial "displays" in active memory. In Kosslyn's account, the image is a quasi-pictorial entity that *depicts* information, in contrast to *describing* it discursively. Thus, images stand in a *nonarbitrary* relation to the object it represents. In the words of Kosslyn and colleagues, "any part of that representation is a representation of the corresponding part of the object" (Kosslyn et al., 1979, p. 536). The image, then, symbolizes by way of resemblance to the object it represents. On this point, Kosslyn stands on the same empiricist foundation as does Paivio. Kosslyn departs, however, from Paivio's conceptualization when he claims that the "surface representations" of imagery are generated from a general and abstract system of deep-structure representations in long-term memory.

Because images are seen to be anchored in more abstract, conceptual representations, the essential property of the intentionality of images seems to have been taken care of. In light of this, Kosslyn takes a surprising turn in his theorizing when he insists on the existence and need for a separate interpretative mechanism (a "mind's eye") that works over ("looks at") the surface image with the purpose of identifying its various properties and sorting them into the proper semantic categories. Why should we have to do a second interpretation by way of "inspecting" an image that is constructed from an underlying conceptual representation? This dubious idea leads Kosslyn to the notion that the image *itself* has (rather than represents) spatial properties (extent, form, etc.) that can be measured. A large part of Kosslyn's research program seems to be aimed at uncovering the spatial properties of the image.

Hebb (1980) and Pylyshyn (1981) have pointed out that it is important to realize that when we have a visual image of an object, the spatial properties we "see" are properties of the object represented and *not* properties of the image *itself.* It is argued that when we have an image of a large tomato, it is the object represented that is large, round, and red—not the image. Although Kosslyn seems to be aware of these problems, the notion of the image as an object to be "inspected" by the "mind's eye" invites just this idea, and Kosslyn explicitly endorses the view that images do have spatial extension. In our view, much of the experimental evidence presented by Kosslyn can indeed be explained by assuming that his subjects interpret the tasks presented to them as requesting that they are to imagine what would happen under real perceptual conditions in relation to a situation specified by the experimenter. This point has been made by Pylyshyn (1981), when he claims that imagery is a process subject to "cognitive penetration."

In the so-called scanning experiments, subjects are asked to form an image of a scene (e.g., a map), which contains different objects at different positions. The subject is instructed to focus on a particular location of the image. Then he or she is asked to verify the existence of different objects at different distances from the focal point of the image. Results show that the decision time increases systematically with the distance to be "scanned." The results are easily explained under the very likely assumption that the subjects take their task to be that of simulating what would happen under actual perceptual conditions.

Kosslyn's counterclaim to this objection is that the distance effect only appears with tasks independently judged to involve imagery, and by subjects reporting that they did use imagery (Kosslyn, 1980). Kosslyn also refers to an experiment by Finke and Kosslyn (1980) where the subjects were asked to image pairs of dots moving toward the periphery and to report when the two dots were no longer distinct. A control group was included and informed about the instructions given to the experimental subjects. The task of the control group was to make the same judgment, and subjects were explicitly told *not* to use imagery. The control subjects were only partly successful in their judgments as to what happened in the imagery condition.

In other experiments, Kosslyn asks his subjects to form small or large images of objects (e.g., a cat); claims that the results show that it takes longer time to verify the existence of properties of small images substantiate the postulated quasi-pictorial properties of images, with the implication that small images are more difficult to "inspect" than are larger ones. What these results may be taken to mean, however, is that more details are brought forward in the construction of large images, which is validated by the finding that it takes longer time to construct larger images. Kosslyn attempts to control for this alternative explanation by comparing the relationship between decision time and association strength of a property to the *noun* of the object. He claims that the fact that the results showing that decision time is systematically related to the size and not to the association strength of a property excludes the alternative interpretation, namely that the decision time is longer for "cat claws" than for "cat head," where the property "claws" is more closely associated with the noun "cat" than is the property of "head." The results from comparing size with association strength to nouns seem to rule out a purely conceptual-propositional interpretation, yet they do not directly support an "inspection" interpretation. A more relevant comparison would be between decision time and the association strength of a property when the subject is *drawing a picture* of the object in question. It is reasonable to assume that subjects under imagery instructions are more likely to generate the property "cat head" than the property "cat claws" for the reason that imaging is more like *drawing* a picture than *seeing* a picture.

In a different series of experiments, subjects are asked to image an object as if it is seen from a long distance and then to imagine that they are gradually moving closer to the object. It is suggested that, at some point, the image will "overflow." At this point, the subject is to "stop" and estimate how far the object seemed to be. Results of these experiments show consistently that smaller objects seemed to overflow at nearer distances than larger ones. From these findings, Kosslyn goes on to make some bold suggestions. Kosslyn claims to have been able to measure the visual angle of the mind's eye, and, furthermore, that the imagery field seems to be round, which is held somehow to be a possible intrinsic property of the image. Again, the results may be interpreted in a less dramatic way. What is shown may only be that people are capable of simulating real physical events under ordinary perceptual conditions. A convenient way of solving the task set by the experimenter would be to simulate what would happen when one looks at the objects at the various distances through a lens and "zooms in" on the objects. The roundness of the imagery field may thus reflect the fact that a lens is round, and not that the image *itself* is round. Again, Kosslyn may be accused of confusing the properties of the image with the properties of the objects and scenes imagined.

It is always possible to find alternative interpretations to the results of a single experiment. The question is, however, whether the evidence from the whole series of experiments tends to support the "inspection" interpretation or the major alternative of the "tacit knowledge" interpretation. It seems clear that there is a third, compromise-alternative, that emerges as more plausible then the two initial positions. It may be true that when we engage in imagery in tasks like those Kosslyn has examined, we do, in fact, attempt to simulate what would happen under actual perceptual conditions. The results of Kosslyn's experiments do not seem to yield to a purely "propositional," "tacit knowledge" interpretation. Thus, we may argue that "inspecting" imagery is a convenient (or, in some instances, necessary) way of judging what happens under ordinary perceptual conditions, and that this is one of the important functions imagery brings to bear in cognition. Results of such experiments indicate that imaginal performance is truly functional and cannot be completely reduced to the utilization of tacit knowledge through a purely propositional representation as Pylyshyn (1981) seems to believe.

The pure "tacit knowledge" interpretation of imagery operations has also been addressed by experiments where the subjects are presented with tasks where the outcome cannot be predicted. Reed, Hock, and Lockhead (1983) performed an imagery scanning experiment where the subjects were given tasks such as scanning a straight line or a spiral. They found that the rate at which the subjects scanned the pattern was dependent on its shape. For instance, the straight line was scanned more quickly than an image of a spiral. With this task the subjects were unable to predict how the different shapes would influence their scanning time. Finke (1989) presented the results of a large number of experiments that converge on the same conclusion: In tasks where the expected outcome would not be obvious to the subjects—such as the McCullough after image effect in imagery—the performance of the subjects seem to indicate that there is a strong equivalence between perception and imagery, even at very low levels of processing.

Neurocognitive evidence seems to support the conclusion that a strong equivalence exists between perception and imagery, as postulated by Kosslyn.

Clinical observations by Luria (1976) and Farah (1988) of neurologically damaged patients show in general that left-hemisphere damage is linked to impairment on verbal tasks, whereas right-hemisphere damage is associated with impairment in the processing of visual material. Roland and Friberg (1985) recorded measurements of regional cerebral blood flow (rCBF) during verbal and visual imagery tasks. The imagery task involved imagining oneself walking through one's neighborhood. The different tasks activated different parts of the cortex. During the visual imagery task, blood flow was most dominant in posterior regions that include the occipital lobe and temporal import for higher visual processing and memory. Goldenberg, Podreka, Steiner, Suess, Deeke, and Willmes (1988) used single photon emission computer tomography PET scan to locate brain activity during imagery and nonimagery tasks. A typical imagery task was the question "Is the green of pine trees darker than the green of grass?" A nonimagery task would be a question like the following: "Is the categorical imperative an ancient grammatical form?" They found that the imagery tasks were associated with high levels of blood flow in the occipital regions and the posterior parietal and temporal visual processing areas. The nonimagery condition did not produce activation of similar brain areas.

As Kosslyn's theory is implemented in a computer program, it should effectively block arguments as to the incoherence of the notion of "mind's eye" operations interpreting a prior and independently formed image. Such a claim has, in fact, been made by Kosslyn et al. (1979).

However, Kosslyn's theorizing here goes far beyond his computer model. The procedure mainly responsible for the interpretive work, FIND, is, in fact, a *common* procedure. LOOK FOR is an inspection routine having the function of activating IMAGE, which is a generative procedure. There is, thus, simply no separate procedure that has the function of interpreting a prior and independently formed image. In the computer model, then, interpretation and construction are strictly commensurate procedures. An image may not, however, be determinate only under the interpretation that it was originally constructed. The image is typically a *dense* representation that may *give rise to* new interpretations. This may be one of the reasons why imagery seems to be such an important working-space in the search processes and restructuring activity needed in creative thinking (see, e.g., Kaufmann, 1980, 1983, 1988, 1993). The challenge, then, is to develop a computer model of imagery that is capable of imagery reconstrual in the sense of creatively generating new interpretations of the image that are not contained in the description that the image was originally constructed under.

A compromise solution of the Kosslyn-Pylyshyn controversy seems, thus, to be the most reasonable one. The idea that the image has, rather than represents, spatial properties is conceptually suspect, and it is not warranted by the empirical findings in Kosslyn's experiments. Pylyshyn's claim that imagery has no special function to fulfill beyond what can be accounted for by appealing to tacit knowledge and reasoning in a purely propositional format does not seem to stand up well against the experimental results presented by Kosslyn. The conclusion seems compelling that imagery is indeed functional and cannot be reduced to purely propositional reasoning based on task-relevant tacit knowledge.

The "double interpretation" process postulated in the theory is unacceptable as it stands in the Kosslyn model. Implementation of the theory in a computer model renders the construction and interpretation together. Thus, the interpretation based on "inspection" that is done by the program is superfluous, and the processes that are contained in the program are not capable of genuine, creative imagery reconstrual. The reconstrual capability of imagery may reflect an important property of the imagery system that distinguishes it from linguistic-propositional representations. We may distinguish between *initial* versus *alternative* content of the image. The primary content is the content as determined under its original intentional description. Yet, by way of its *perceptual* content, we may argue that there are "dormant," potential interpretations that are not "mentioned" in its original intentional formulation, and that can be discovered by inspecting its perceptual content (cf. Kaufmann, 1986, for an elaboration of this idea, and Brandimonte, this volume, for a similar view). This secondary content may be justifiably and aptly be described as being "seen" with the "mind's eye."

Thus we may reconcile the Propositional and Pictorialist theories by affirming *both* that images come in interpreted form as the propositionalist claim, *and* that images may be reinterpreted by way of a quasi-perceptual inspection process of the kind that the pictorialists posit.

In his Equivalence Model of imagery, Finke (1989) pursues the same track as Kosslyn (1980, 1983). Finke defines "mental imagery" as "the mental invention or re-creation of an experience that in at least some respect resembles the experience of perceiving an object or an event, either in conjunction with, or in the absence of, direct sensory stimulation" (Finke, 1989, p. 2). In practice, Finke takes the position that a close resemblance exists between perception and imagery. The conceptual point of departure for Finke's research program is formulated in the principle of "perceptual equivalence," which means that "imagery is functionally equivalent to perception to the extent that similar mechanisms in the visual system are activated when objects or events are imagined as when the same objects or events are actually perceived (Finke, 1989, p. 41)." From a series of experiments, Finke arrives at the conclusion that the correspondence between perceiving and imaging is indeed close, and may extend to an impressively low level of processing.

Finke has been able to demonstrate that a strong degree of equivalence *may* obtain between perception and imagery, yet Finke's research program may be criticized for being biased by focusing mainly on *similarities* of imaging and perceiving. Searching selectively for *differences* between the two kinds of mental activities might lead one to the opposite conclusion. Besides, his model seems to suffer from the same serious limitation as the Kosslyn model. It seems clearly to be a "special case" type of model, where there is no qualitative principle that distinguishes perception and imaging. Finke, like his Empiricist philosophical predecessors, seems clearly to contend that the distinction between the two kinds of phenomena is a matter of degree of intensity, in terms of vividness and detail in content.

The equivalence of imagery and perception is taken to such an extreme as to deny any distinction in terms of qualitative principles. Thus, there is no conceptual basis for making the required distinction between imagery and sensation. An unacceptable consequence of both Kosslyn's and Finke's theory is that the imager is left in a continuous "Perky state" (cf. Segal, 1972). By this is meant a state where the imager is fundamentally unable to distinguish between percepts and images. This would be the case if the only distinction between imagery and perception is the fragile difference in vividness.

We know that this is a special case, as with hallucinations or under special experimental conditions (Segal, 1972). Under ordinary circumstances, we are quite able to make this distinction. A basic requirement of a theory of imagery is that it contains a specification of those mechanisms that enable us to do so. A "weak percept" conception of images seems not to be sufficient in this regard.

THE DESCRIPTIONALIST THEORY

Propositional Representations and the Conceptualist Theory in Philosophy

A radically different account of the nature of imagery draws its main intellectual inspiration from what may be termed the Conceptualist theory, which is mainly rooted in Rationalist epistemology (see Price, 1969). According to the Conceptualist, the basic work in cognition is not mediated by either images or words. Rather, thinking is held to be a unique type of cognitive activity that may accompany and be expressed in language or imagery, and that may also occur in the *absence* of these. The proper substance of thinking is made up of mental entities of a special and abstract sort, variously described as "concepts," "abstract ideas," "deep units,", etc. Imagery is thus placed in a purely external and adventitious relation to the act of thinking and is either regarded as epiphenomenal or assigned a secondary, auxiliary function. The basic assumption behind theories in this category is that the content of an image may be completely assimilated to the intentional description under which it is constructed. No surplus meaning in terms of its sensory-perceptual content is allowed for.

The Logical Grammar of Imaging

It is noteworthy that the mental image has had a different fate in recent philosophical discussions compared to the empirically based treatment in psychology. Although the pro-imagery stance seems to dominate in psychology (e.g., Anderson, 1990), Dennett's claim that being able to dispose of mental images would be "a clear case of good riddance" (Dennett, 1969, p. 141) seems the more representative of the philosophical position. Contemporary philosophers try to establish the nature of mental concepts by charting the logical geography of these concepts (cf. Ryle, 1949). This is normally done through the Wittgensteinian procedure of probing the logical grammar of the concept in question (e.g., Wittgenstein, 1953). In the case of imagery, the aim of the analysis is to find the most appropriate conceptual analogies that can be used to express the facts about imaging.

As far as the negative claim about imagery is concerned, Shorter's (1952) influential Wittgensteinian analysis of the nature of imagery proceeds along the same track. According to Shorter, mental images are *not seen,* they are *not objects,* and therefore they *do not exist* (in the technical sense of not being independent objects). These counterintuitive claims are held to be forced upon us both by logical and empirical considerations. Expressions like "seeing a mental picture" have no logical use. Besides, it is held to be a matter of empirical fact that there is nothing we can literally see in imagery, not even in a lax and metaphorical sense of "seeing." A basic premise of these conclusions is that there is a radical distinction between imaging and perceiving. The basis of this distinction is: Whereas imaging is a "doing," perceiving is a "getting." This is because perceiving is a *relational* expression, in the sense that perception relates to an interpretively neutral object, whereas imaging relates to an intentionally constructed description that forms its essential content (see also Chambers & Reisberg, 1985; Dennett, 1982; Heil, 1982). Thus, the reality of the image is the *thought* of what the image is an image *of.* The conclusion follows that we cannot have an image of X without knowing that the image is *of* X, whereas we can perceive an object without knowing what the object is. Thus, "having an image" could not possibly be placed in the same logical category as "perceiving a picture." One important consequence of such arguments is that an image is totally fixed under its intentional description and cannot be ambiguous.

Are the experiments designed by psychologists to examine the issue of image detection and image reconstrual to be regarded as a philosophically naive ploy with a foregone logical conclusion? This implication clearly seems not to be valid. The point that imaging is more of a doing than perceiving and that images, at least in the paradigmatic case, are constructed under intentional descriptions are both well taken. These arguments do not, however, warrant the conclusion that the mental image is *entirely* determined by its descriptional content. On the contrary, the argument to this effect seems a clear case of begging the question, in the sense that it assumes as premise what is to be shown in the conclusion. In fact, the conclusion that the image is strictly commensurate with the thought of what the image is *of* seems to strip the mental image of its conceptual autonomy. Besides, by assimilating imagery strictly to thought, any special functional value of imagery as a self-contained form of cognition seems denied—a conclusion that clearly goes against the massive amount of empirical evidence that seems to attest for an important and independent functional role of imagery in cognition.

The Conceptualist theory was brought into experimental psychology by the members of the Wurzburg school (see Mandler & Mandler, 1964). In their kernel idea of "imageless thought," thinking is seen as a fresh mental category that does not require representation through any kind of symbolic particulars (i.e., images and words). The basic elements of thought are "abstract ideas," rather than concrete images.

Within the Conceptualist theory there is no problem in accounting for the semantic and conceptual content of images, since images are seen as the *products* of more basic, abstract mental processes that are conceptual in nature. It also escapes the problem of identifying thinking with the mere occurrence or production of symbols in "full dress," which burdens a mediational theory of the Paivio type. After all, it is extremely rare for thinking to be constantly formulated in words, in a kind of well-articulated inner speech. Nor does it happen very often that thinking occurs through a constant stream of full-fledged images.

This does not, of course, prove the Conceptualist theory to be correct. After all, the notion of thinking as a "unique," "impalpable" experience is rather abstruse, and the Wurzburg theorists never managed to develop it in a satisfactorily clear and constructive way.

Let us now examine the contemporary variants of the Conceptualist theory. Here we may distinguish between "hard-nosed" versions, where the image is seen as epiphenomenal, and "soft-nosed" versions, where imagery is assigned a secondary, supportive function in cognition.

An articulate defense of the hard-nosed version is provided by Pylyshyn (1973) in his comprehensive and thorough criticism of the systematic status assigned to the concept of imagery in mediational models. According to Pylyshyn, images are pre-interpreted, selected, and may be abstract, and the general notion that "all learning and memory—and indeed all cognition—takes place exclusively through the medium of either words or images" (Pylyshyn, 1973, p. 4) is seen as totally misguided. Rather, cognition is mediated by "something quite different" from either words or images. This something else is variously described as "concepts" or "abstract ideas." Thus, reference is made to an abstract and amodal representational format of a purely conceptual nature. The existence of images is, of course, not denied, but they are regarded as epiphenomenal ripplings on the surface, devoid of functional value. As far as language is concerned, it is mainly assigned a labeling function in thought, and is conceived primarily as an instrument for communication of the preformed nonverbal mental concepts (Pylshyn, 1973, p. 7). The close kinship of Pylyshyn's views to the orthodox Conceptualist theory is clearly seen.

To buttress his claim, Pylyshyn seeks support in the work of the philosopher Frege (1960, originally published, 1879). From the example of two sentences that express the same thought, Frege makes the following comment, which Pylyshyn takes to heart: "I call the part of the content that is the same in both *the conceptual content. Only this* has significance for our symbolic language; we need therefore make no distinction between propositions that have the same conceptual content" (Frege, 1960, p. 3, originally published, 1879). For Pylyshyn, this is tantamount to saying that the concept in question must be a *mental* entity. As we can express the same thought in different sentences, there must be an underlying mental entity of a different nature than the words used to express it.

However, here Pylyshyn mistakes his prosecutor for his defense lawyer. Frege explicitly opposed, and, indeed, rebelled against the identification of a concept with a mental entity. For Frege, the concept in question was an *abstract* and *objective* entity, and *not* a mental and subjective entity (see also Putnam, 1975). The sentences may express the same thought in much the same way as two different instruments may be brought to perform the same function. The direct move from the existence of abstract entities to the necessary existence of linguistically neutral abstract *mental* entities existing in an elusive conceptual medium at the deep-structure level of the mind is, thus, not legitimate. We believe that the temptation to make this move from the considerations that Pylyshyn expresses is a primary motive or postulating the sort of abstract, amodal representational system that has won such appeal in current cognitive theories (see Anderson, 1976, 1980; Anderson & Bower, 1973; Kintsch, 1974; Lindsay & Norman, 1977; Marschark, Richman, Yuille, & Hunt, 1987; Norman & Rumelhart, 1975). We regard this as an unfortunate move, because, as has been pointed out by Harman (1975), it only pushes the problem back one step (see also Kosslyn & Pomerantz, 1977).

Now we have to explain how meaning is established in the amodal, conceptual representations. We agree with Harman when he claims that "One cannot continue forever to translate one system of representation into another," and that this kind of theory "only delays the moment of confrontation" (Harman, 1975, p. 282), where we realize that a different account is needed. The only way to save this kind of theory seems to be that the underlying conceptual language that we are supposed to think in is, somehow, *intrinsically intelligible*. But Pylyshyn has another card up his sleeve that must be considered. The existence of an amodal conceptual representation is held to be necessary to explain other problems related to the meaning function. Claims Pylyshyn: "As long as we recognize that people can go from mental pictures to mental words, or vice versa, we are forced to conclude that there must be a representation (which is more abstract and not available to conscious experience) which encompasses both. There must in other words be some common format or interlingua" (Pylyshyn, 1973, p. 5).

But nothing forces us to follow Pylyshyn in this assumption. On the contrary, since the units in the underlying propositional representations are regarded as fundamentally different from words and images, it can be shown that Pylyshyn's argument is logically incoherent. To be able to translate from Code 1 to Code 3, we must postulate a Code 4, etc. An infinite regress has been generated and nothing has been explained by resorting to an abstract, underlying metalanguage (see also Kosslyn & Pomerantz, 1977).

Anderson (1978), who favors the propositional theory of representation, nevertheless accepts the validity of this argument. The conclusion he draws is, however, surprising indeed: "It is simply not the case that it is necessary to have a propositional or any other intermediate code for translation. By careful analysis, it might be possible to show that an interlingua makes the translation process more efficient, but such an analysis has not been forthcoming" (p. 256). But what the argument shows is not that an interlingua is not *necessary* to effect the translation, but rather that it is *not possible* to solve the translation problem by postulating an interlingua at a deep-structure level, which is fundamentally different from words and images. When an infinite regress is generated, it means that the idea in question is logically corrupt. The translation problem is, in a sense, real enough. And a sound theory of representation has to offer a convincing solution to it. None of the theories we have considered so far, however, seem adequately developed to cope with the problem.

Disregarding such conceptual problems as those outlined above, and viewing matters in more strictly empirical terms, it also seems that the hard-nosed theory runs into serious difficulties in explaining imagery effects in cognitive performance, such as modality-specific interference effects (Atwood, 1971; Brooks, 1967; Byrne, 1974; Salthouse, 1974, 1975), memory for modality information (see Kieras, 1978, for a more general review), the mental rotation phenomenon (Shepard, 1978a, 1990; Shepard & Cooper, 1982), and many other phenomena (Kosslyn, 1980, 1983; Kosslyn, & Pomerantz, 1977, and Paivio, 1975a, 1975b, 1983a, 1986, for detailed discussions of the empirical side of the issue). Although Anderson (1978) has been clever in pointing out how the propositional model may accommodate many of these findings, we agree with Hayes-Roth (1979) that the propositional account is notoriously ad hoc, and that Imagist theories gain the upper hand in having predicted the results.

This upper hand is conditional, of course, on the assumption that these results are not determined artifactually by the same tacit theories and knowledge being shared by subjects and investigators. This general state of affairs in the field has consequently fostered compromise variants of the propositional theory, where imagery is given a functionally autonomous role in cognition. As an example we may choose the model advocated by Yuille and Catchpole (1977), which is mainly inspired by Piaget's theory of symbolic representation.

According to Yuille and Catchpole we have to assume the existence of two *distinct* levels of cognitive functioning, which are referred to as the *representational* and the *abstract* planes. Since, in their view, "images and words are too concrete to serve as the basis for most cognitive operations (Yuille & Catchpole, 1977, p. 177), the fundamental cognitive processes are done "off-stage" at the abstract level "in a form and symbolism unique to the mind" (p. 177). Basic knowledge is also seen to be stored in the abstract coding system. Imagery is located at the representational level and assigned several supportive functions, such as the temporary maintenance of a constructed representation, reconstruction of ideas, memories, feelings, etc., from the abstract code, as well as making possible a more direct recovery of past experience.

Such a hybrid model has the merits of attempting to deal constructively with both the semantic/conceptual and the sensory/perceptual aspects of imagery. Despite its merits, this liberalization of the propositional theory does not solve its basic problems. Because we are dealing with distinct levels in cognition, where the basic processing occurs at the abstract level, in a representational system composed of units that are different from words and images, it follows, as Yuille and Catchpole point out, that "the contents and activities of the abstract plane are not available to conscious inspection. . . . [C]onscious inspection of an abstract idea requires its translation into a representational mode" (p. 179). In other words, our thoughts are hatched out at a deep-structure level in a unique "language of thought" beyond conscious access. Then, somehow, they are translated into a concrete representation (in images or words) and made accessible to consciousness.

In our opinion, this is a highly problematic implication of the model. In the first place, such dissection of thinking into two distinct spheres (generation at an amodal deep-structure level and representation in conscious surface symbols) really implies that our thoughts should constitute a continuous source of potential surprise to us. There are elements of this feature in our mental experience, particularly in the case of "unbidden images." However, because this is normally not the case, there seems to be something fundamentally wrong with the ontological division between the abstract and the representational level.

Apart from such perplexing implications of the theory, a logical impasse blocks the road from the abstract to the representational level. As these two levels are distinct, and the abstract, underlying representational system is *different* from words and images, we have to postulate a sort of "mental link station,", i.e., the two codes must be interconnected by a translator code that somehow encompasses both. But to move from the abstract code to the translator code, we would need a new translator code, and so on. Again we are involved in an infinite regress, and there seems to be no way of reaching the representational level from the abstract code.

It should be emphasized that the translation required on the theory of an amodal, underlying representation is different from translating from one language to another. Here the primary language is learned and then linked to the secondary language. It is difficult to see that an amodal language that is prior to the natural language we speak could be learned. Thus, the postulation of a pre-existing amodal language of thought naturally leads to the conclusion advocated by Fodor (1976), who claims that our basic conceptual knowledge (left unspecified) is *innate*. But the idea that such concepts as "electron" and "xylophone" are innate hardly seems an attractive one. (For a comprehensive critical discussion of Fodor's theory of the language of thought, see Kaufmann, 1980.)

Regardless of how attractive the cognitive theories may seem in many important respects, the conclusion nevertheless seems inevitable that there is something fundamentally wrong with their conceptual foundation.

Thus, it seems that a sound conceptual basis for a theory of symbolic representation has yet to be found.

Meaning and Concepts as Nonverbal Mental Entities

Delving into the nature of underlying, conceptual representations may seem to be a detour on the course to a viable psychological theory of the nature and functional role of mental imagery in cognition. I will challenge this assumption, and argue that a proper perspective on the conceptual status of and the relationships between mental codes is a prerequisite to understanding the particular role of mental imagery in this context. Moreover, it will be argued that the solution proposed entails specific, empirically testable hypotheses on the functional role of imagery in cognitive performances.

A major source of confusion for the theories discussed above may be found in the implicit assumption that meanings and concepts must be identified with some sort of nonverbal mental entity.

The Imagist-inclined theorist points to the image as the central substance of meaning. But as we have seen, the image cannot fulfill any basic meaning function. The conceptualist theorists treat meaning as some sort of abstract idea or amodal proposition. This purely cognitive substance is held to provide semantic life to otherwise dead words and a semantic anchor for otherwise basically ambiguous images.

But this move to the deeper abstract level of mind seems not to move us any further to a constructive solution, since it is by no means clear what is meant by such an "abstract idea" or "concept" and how its meaning function is established. Moreover, there seems to be no escape from a vicious infinite regress in translating from one code to another under the assumption that the language of thought is amodal.

In contemporary philosophy Wittgenstein (1953) has taken the lead in an effort to develop a new theoretical account of meaning. In this theoretical position the negative claim is that meaning should not be identified either with the object a symbol "stands for" or with a mental entity behind the symbol that represents the object, i.e., an image, an abstract idea, or a "concept." According to Wittgenstein, then, "meaning" does not stand for any entity at all. Rather, the term "meaning" is seen as a circumscription for statements about the *use* of signs (see Specht, 1963, for a lucid exposition of Wittgenstein's theory of meaning). From the Wittgensteinian perspective, linguistic activity stands in no need of a mental correlate in the form of images or abstract mental ideas or processes to be meaningful.

More recently, Black (1972) makes a similar point and claims: "The 'life' of the words, we might say, is not in some supposed mental afflatus, but rather in the capacity of the particular utterance to interact with, and provide a point of departure for, further symbolic activity" (p. 30). Thus, rather than referring to a mental entity in the form of an image or an abstract idea, "meaning," in the psychological sense, refers to our *ability* to handle interrelated and coordinated functions of signs.

Wittgenstein's analysis, however, may primarily be seen as relevant to the level of meaning related to communication and to the use of language in certain institutions, rituals, and practices of a group of speakers, as suggested by Harman (1968).

Even more important, perhaps, is the point of distinguishing between different meanings of the term "meaning."

Luria (1982) makes an interesting distinction between "meaning" and "sense," and points out that it is only recently that these concepts have been differentiated by Western researchers.

"Meaning" refers to the system of semantic relations connected with a word (or other sign) that has evolved during social history. Meaning reflects general human experience, and can be used not only to refer to an object but also as a basis for analyzing the object in question by reference to a system of objective associations. This system is the same for everyone. This may be seen as the *objective* aspect of meaning, and the one we have in mind when we ask such questions as "What is really the meaning of X?" By "sense," Luria understands the signification of an individual instance of a word, which is, in part, determined by the particular interest or need of a user in a given situation. According to Luria, "sense" is a selection from the list of all possible meanings of that or those which the person needs in a given situation, as determined by his or her pragmatic concerns on that occasion.

It should be emphasized, however, that such a meaning determined by the situation should not be seen only as a selection from the objective repertoire of meanings. Often it will be more appropriate to speak of an *adaptation* rather than a selection. When tailored to a specific need in a particular situation, the meaning of a word is often changed and expanded in the process in a way that transcends its objectively established use. In this connection, we want to underscore the point that meanings and concepts are normally open-textured, rather than rigidly specified through necessary and sufficient conditions. This has the important asset of ensuring flexibility in adaptation to new situations, and makes for a continuous growth of language to accommodate the constant stream of new experiences. A concept functions not only as a summary abstraction of previous experiences. Equally important is its function as a model to anticipate and accommodate new experiences. Furthermore, Luria seems to confuse the specific adaptation in meaning to a given situation with the individual's subjective representation of meaning. This is evident when he points out that a word like "ugol" has different meanings for a housewife, a scientist, and a child.

In an important paper, Putnam (1975) points out that it is hardly ever the case that one individual knows the full range of (objective) meanings associated with a word. Rather there is a "division of linguistic labor," where different individuals are carriers of different aspects of the total meaning, which is only realized by the collective linguistic body. The point made by Putnam brings out the need for singling out a third aspect of meaning. This will be referred to here as "subjective meaning" and signifies the individual representation of the meaning of a word. This seems to be the aspect of meaning addressed by Harman (1975,

1977), when he discusses the nature of meaning *in thought*. According to this analysis, the meaning of a word (sign) or sentence is its *role in the individual's conceptual scheme*.

The point we want to make is that there may be no conflict between the different views of meaning discussed above. Rather, the different theorists are focusing on different aspects of the concept of meaning. Wittgenstein is concerned with giving an analysis of objective meaning when he suggests that meaning does not refer to any entity, but is a circumscription for statements of the uses of a sign in the various language games it enters into. Wittgenstein also emphasizes the point made by Luria concerning the *sense* of a word, which is the situation-adapted meaning of a word determined by the pragmatic concerns of a user on a specific occasion. Harman is concerned with the meaning in thought, which is the individual's subjective representation of the meaning of a sign. This is the aspect of meaning that is of the greatest concern to cognitive psychologists.

In mainstream cognitive psychology, the part of the meaning complex that has to do with the subjective interpretation of meaning is frequently analyzed in terms of the concept of a *schema* (or related concepts, like "frame" or "model").

The "substance" or units of the underlying meaning structures are generally held to be *conceptual* entities, which are "abstract symbolic representations" of knowledge. Such abstract, conceptual representations are seen to be expressed and described in language, but are *not themselves linguistic* (see, e.g., Rumelhart and Ortony, 1977, p. 111; Potter & Kroll, 1986).

This particular notion represents a clear commitment to the traditional Conceptualist theory, where concepts are seen as purely "cognitive," abstract, nonlinguistic ideas.

The Appeal to the Other Language

Harman (1981) distinguishes between two main approaches to language learning, which is clearly relevant to our present discussion of the nature of conceptual representations.

Under the assumption that there is an "inner language" of thought that may or may not be distinct from the "outer language" we speak, Harman distinguishes between two major views in this domain.

The Code Breaking (CB) Theory

According to *code breaking theory* (CB), "One's inner language, which one thinks in, is distinct from one's outer language, which one speaks. Communication involves coding or translation between inner and outer languages. Learning language is a matter of learning an outer language and involves acquiring the ability to do such coding or translation" Harman, 1981, p. 38). Within this view, then, underlying, conceptual representations are linguistically neutral, semantic representations.

The Incorporation View (IV)

The *incorporation view* (IV) represents the opposite view, and builds on the following basic thesis: "Knowledge of a language is the ability to use that language; and the primary use of language is in thought. Knowing a language is being able to think in it. Learning an outer language involves the incorporation of that language into one's inner language" (Harman, 1981, p. 38).

It is readily seen that the CB conception is a statement of the Conceptualist theory with its claim for the existence of underlying representations of a nonlinguistic, conceptual kind. This is the view found in contemporary mainstream cognitive psychology. One reason for assuming this position to be the correct one may be that learning and understanding a language must involve a mapping of language expressions to preexisting, underlying semantic representations. Thus, Kosslyn (1983) claims that underlying propositional representations could not be linguistic since learning the first word requires the existence of an underlying representation that is not linguistic. This is to assume that the only possible model is CB, where learning a language involves translation between linguistic expressions and underlying, linguistically neutral, semantic representations. But this is not necessarily so.

According to the IV model, the meaning of a word is acquired by way of learning how to *use* it in the proper way. A translation to an underlying, linguistically neutral semantic representation is not required in this view. According to IV the resultant internal representation of the meaning of a word is an incorporation of the language we speak. Moreover, as have been pointed out above, the CB argument entails a danger of infinite regress. At some point the translation process must come to an end. It seems that we are left with two major options: One is to assume that there exists an innate language, where basic concepts are given from which all other concepts can be constructed. This is the position taken by Fodor (1976). The other option is to give an alternative analysis of the meaning function at some point so as to stop the regress. This is the position advocated by Harman in his conception of meaning as a matter of the role of a sign in the individual's conceptual structure.

Harman also points to the problem of translation relations that is somewhat embarrassing for the CB model.

On the assumption that there exists linguistically neutral, semantic representations, the same thoughts should be perfectly translatable in different languages. If the thought expressed by X is the same as that expressed by Y, which, in turn, is the same as that expressed by Z, it follows, on the premise of transitivity of identity, that the thought expressed by X is the same as that expressed by Z. This is to say that, in the CB model, the translation should be an equivalence relation. However, the normal case is that such translation relations are *matters of degree.* As shown by Quine (1960), there are different schemes of translation, and these may compete with each other. Since CB implies that thoughts are linguistically neutral states that may be expressed in different languages without being relative to translation, the IV model looks more promising since it does not rest on the equivalence thesis, and may account for the relativity of translations that exist.

In the context of cognitive functioning we will, then, suggest that the analysis of meaning in terms of *conceptual role* advocated by Harman (1975, 1977) may be the appropriate one, with reference to the work of the philosopher Wilfrid Sellars (1963), who argued that the meaning of a symbolic expression should be conceived as its potential role in the "evidence-inference-action language game of thought." By this, Sellars seems to mean that the essence of thinking is the processing of inferences to obtain evidence related to the content and purpose of the thought process—e.g., the solution to a problem. The meaning of a sign or sentence is its role in the system of thought, or, more specifically, its role in the individual's conceptual scheme.

Thus, it seems natural and promising to follow the line advocated by Harman (1970, 1975, 1977), leading to the view that the primary use of language is in *thought,* and that its use in communication is secondary and derived. In this view, learning a language is learning *a new way of thinking,* which enables us to acquire a vast repertoire of propositional attitudes and conceptual resources that we would not have *without* language. Taking this a step further, we will suggest that the acquisition of language is primarily the acquisition of a representational system that makes genuine conceptual and discursive thinking possible. Within this scheme, the underlying conceptual representations used in cognition may be seen to consist in deep structures, or tokens of such deep structures, where the tokens in the language of thought are *type-identical* to the tokens in the language we speak. It may be argued that it seems strange to talk about type-identity between internal tokens and spoken or written tokens, since there cannot be much of a physical resemblance between the internal tokens used in thought and the spoken or written tokens of natural language.

However, as the philosopher Hartry Field (1981) argues, this is a very bad argument. The type-identity in question is no more mysterious than the type-identity that exists between spoken and written tokens, which bear little physical resemblance to each other. Furthermore, the *abstractness* and *conceptual nature* of the underlying representations in cognition may be seen to reside in the *schematic form* that the underlying units are organized in, rather than in the *content* of the representational units themselves.

In my view, then, the move to the nonlinguistic, purely "amodal" and "conceptual" level is unwarranted and may turn out to be a serious mistake. The abstractness of a conceptual representation can be seen to reside in the *schematic form* of the internal representations, and not necessarily in the *content* of the units of which the conceptual representations are composed. We do not need a double reason to account for the abstractness and conceptual nature of internal representations. This onus is fully discharged under the assumption that linguistic (and supporting imaginal) units are arranged in a *schematic form* and meaning can be conceived as the *role* of linguistic (and imaginal) units in the individual's conceptual scheme. The resort to purely conceptual, "imageless ideas" is, in our view, apt to obscure, rather than clarify, the debate over the nature of representations of knowledge. Such entities have never been described in a satisfactory way either in the early Wurzburg psychology or in contemporary information-processing psychology, and they are not needed for conceptual or empirical reasons. I will therefore suggest that the "language of thought" is not a system of representation composed of purely conceptual, nonlinguistic, nonimaginal representational units. Rather, the language of thought that is used in thinking and reasoning can more profitably be seen as a *conceptual abstraction of the language we speak,* which is structured in a schematic *form.*

I therefore conclude this discussion by suggesting that the concept of a schema, as an organized packet of information, applies to the level of the *form* of a representation and should not be confused with the question pertaining to the *content* of the units that representations are composed of. That is, rather than searching for the conceptual in the abstractness of the *content* of an elusive "amodal" code, we should look for the conceptual properties of symbolic representations in the way symbols are organized into conceptual *patterns* in the mind. The failure to distinguish between these two aspects of representations is common to both Symbolist- (e.g., Paivio, 1986) and Conceptualist-inclined theorists (e.g., Norman & Rumelhart, 1975; Potter & Kroll, 1986; Rumelhart & Ortony, 1977), and is, in our view, a major source of confusion in the current debate over the nature of mental representations.

Closely akin to this confusion is the confusion over *levels* of representations. In my view the imagery-proposition debate is a straw-man debate in the sense that we are dealing with representations at different levels. Imagery is at the level of *conscious* representations, whereas propositions are at the level of *underlying* representations. They are both real and both functional, but in different roles and capacities on different levels of representations. The confusion over levels of representations also seems to be implied in Johnson-Laird's triple-code theory (Johnson-Laird, 1992) that argues for the existence of three major representational systems: *propositions, mental models,* and *images.*

According to the theory, propositions have a predicate structure, whereas mental models and images have an analog and spatial structure. The distinction between mental models and images is said to be necessary because mental models can be abstract, whereas images are concrete.

It seems to me that Johnson-Laird's theory, as it stands, is clearly fallacious. On the level of the primary distinction, mental models and images are strictly commensurate in terms of properties and characteristics. The best argument one could possibly make would be to see images as a subdivision under mental models. However, this is not a very attractive nor parsimonious solution. In my view, a more coherent interpretation would be to see images aligned with linguistic representations on the level of conscious representation, and propositions as representations underlying linguistic representations while mental models are underlying representations for mental images on the conscious level. The distinction between abstract and concrete would then be a continuum within the mental model–mental imagery system. In the last section of this chapter I will describe a general model of symbolic representations along these lines.

In conclusion, I will suggest that the concept of a schema, as a structured whole, may be seen as a representational unit for the concept of a "game," which is a more or less organized and rule-governed activity that words (signs) enter into. While objective meaning, as defined above, may be well captured in the Wittgensteinian analysis of meaning as a matter of function in a game, a word's role in the individual's conceptual scheme may be seen as its representational equivalent, referring to subjective meaning, as defined above. The individual's understanding of the meaning of a word may thus be conceived as a function of the extensiveness and accuracy of representation in the individual's relevant conceptual scheme. According to the analysis advocated here, level of understanding would be determined both by the degree of elaboration of the scheme in question and by the appropriateness of the role assignments in the relevant conceptual scheme.

PROCESS THEORIES

In this category we find theories that circumvent many of the issues discussed above by emphasizing the point that, rather than treating images as static entities, we should focus on the *act of imaging* and on its proper function in ongoing cognitive activities.

From a philosophical stance, Ryle (1949) claims that expressions like "seeing a mental image" have no valid use. Thus, the common sense view of imagery reflects a distorted view of the nature of the mental image. According to Ryle, an image is not an object. It lacks size, shape, temperature, cannot be given a specific location in space, and is not *found* existing anywhere. Because the concept of "seeing" logically requires an object to be seen, it follows that there is nothing to be "seen" in images. In Ryle's theoretical scheme, images do not exist but the *act of imaging* does. Ryle (1949) goes on to suggest a dispositional analysis of the process of imaging. Here imagery is conceived as a form of expecting to see something, except that the expectations involved in imaging are not fulfilled. Rather, it is like a rehearsal of them being fulfilled. This conception of imagery has been further developed in psychology by Neisser (1976, 1978; cf. Kaufmann, 1980, 1986 for a more detailed treatment and critique). Still, there is definitely some sort of visual experience involved in imagery. This aspect of imaging is hardly properly accounted for in a purely dispositional analysis along Rylean lines.

Recently, Neisser (1976) has presented a theory of imagery that is clearly in this tradition. Neisser rejects both the analog theory and the propositional theory of imagery. The analog theory is said to entail serious internal inconsistencies (e.g., implying undischarged homunculi). Furthermore, both theories are claimed to be unable to explain basic facts about imagery (e.g., why images and percepts are not systematically confused).

According to Neisser, the true nature of the image is captured when we see it not as a static entity, but as a process in on-line cognitive activities. More specifically, Neisser links the function of imagery primarily to its role in perception. More specifically, Neisser argues that imaging be regarded as a form of *percep-*

tual anticipation. The primary purpose of imaging is in "preparing for extero-spection" (1978, p. 173). The very essence of imagery, then, is *perceptual readi-ness.* "To have a perceptual set for something is to have an image. The more precisely that image anticipates the information to come, the more effective the set should be" (Neisser, 1976, p. 145).

But this conception of imagery also seems problematic in many respects. Whereas a limited class of imaging may perhaps, be validly described as percep-tual anticipations, it seems to us that in the normal case of imagery it is quite the *opposite* that is happening: When we are imaging, we do it rather as a *substi-tute* for real perceptual experience, and precisely because we do *not* anticipate any "exterospection." Suppose that we were to describe the looks of a deceased relative. As we certainly cannot expect any perceptual input, we may summon up an image of the person to aid us in our task. Neisser is aware of this problem, but his attempt to show that it makes sense to speak of anticipations even in the cases where we do not anticipate anything is simply not successful.

Matching the grammar of the concept of perceptual anticipation with the grammar of the concept of imaging, we clearly see that they are fundamentally different phenomena. In a thoroughly justified criticism of Neisser's theory, Hampson and Morris (1978a) refer to a critique by Hannay (1971) of Ryle's dispositional account of imaging, which transfers with full force to Neisser's theory. Where a perceptual anticipation goes unfulfilled, according to Hannay, we always experience surprise or disappointment. Such a description does not fit images in the same way. Consequently, images cannot all be perceptual anticipa-tions. In a reply to Hampson and Morris, Neisser (1978) claims that this is de-monstrably wrong, since many kinds of anticipations are unfulfilled without sur-prising or disappointing anyone. To substantiate this claim, Neisser refers to the example of a seed described as "a highly structured set of anticipations—it is ready for the warmth and nutrients that will enable it to grow—but no one supposes that seeds are capable of surprise" (1978, p. 171). Of course, no one supposes that seeds are capable of surprise, but that is because no one should suppose that seeds are capable of having anticipations in the first place! Speaking of seeds as having "anticipations" is just as misleading and erroneous as describ-ing a magnet as "recognizing" the magnetic meridian, or of the lymphocytes of the body "remembering" a smallpox injection (the examples are borrowed from Toulmin, 1971, where a general discussion of the appropriate conditions for em-ploying cognitive terms is found).

In the case of the seed having "anticipations," the context of purposive behav-ior where it is appropriate to assign cognitive terms to the behavior of organisms is completely absent. (The same argument applies to another example of Neis-ser's where the military system is endowed with "anticipations.")

Thus, it seems that Neisser has not been able to meet the serious challenge presented to him by Hampson and Morris. He merely circumvents it by stepping outside the logic of the concept of anticipation.

Moreover, no empirical evidence has been forthcoming to support the notion of imaging as anticipations of upcoming visual stimuli. Given the time parame-ters involved in perception and imaging, with perception being fast as compared to the "sluggishness" of imaging, the idea that imaging has its primary role in preparing for future visual perceptions seems highly unlikely. It seems more likely that this particular function of imaging is involved in preparing for motor actions (e.g., Reisberg, this volume) and in problem-solving activities (e.g., Kaufmann, 1986, 1988, 1993). The core of Neisser's argument that we refocus our considerations on imagery from static, isolated entities to an active imaging process as an auxiliary in the context of other ongoing cognitive activities seems well taken (cf. Kaufmann & Helstrup, 1993). However, isolating its function to anticipation only seems too narrow, and mainly due to a particular theoretical emphasis on its role in the act of perception. By projecting the perspective on imagery onto a wider range of cognitive activities, a more diversified perspective on different functions of imaging will appear, as will be argued in the final section of this chapter.

A SUGGESTED SOLUTION AND AN ALTERNATIVE MODEL

Nature of Imagery

It seems to us that both the Descriptionalist and the Pictorialist theories fail by pressing the case for their contrasting views toward their cherished extremes. On the basis of logical as well as empirical considerations, time should be ripe for conceding that images are not *either* descriptions *or* mental pictures. This is probably the point Fodor (1976) has in mind when he claims that as far as images go, there is an "infinite range from paragraphs to photographs" (Fodor, 1976, p. 190). Marks (1983) argues that there is a continuum from the lowest levels, which produce vivid quasi-perceptual imagery, to the highest levels, where imagery is abstract and conceptual.

From my point of view, images are neither pure symbols nor pure perceptual experiences, but a typical hybrid mental concept with both symbolic and perceptual properties. In principle, images should be seen as located across the boundary between thought and sensation. Also, we agree with the view of "functional images" advanced by Bartlett (1921, 1925, 1927). Images normally put to use are far more sketchy and fleeting than most current models of imagery suggest. This is in line with the claim made by Anderson (1990) that most images may be *spatial* rather then visual or pictorial in nature.

In Figure 3.1 an alternative conceptual model of the nature of the imagery phenomenon is suggested, which is believed to capture its full range. Based on the arguments set forward above, we also indicate the relative frequencies of the various types of images along the relevant conceptual dimension with the two polar activities of thought and sensation.

As is seen from Figure 3.1, the model implies that images have intentional properties (in the sense of reference and abstraction), and perceptual-experiential properties (intensity and duration). The model thus clearly distinguishes images from both pure symbols and pure perceptual experiences, which is logically re-

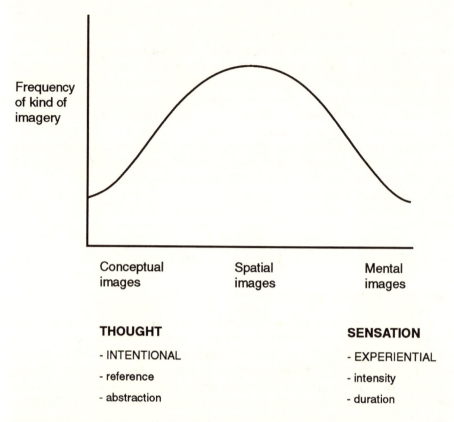

FIGURE 3.1. Postulated frequency of kinds of imagery along a continuum ranging between the polar concepts of thought and sensation.

quired if imagery is to be considered an autonomous mental activity. We believe that this conceptual model allows for a new and more refined analysis of the concept of imagery. It is intended to be used as a framework for constructing more specific, explanatory theories of the nature and function of mental imagery.

If one grants that images have a "getting" (i.e., an autonomous perceptual layout) and a "doing" aspect (i.e., intentional content), the model explicitly implies that reconstrual of images is possible. Interpretations of images could go in the mode of "doing" from description to image and in the mode of "getting" from "inspection" of uninterpreted parts of the image to new description. This implication of the model seems patently invalidated by the results of a series of experiments performed by Chambers and Reisberg (1985).

In five experiments, Chambers and Reisberg presented certain classical ambiguous figures, like the duck-rabbit figure, to their subjects. The task given to the subjects was to internalize the figure as a mental image, inspect the image, and try to detect the alternative meaning configuration. Despite variations in procedure, and extensive prompting in five experiments, not a single subject was able to find the *rabbit* when they had initially seen the *duck* or vice versa. Reisberg and Chambers (1991) corroborated these results in a new series of experiments involving different ambiguous figures (also see Chambers, 1993; Reisberg & Logie, 1993). What is natural and easy in perception thus seems impossible in imaging. Are images, after all, conceptually and functionally radically different from percepts?

Based on their experimental evidence, Chambers and Reisberg (1985) took the strong stand that images are radically different from percepts. They claim that images are "saturated" with our understanding of their form, and, indeed, that images have no existence independent of our understanding. That is, images are exclusively determined by the intentional description under which they are constructed.

However, in terms of the conceptual model advocated here, the pictures used by Chambers and Reisberg hardly represent paradigmatic cases of functional images. In its detailed outline, the duck-rabbit figure is more like the polar case of mental *pictures*. Besides, mental images are dynamic. To inspect a mental image in many respects resembles the construction of this image. Mental images therefore have sharp details in focus, and vague parts in the periphery (cf. Finke, 1989). The duck-rabbit figure is more like a picture than an image. Pictures are sharp in all details, and they differ from images in lacking unfocused vague points. Being able to form images with detailed picture-like qualities may thus require extremely high imaging ability. This is a particularly relevant consideration in relation to the task to be performed in the image reconstruals required, since successful performance may depend on being able to preserve crucial details of the pictures in question (cf. Peterson, 1993).

As shown by Kosslyn, 1980, mental images suffer considerable fading in the normal case. The mental-picture aspect of imagery is therefore designated in our model as a low-frequency instance of imagery. As such, our model implies that, although reconstrual should be possible, it should be difficult under the Chambers and Reisberg conditions. Consequently, successful performance may depend on more specific instructions, as shown by Hyman (1993), or facilitating demonstrations, as shown by Peterson (1993). Under these conditions, image reconstrual is not only possible but quite common.

In the most recent development of the original Chambers and Reisberg theory, Reisberg and Logie (1993) take account of the discrepant findings on image reconstrual. It is now argued that imagery is like perception in requiring, and operating, within a frame of reference. The "Frame-of-Reference" model reaches further than the "Figure-Caption" model developed by Reisberg and Chambers (1991). Besides the intentionally conferred meaning, the concept extends to such organizational factors as figure and ground, parsing, orientation, etc. Such specifications provide the frame of reference that serves as the basis for the interpretation of the stimulus geometry involved in perceiving and imaging. As support for the revised theory, Reisberg and Chambers (1991) report findings where the subjects are asked to image shapes. One of the shapes, presented in the latter part of the series, is a schematic map-representation of Texas, presented upside-down. The subjects are then asked to rotate the figure 180 degrees. Given that they are able to do this adequately, they are then "staring" at a map of Texas. When asked to determine what they "see," and told that it resembles a "familiar geographic form," the zero finding of the original Chambers and Reisberg results was replicated; that is, none of the subjects are able to see Texas in their images. This is in clear contrast to the condition where the subjects draw their images. With this stimulus support more than half of the subjects were able to interpret the figure successfully. The frame of reference is here thought to be *orientation*. When the subjects were informed that the bottom was the top subsequent to image reversal, a significant number of subjects were able to detect Texas in their image.

The theoretical model developed by Reisberg and Logie (1993) to account for such findings is not entirely clear, however. It is argued that images, like percepts, are obligatorily accompanied by a perceptual reference frame and can only be understood within this frame. This is taken to be different from the case of pictures. But now we seem to have a theory that affirms a strong *equivalence* between perception and imagery, whereas the starting point for the whole discussion about image ambiguity was to drive a wedge between perception and imagery by pointing to the fundamental difference between percepts that can be ambiguous and images that, by definition, are unambiguous.

I must confess that I do not understand how percepts and images can be aligned as two instances of the same species in contrast to "pictures." A picture is not a self-contained entity that can be meaningfully conceptualized apart from perception. Strictly, a "picture" is an object that portrays information and can only be meaningfully understood as an object of perception, not as an entity in and of itself. And perception cannot be treated as a "freewheeling" process, severed from its object. That is, perception cannot be *contrasted* with its very object. Thus, because a picture is the object of perception, and thus an integral part of perception, by Reisberg and Logie's own definitions, a picture necessarily must exist within a frame of reference. And then the distinction between perception and imagery stands in danger of being totally blurred. To salvage the distinction between perception and imagery, it seems that we are thrown back to a familiar argument that in perception there is an *independent* object that may serve to redefine the original frame of reference for an object, by allowing for closer examination, whereas there is no comparable object in imaging (cf. Dennett, 1982; Heil, 1982).

Put another way, perception is a *relational* concept and imagery is not. Thus, the image is bound to its original intentional description. Image reconstrual, then, is only possible if the original frame of reference is altered, as in the experiments referred to above that used instructions and demonstrations apt to alter the frame of reference that surrounds the image.

A crucial test of the revised theory may lie in demonstrating that reconstrual may occur under *uncued* conditions, where *no* hints are made to the effect of altering the frame of reference of the image. Our model suggests that successful, uncued performance with the duck-rabbit kind of stimulus should occur. But because reconstrual is dependent on the ability to retain crucial details of the target figure (cf. Peterson, 1993), it may require superior visualization ability. Thus, we (Kaufmann & Helstrup, 1993) decided to replicate the Chambers and Reisberg experiment using the same ambiguous figures. In contrast to Chambers and Reisberg, who used ordinary university students as subjects, we employed a group of art students who were self-selected as pronounced visualizers and who employed visualization regularly in their work.

According to the predictions made from our model, the results showed that uncued reconstrual is, in fact, possible. A significant proportion of subjects (15.4%, $p = .055$, Fischer's exact probability) was able to reconstrue the duck-rabbit figure in imaged form. A highly significant proportion of the subjects (28%) was able to reconstrue either duck-rabbit or dog-chef, or both ($p = .0048$, Fischer's exact probability).

Consistent with our findings, Brandimonte (this volume) also reports that imagery reconstrual is significantly enhanced (ca. 50% reconstrual rate) under articulatory suppression, which is thought to suppress spontaneous verbal recoding of the image. Brandimonte's striking findings may be interpreted in at least two ways:

1. Because, by its very nature, an image is interpreted, any experimental manipulation that disrupts the linguistic process that may be crucial to the forming of a frame of reference turns the image into a "no-image," that is, an artificial, experimentally created entity that is not a representative instance of the generic class of images. Thus, the results merely *prove* the point that a true image is obligatorily accompanied by an interpretation in the form of a frame of reference for understanding.

2. The experimental manipulation allows the creation of an imagery state that is closely related to "unbidden images" like hypnagogic images (i.e., images preceding sleep), which seem to come uninterpreted and are assigned meaning after its generation—a phenomenon that seems to require extending the language to such expressions as "seeing" and "inspecting" images in "the mind's eye" (cf. Flew, 1956).

The first interpretation may be regarded as pure sophistry, and, more seriously, an example of defending a theory by means of begging the question in favor of a particular theory. Thus, the second interpretation seems more probable, and clearly speaks against the Reisberg and Logie theory, as no aid in altering the frame of reference is made here.

Reisberg and Logie (1993) admit that somehow the individual may be able to alter the frame of reference spontaneously, without prompting or externalization. Making this move has the virtue of adapting the theory to fit all the evidence that has been accounted for. However, the question that now looms large is whether *any* kind of empirical evidence can possibly be specified that is clearly ruled out by the theory. What we now have seems to be a theory that is approaching the state of being totally unconstrained and untestable.

Thus, imagery reconstrual clearly seems to be within the range of possible imagery operations, also under uncued conditions. The distinction between percepts and images seems to be more fluid than the Reisberg and Logie theory allows for.

This brings us back to the perennial issue about images as *objects.* Clearly, and trivially, it is true that an image is not a full-fledged object like a physical picture. It cannot be torn apart, hung on the wall, burned in the fireplace, and so on. But this line of reasoning does not prove that an image cannot be described as an object in *any* sense of the concept. The question is if it makes sense to talk about "mental objects." If it can be shown that the image may serve as an *independent source of information,* enough is left to qualify as an "object," and then it makes perfect sense to talk about "inspecting" and "seeing" images.

The Functions of Imagery

It was argued above that resolving the conceptual issues related to the question of the nature of structural relationships between different mental codes would provide us a platform on which to build a psychological theory of the functional role of mental imagery in cognition. The major conceptual questions surrounding the concept of imagery now seem to have satisfactory solutions, in the sense that they are *possible* solutions:

1. Since, in my theory, the "inner" language that we think in incorporates the "outer" language that we speak in, and thinking is held to be internally related to its symbolic expression, no difficulty arises in translating from the "abstract" to the "representational" level. Also avoided are the problems involved in identifying thinking with verbal-imaginal mediational processes, or with an autonomous mental process at an abstract level.

2. Since imagery is seen to be nested into language as a subsidiary representational system, no difficulties are involved in accounting for its semantic and conceptual content, and the "intercode" translation problem is also handled.

3. The theory recognizes the quasi-perceptual aspect of imagery and its potential functional value in cognition. Expressions like "seeing" and "inspecting" images in the "mind's eye" are perfectly legitimate. They may be seen as appropriate extensions of the language that we use to describe some aspects of imagery experience. Owing to their capacity to serve as an independent source of information, images do qualify as "objects," and they do exist in the technical-philosophical sense of the term.

4. Since, in our theory, language is held to be a superordinate form of representation, it follows that verbal and visual codes are not independent nor functional equals. Rather, the theory that flows from our considerations may be termed a Nested Representational Model. The general place of imagery in cognition may be characterized as *subsidiary* in the sense of being an *auxiliary representational system* operating mainly within and under conceptual control of the superordinate linguistic-propositional symbolic system.

In this capacity, imagery may harbor important functions for cognitive performance. We will argue that these functions are specifically due to its *quasi-perceptual* properties. Our considerations on the conceptual side give rise to a general view on the functional role of imagery in cognition. In general terms the basic premise of the theory can be stated as follows: *Imagery is a subsidiary, auxiliary representation assisting linguistic-conceptual representation through its quasi-perceptual properties.*

In the following section we will spell out a possible application of this theory in the domain of thinking and problem solving.

Morris and Hampson (1983, 1990) have developed a model based on the thesis that the functions of consciousness are to monitor and control processing that does not proceed automatically. They argue that, because imagery is a form of conscious representation, it should be particularly useful under novel task conditions. A potential limitation of their model is that it does not distinguish between the role of imagery and other forms of conscious representation, like verbalization, in regard to task novelty. Nor do they go into the level of underlying representations. Their model is therefore incomplete in several respects. The present theory aspires to the status of a general model of symbolic representation that places the different codes that are treated in other theories in a coherent model that distinguishes between the level of conscious representation and the level of underlying representation. On the conscious level of representation the theory postulates two major symbolic systems: The Linguistic representational system and the Imagery system, where *visual* imagery is held to be the major system in human cognition.

At the level of underlying representation, the theory distinguishes between Propositions that are abstracted and schematic versions of Linguistic representations, with a predicate structure, and Mental Models that are abstract forms of imagery, with a visuo-spatial structure. The two systems can "talk to each other" in the sense of the Linguistic-Propositional system providing semantic content to Imagery-Mental models, while the Imagery-Mental Model system provides visuo-spatial information to the Linguistic-Propositional system.

The theory is probably most closely affiliated with the latest version of Paivio's Dual Coding theory (Paivio, 1986, 1991). In agreement are the ideas of two major symbolic systems, and different levels of representations. However, there are also some important differences between the theories. In Paivio's theory the two symbolic systems differ only in the qualitative sense of being linked to different modes of information processing. Thus, the two systems are "equitable" and related in a symmetrical way. In the present theory, it is argued that there is also a distinction to be made along the dimension of level of processing. Specifically, it is argued that the Linguistic system is superordinate, in the sense of being linked to the more powerful computational mode of processing, whereas imagery is tied to the weaker kind of perceptual mode of information processing. Thus, imagery is seen as an ancillary symbolic system. In this capacity, it may, however, serve important information-processing functions, to be specified below.

In the Paivio model, imagery is seen as self-contained in regard to its intentional and semantic properties. In my theory, imagery is seen as dependent on linguistic-propositional representations for its meaning functions. In line with this thesis, there is consistent empirical evidence showing an asymmetrical relationship between the imagery variable *(I)* and verbal meaning *(m)* in a wide range of cognitive tasks. If the semantic meaning of an image is contained in its linguistic-propositionally derived meaning, the image contains both meaning shared with its corresponding verbal symbol plus an additional perceptual content. Thus, we should expect an asymmetrical effect of *I* and *m* in cognitive tasks, in the way that when *m* is partialled out, *I* still has a significant effect on performance. When *I* is partialled out, both the shared meaning and the unique perceptual content is eliminated and we would not expect a remaining effect for *m*. This is precisely what the research evidence shows in a wide array of tasks, ranging from single word through word-pairs and sentences to text units (Kaufmann, 1993).

Another major difference between the Paivio model and the present model is that the Paivio theory is primarily developed to account for memory and learning functions, whereas the present theory is more specifically developed for functions of thinking and problem solving. I will now describe the specifics of the theory as it relates to the functional role of the Linguistic-Propositional and the Imagery-Mental Model mode of symbolic representations in thinking and problem solving.

In our theory of symbolic representation in thinking and problem solving (Kaufmann 1980, 1981, 1985, 1988; Kaufmann & Helstrup, 1993), the symbolic strategies of verbalization and visualization are linked to low programmed tasks via the concept of the general functions of consciousness in cognitive processes, as proposed by Morris and Hampson (1983, 1990). However, the theory also prescribes a division of labor between linguistic and imagery representation *within* the task novelty dimension. Specifically, it is argued that visual imagery is linked to the high-novelty end of the continuum through its capacity to access a set of simpler processes of a perceptual kind. Such simpler processes are seen to be needed in low programmed tasks, where computational processes in the form of rule-governed processes are difficult or impossible to perform. The theory is outlined in Table 3.1.

The basic assumptions of the theory are founded on the empirically and well-established problem-solving principle that when a task is low in programming, the individual has to resort to so-called *weak methods* (Newell, 1969; Simon, 1978). Weak methods are general, pragmatic strategies that may be applied to a wide range of problems. They are "weak" in the sense that they lack precision and do not guarantee success. In contrast, strong methods are precise, tailor-made to the situation, and grant a safe and fast solution of the task. It is argued that this principle may be transferred to the domain of representational methods.

The basic thesis of the theory is as follows: A linguistic-propositional-representational format is a strong one in the sense that great precision may be achieved in the form of explicit descriptions. It is easily and quickly manipulated and allows in principle the full range of computational operations to be actual-

TABLE 3.1. Kaufmann's theory of symbolic representations in problem solving.

Conscious representations	Verbal		Imaginal	
Mode of Operation	Computational Transformations (Rule-Governed Inferences)		Perceptual Simulations (Mental Modeling)	
Main information-processing categories	Deductive reasoning	Inductive reasoning	Perceptual comparisons	Perceptual anticipations
Underlying representations	Propositional		Analog	

ized. In contrast, imagery is more ambiguous, sluggish, and less easily manipulated. Moreover, imagery mainly actualizes simpler cognitive operations of a perceptual kind, like anticipation and comparisons. Perceptual operations may, however, be useful and even necessary in low programmed task environments, where computational operations are difficult or impossible to perform.

More specifically, limitations of the possibility of using computational operations may be due to lack of experience with the task at hand, where computational processes break down because of a lack of rule-based information to operate on (novelty). Limitations of computational operations may also result from strain on working memory due to high information load (complexity). Finally, uncertainty as to which rule or procedure should be used may lead to computational dysfunction (ambiguity). In this perspective, images may be best described as perceptual-like, conscious representations of mental models. Such perceptual mental models allow a transformation from computational to perceptual operations. More specifically, we have suggested that deductive operations may be converted into simple, quasi-perceptual comparisons, where certainty of judgment may be reached. The imagery-parallel to inductive operations may be found in quasi-perceptual anticipation, where a future state of affairs may be imagined on the basis of a previous sequence of events (cf. Kaufmann, 1990, for a more detailed discussion).

In agreement with the theory, extensive reviews of the relevant experimental literature suggest strongly that imagery gains increasing importance in direct inverse proportion to the degree of structure of the task. With highly novel, complex, or ambiguous task environments, the subject tends to switch from a linguistic-propositional to an imagery-based strategies (Kaufmann, 1984b, 1990).

The basic premise of the theory rests on the assumption that linguistic-propositional and imagery based representations are clearly distinguishable in terms of the kinds of operations that may be most readily executed through these various forms of symbolic modes of representation. Specifically, it is held that the sensory-perceptual properties of imagery have functional value. Level of processing of the task, among other conditions, may determine the functional usefulness of the perceptual properties of imagery. By implication a major role is assigned to the processing required in the typically low programmed task environments characteristically dealt with in creative thinking.

However, problem solving may be seen as a superordinate cognitive activity that is also involved in lower-level processing tasks as well (cf. Kaufmann, 1979). Even in relatively simple cognitive tasks, like short-term memory, there will be strategic considerations related to means-ends analyses—a core of problem-solving activity (cf. Helstrup, 1974, 1987). From this perspective, we have examined imagery effects ranging from simple to complex tasks (Kaufmann, unpublished findings). The task considered falls on a continuum of complexity ranging from memory for individual words, word-pairs, sentences, text, and concept formation, to tasks of problem solving and creativity. In line with the theory presented above, imagery seems to increase in importance as we move up on the dimension of complexity. Interestingly, variations in degree of structure (novelty, complexity, ambiguity) *within* each category of tasks also seem to determine systematically the need for and usefulness of imagery as a representational system.

There is, of course, a clear limitation involved in analyzing results from a diverse area of research originating from quite different questions than the ones in which we are interested. On the other hand, there is an advantage in the sense of having a neutral basis for analysis. Nevertheless, it is necessary to replicate such findings in a uniform, more standardized, and well-controlled research program that would permit a more direct comparison of imagery effects on cognitive performance as a consequence of variations in the parameters held to be important in the theory presented here.

REFERENCES

Anderson, J. (1990). *Cognitive psychology and its implications* (3rd ed.). New York: Freeman.

Anderson, J. R. (1976). *Language, memory and thought.* Hillsdale, NJ: Erlbaum.

Anderson, J. R. (1978). Arguments concerning representations for mental imagery. *Psychological Review, 4,* 249–277.

Anderson, J. R. (1980). *Cognitive psychology and its implications.* San Francisco: W. H. Freeman.

Anderson, J. R., & Bower, G. H. (1973). *Human associative memory.* Washington, DC: Hemisphere.

Atwood, G. (1971). An experimental study of visual imagination and memory. *Cognitive Psychology, 2,* 290–299.

Baker, G. P., & Hacker, P. M. S. (1980). *Wittgenstein: Understanding and meaning.* Oxford: Basil Blackwell.

Bartlett, F. C. (1921). The function of images. *British Journal of Psychology, 11,* 320–337.

Bartlett, F. C. (1925). Feeling, imagery and thinking. *British Journal of Psychology, 16,* 16–28.

Bartlett, F. C. (1927). The relevance of visual imagery to thinking. *British Journal of Psychology, 18,* 23–29.

Black, M. (1972). *The labyrinth of language.* London: Pelican Books.

Berkeley, G. (1710). A treatise concerning the principles of human knowledge. In R. M. Hutchins (Ed.), *Great books of the Western world.* London: Encyclopedia Britannica, 1952. (Original work published 1710)

Block, N. (1983). Mental pictures and cognitive science. *The Philosophical Review, 92,* 499–541.

Brooks, L. R. (1967). The suppression of visualization by reading. *Quarterly Journal of Experimental Psychology, 19,* 289–299.

Bruner, J. S. (1964). The course of cognitive growth. *American Psychologist, 19,* 1–15.

Bruner, J. S., Olver, R. R., & Greenfield, P. M. (1966). *Studies in cognitive growth.* New York: John Wiley.

Bugelski, B. R. (1977). Imagery and verbal behavior. *Journal of Mental Imagery, 1,* 39–52.

Bugelski, B. R. (1982). Learning and imagery. *Journal of Mental Imagery, 6,* 1–92.

Byrne, B. (1974). Item concretness and spatial organization as predictors of visual imagery. *Memory & Cognition, 2,* 53–59.

Chambers, D. (1993). Images are both depictive and descriptive. In B. Roskos-Ewoldsen, M. J. Intons-Peterson, & R. E. Anderson (Eds.), *Imagery, creativity and discovery* (pp. 77–97). Amsterdam: Elsevier Science.

Chambers, D., & Reisberg, D. (1985). Can mental images be ambigous? *Journal of Experimental Psychology: Human Perception and Performance, 11,* 317–328.

Chase, W. G., & Clark, H. H. (1972). Mental operations in the comparisation of sentences and pictures. In L. W. Gregg (Ed.), *Cognition in learning and memory* New York: John Wiley.

Dennett, D. C. (1969). *Content and consciousness.* New York: Humanities Press.

Dennett, D. C. (1982). Two approaches to mental images. In N. Block (Ed.), *Imagery* (pp. 87–107). Cambridge, MA: MIT Press.

Dreyfus, H. L., & Dreyfus, S. E. (1986). *Mind over machine.* New York: The Free Press.

Farah, M. J. (1988). Is visual imagery really visual? Overlooked evidence from neuropsychology. *Psychological Review, 95,* 307–317.

Field, H. H. (1981). Mental representation. In N. Block (Ed.), *Readings in philosophy of psychology* London: Methuen.

Finke, R. A. (1989). *Principles of mental imagery.* Cambridge, MA: MIT Press.

Finke, R. A., & Kosslyn, S. M. (1980). Mental imagery acuity in the peripherial visual field. *Journal of Experimental Psychology: Human Perception and Performance, 6,* 126–139.

Flew, A. G. N. (1956). Facts and "imagination." *Mind, 65,* 392–399.

Fodor, J. A. (1976). *The language of thought.* Hassocks, Sussex: Harvester Press.

Frege, G. (1960). Begriffschrift. In M. B. P. Geach (Ed.), *Translations from the philosophical writings of Gottlob Frege.* Oxford: Basil Blackwell. (Original work published 1879)

Galton, F. (1883). *Inquiries into human faculty and its development.* London: Macmillan.

Geach, P. (1971). *Mental acts.* London: Routledge.

Goldenberg, G., Podreka, I., Steiner, M., Suess, E., Deeke, L., & Willmes, K. (1988).

Regional cerebral blood flow patterns in imagery tasks—results of single photon emission computer tomography. In J. E. M. Denis & J. T. E. Richardson (Eds.), *Cognitive and neuropsychological approaches to mental imagery.* Dordrecht/Boston/Manchester: Martinus Nijhoff.

Hampson, P. J., & Morris, P. E. (1978a). Unfulfilled expectations: A criticism of Neisser's theory of imagery. *Cognition, 6,* 79–85.

Hampson, P. J., & Morris, P. E. (1978b). Cyclical processing: A framework for imagery research. *Journal of Mental Imagery, 3,* 11–22.

Hampson, P. J., & Morris, P. E. (1990). Imagery, consciousness, and cognitive control: The BOSS model reviewed. In P. J. Hampson, D. E. Marks., & J. T. E. Richardson (Eds.), *Imagery: Current developments* (pp. 78–102). London: Routledge.

Hannay, A. (1971). *Mental images: A defence.* London: George Allen & Unwin.

Harman, G. H. (1968). Three levels of meaning. *The Journal of Philosophy, 65,* 590–602.

Harman, G. H. (1970). Language learning. *Nous, 1,* 33–34.

Harman, G. H. (1975). Language, thought and communication. In K. Gunderson (Ed.), *Language, mind and knowledge (Minnesota Studies in the Philosophy of Science)* Minneapolis: University of Minnesota Press.

Harman, G. H. (1977). *Thought.* Princeton, NJ: Princeton University Press.

Harman, G. (1981). Language learning (pp. 38–44) In N. Block (Ed.), *Readings in philosophy of psychology. Vol. 2.* London: Methuen.

Hayes-Roth, F. (1979). Distinguishing theories of representation: A critique of Anderson's Arguments Concerning Representations for Mental Imagery. *Psychological Review, 4,* 376–382.

Hebb, D. O. (1980). *Essay on mind.* Hillsdale, NJ: Erlbaum.

Heil, J. (1982). What does the mind's eye look at? *The Journal of Mind and Behavior, 3,* 143–149.

Helstrup, T. (1974). *Kognitive prosesser i kort tids hukommelse.* Unpublished doctoral dissertation, University of Bergen, Norway.

Helstrup, T. (1987). One, two, or three memories? A problem solving approach to memory for performed acts. *Acta Psychologica, 66,* 37–68.

Horowitz, L. M. J. (1970). *Image formation and cognition.* London: Butterworths.

Humphrey, G. (1959). *Thinking.* London: Methuen.

Hyman, I. E. Jr. (1993). Imagery, reconstructive memory and discovery. In B. Roskos-Ewoldsen, M. J. Intons-Peterson, & R. E. Anderson (Eds.), *Imagery, creativity and discovery* (pp. 77–97). Amsterdam: Elsevier Science.

Johnson-Laird, P. N. (1992). Images, models and propositional representations. *Fourth European Workshop on Imagery and Cognition,* 211–218.

Kaufmann, G. (1979). *Visual imagery and its relation to problem solving. A theoretical and experimental inquiry.* Oslo: Norwegian University Press.

Kaufmann, G. (1980). *Imagery, language and cognition.* Oslo: Norwegian University Press.

Kaufmann, G. (1981). The functional significance in ideational fluency performance. *Journal of Mental Imagery, 5,* 115–120.

Kaufmann, G. (1983). How good are imagery questionnaires? *Scandinavian Journal of Psychology, 24,* 59–64.

Kaufmann, G. (1984a). Mental imagery and problem solving. In A. Sheikh (Ed.), *International review of mental imagery* (Vol. 1). New York: Brandon House.

Kaufmann, G. (1984b). Can Skinner define a problem? *The Behavioral and Brain Sciences, 7,* 599.

Kaufmann, G. (1985). A theory of symbolic representation in problem solving. *Journal of Mental Imagery, 9,* 51–70.

Kaufmann, G. (Ed.). (1986). On the conceptual basis of imagery models: A critique and a theory. In D. Marks (Ed.), *Theories of imagery formation.* New York: Brandon House.

Kaufmann, G. (1988). Mental imagery and problem solving. In J. E. M. Denis & J. T. E. Richardson (Eds.), *Cognitive and neuropsychological approaches to mental imagery.* Dordrecht/Boston/Manchester: Martinus Nijhoff.

Kaufmann, G. (1990). Imagery effects on problem solving. In P. J. Hampson, D. E. Marks., & J. T. E. Richardson (Eds.), *Imagery: Current developments* (pp. 169–194). London: Routledge.

Kaufmann, G. (1993). The content and logical structure of creativity concepts: An inquiry into the conceptual foundations of creativity research. In S. G. Isaksen, M. Murdock, R. Firestien, & D. Treffinger (Eds.), *Understanding and recognizing creativity.* Norwood, NJ: Ablex.

Kaufmann, G., & Helstrup, T. (1993). Mental imagery: Fixed or multiple meanings? Nature and function of imagery in creative thinking. In B. Roskos-Ewoldsen, M. J. Intons-Peterson, & R. E. Anderson (Eds.), *Imagery, creativity and discovery* (pp. 77–97). Amsterdam: Elsevier Science.

Kieras, D. (1978). Beyond pictures and words: Alternative information-processing models for imagery effects in verbal memory. *Psychological Bulletin, 85,* 532–554.

Kintsch, W. (1974). *The representation of meaning in memory.* Hillsdale, NJ: Erlbaum.

Kosslyn, S. M. (1980). *Image and mind.* Cambridge, MA: Harvard University Press.

Kosslyn, S. M. (1983). *Ghosts in the mind's machine: Creating and using images in the brain.* New York: Norton.

Kosslyn, S. M., & Pomerantz, J. R. (1977). Imagery, propositions, and the form of mental representations. *Cognitive Psychology, 7,* 52–76.

Kosslyn, S. M., Pinker, S., Smith, G. E., & Schwartz, S. P. (1979). On the demystification of mental imagery. *The Behavioral and Brain Sciences, 2,* 535–581.

Lindsay, P. H., & Norman, D. A. (1977). *Human information processing.* New York: Academic Press.

Luria, A. R. (1976). *Cognitive development: Its cultural and social foundations.* Cambridge: Harvard University Press.

Mandler, J. M., & Mandler, G. (1964). *Thinking: From association to gestalt.* New York: John Wiley.

Marks, D. (1977). Imagery and consciousness: A theoretical review from an individual differences perspective. *Journal of Mental Imagery, 2,* 275–290.

Marks, D. (1983). Mental imagery and consciousness: A theoretical review. In A. A. Sheikh (Ed.), *Imagery: Current theory, research and application.* New York: John Wiley.

Marschark, M., & Cornoldi, C. (1990). Imagery and verbal processing. In C. Cornoldi, & M. McDaniel (Eds.), *Imagery and cognition* (pp. 133–182). New York: Springer-Verlag.

Marschark, M., Richman, C. L., Yuille, J. C., & Hunt, R. R. (1987). The role of imagery in memory: On shared and distinctive information. *Psychological Bulletin, 102,* 28–41.

McKellar, P. (1957). *Imagination and thinking.* New York: Basic Books.

Morris, P. E., & Hampson, P. J. (1983). *Imagery and consciousness.* New York: Academic Press.

Morris, P. E., & Hampson, P. J. (1990). Imagery, consciousness, and cognitive control: The BOSS model reviewed. In D. M. P. J. Hampson & J. T. E. Richardson (Eds.), *Imagery: Current developments.* London: Routledge.

Neisser, U. (1976). *Cognition and reality.* San Francisco: W. H. Wheels & Co.

Neisser, U. (1978). Anticipations, images and introspection. *Cognition, 6,* 169–174.

Newell, A. (1969). Heuristic programming: Ill. Structured problems. In J. Aronsky (Ed.), *Progress in operations research* (Vol. 3). New York: John Wiley.

Norman, D. A., & Rumelhart, D. E. (1975). *Explorations in cognition.* San Francisco: W. H. Freeman.

Paivio, A. (1971a). Imagery and deep structure in the recall of English nominalizations. *Journal of Verbal Learning and Verbal Behavior, 10*(b), 1–12.

Paivio, A. (1971b). *Imagery and verbal processes.* New York: Holt.

Paivio, A. (1972a). Imagery and language. In S. J. Segal (Ed.), *Imagery: Current cognitive approaches.* New York: Academic Press.

Paivio, A. (1972b). A theoretical analysis of the role of imagery in learning and memory. In P. W. Sheehan (Ed.), *The function and nature of imagery.* London: Academic Press.

Paivio, A. (1975a). Imagery and synchronic thinking. *Canadian Psychological Review*(a), 147–163.

Paivio, A. (1975b). Neomentalism. *Canadian Journal of Psychology, 29,* 263–291.

Paivio, A. (1976a). Imagery in recall and recognition. In J. Brown (Ed.), *Recall and recognition.* London: John Wiley.

Paivio, A. (1976b). Images, propositions, and knowledge. In J. M. Nicholas (Ed.), *Images, perception and knowledge.* Dordrecht: Reidel.

Paivio, A., & Begg, I. (1981). *Psychology of language.* Englewood Cliffs, NJ: Prentice-Hall.

Paivio, A. (1983a). The empirical case for dual coding. In J. C. Yuille (Ed.), *Imagery, memory and cognition.* Hillsdale, NJ: Erlbaum.

Paivio, A. (1983b). The mind's eye in art and science. *Poetics, 12*(b), 1–18.

Paivio, A. (1986). *Mental representations.* New York: Oxford University Press.

Peterson, M. J. (1993). Imagery's role in creativity and discovery. In B. Roskos-Ewoldsen, M. J. Intons-Peterson, & R. E. Anderson (Eds.), *Imagery, creativity and discovery* (pp. 1–38). Amsterdam: Elsevier Science.

Pinker, S., & Kosslyn, S. M. (1983). Theories of mental imagery. In A. A. Sheikh (Ed.), *Imagery: Current theory, research and application* New York: John Wiley.

Potter, M. C., & Kroll, J. F. (1986). Pictures in sentences: Understanding without words. *Journal of Experimental Psychology: General, 115,* 281–294.

Price, H. H. (1969). *Thinking and experience.* London: Hutchinson.

Putnam, H. (1975). The meaning of "meaning." In K. Gunderson (Ed.), *Language, mind and knowledge.* Minneapolis: University of Minnesota Press.

Pylyshyn, Z. W. (1973). What the mind's eye tells the mind's brain: A critique of mental imagery. *Psychological Bulletin, 80,* 1–23.

Pylyshyn, Z. W. (1981). The imagery debate: Analogue media versus tacit knowledge. *Psychological Review, 88*(1), 16–45.

Quine, W. (1960). *Word and object.* Cambridge: M.I.T. Press.

Reed, S. K., Hock, H., & Lockhead, G. R. (1983). Tacit knowledge and the effect of pattern recognition on mental scanning. *Memory & Cognition, 11,* 137–143.

Reisberg, D., & Chambers, D. (1991). Neither pictures nor propositions: What can we learn from a mental image? *Canadian Journal of Psychology,*

Reisberg, D., & Logie, R. (1993). The ins and outs of working memory: Overcoming the limits on learning from imagery. In B. Roskos-Ewoldsen, M. J. Intons-Peterson, & R. E. Anderson (Eds.), *Imagery, creativity and discovery* (pp. 39–76). Amsterdam: Elsevier Science.

Roland, P. E., & Friberg, L. (1985). Localization of cortical areas activated by thinking. *Journal of Neurophysiology, 53,* 1219–1243.

Rorty, R. (1980). *Philosophy and the mirror and nature.* Oxford: Basil Blackwell.

Rumelhart, D. E., & Ortony, A. (Eds.). (1977). *The representation of knowledge in memory.* Hillsdale, NJ: Erlbaum.

Ryle, G. (1949). *The concept of mind.* London: Hutchinson.

Salthouse, T. (1974). Using selective interference to investigate spatial memory representation. *Memory & Cognition, 2,* 749–757.

Salthouse, T. (1975). Simultaneous processing of verbal and spatial memory representation. *Memory & Cognition, 3,* 221–225.

Segal, S. J. (1972). Assimilation of a stimulus in the construction of an image. The Perky effect revisited. In P. W. Sheehan (Ed.), *The function and nature of imagery.* New York: Academic Press.

Sellars, W. (1963). *Science, perception and reality.* London: Routledge.

Shepard, R. N. (1978a). The mental image. *American Psychologist, 37,* 125–137.

Shepard, R. N. (1978b). Externalization of mental images and the act of creation. In W. E. C. B. S. Randawa (Ed.), *Visual learning, thinking, and communication* (pp. 133–189). New York: Academic Press.

Shepard, R. N. (1990). On understanding mental images. In H. Barlow, C. Blakemore, & M. Weston-Smith (Eds.), *Images and understanding.* Cambridge: Cambridge University Press.

Shepard, R. N., & Cooper, L. A. (1982). Mental images and their transformations. Cambridge, MA: MIT Press.

Shorter, J. M. (1952). Imagination. *Mind, 61,* 527–542.

Simon, H. A. (Ed.). (1978). *Information processing theory of human problem solving.* Hillsdale, NJ: Erlbaum.

Specht, E. K. (1963). *The foundations of Wittgenstein's late philosophy.* New York: Manchester University Press.

Titchener, E. B. (1910). *A textbook of psychology.* New York: Macmillan.

Titchener, E. B. (1914). *A primer of psychology.* New York: Macmillan.

Toulmin, S. (Ed.). (1971). *The concept of "stages" in psychological development.* New York: Academic Press.

Tye, M. (1991). *The imagery debate.* Cambridge, MA: MIT Press.

Wittgenstein, L. (1953). *Philosophical investigations.* Oxford: Basil Blackwell.

Yuille, J. C., & Catchpole, M. F. (1977). The role of imagery in models of cognition. *Journal of Mental Imagery, 1,* 171–180.

CHAPTER 4

The Nonambiguity of Mental Images

Daniel Reisberg

Scholars interested in mental imagery spent roughly a decade debating the fundamental nature of imagery. Broadly speaking, the question in this debate hinged on whether we should think of imagery as *depictive* in nature, so that mental images were, in some deep sense, just like pictures, or whether images were instead *descriptive* in their nature, so that mental images were best thought of as basically propositional in character.

One would seek in vain for a published resolution of the imagery debate, but, in the eyes of most psychologists, the resolution has long been clear: In brief, both sides had it right. Images do have depictive qualities, and imaging does have much in common (both functionally and anatomically) with perceiving (Farah, 1988; Finke, 1985, 1989). At the same time, though, other evidence reveals how images are "cognitively penetrated" in one way or another, and therefore *not* picture-like.

In this chapter I will describe several lines of evidence pertinent to these claims, arguing for a "duplex" conception of imagery. In essence, I will propose that mental images are neither pictures nor propositions, but something in between. Moreover, I will argue that this character of imagery has important consequences, not just for our theorizing but also for the *function* of, and indeed, the *limits on* the function of mental images.

As a way of entering this discussion, it should be acknowledged that, on anyone's account, images do have much in common with pictures. Thus, in many regards, images surely are depictive. For example, various studies show that the pattern of what information is available in a mental image, and what information is salient, resembles the pattern one would expect with a pictorial representation;

this pattern of information availability is, correspondingly, rather different from what one would expect with a descriptive representation (e.g., Kosslyn, 1976). Likewise, chronometric studies show that the time needed to scan across, or to rotate, or to zoom in on a mental image all correspond to what one would expect with a pictorial representation (Kosslyn, Ball, & Reiser, 1978; Shepard & Cooper, 1982). These findings, showing that images preserve the metric properties of space, speak directly to the claim that images are indeed depictive. Moreover, and directly relevant to present concerns, there is also a great deal of evidence, including both historical and laboratory evidence, to show that one can be reminded by, or instructed by, or surprised by one's own mental images, implying in each case that one can "read off" information from a mental image in about the same way that one can "read" information from a picture (Finke, 1989, 1990; Kosslyn, 1983; Richardson, 1980). Once again, this implies a depictive quality for images, but, in addition, suggests an important function for images—as a rich source of discovery about appearances and spatial relations.

It was against this backdrop that, in 1985, Chambers and I published some data indicating a *contrast* between images and pictures, and, in particular, data suggesting important limits on what subjects could discover from their mental images (Chambers & Reisberg, 1985). Subjects were shown the form in Figure 4.1—the ambiguous duck/rabbit—for 5 seconds. This turns out to be enough time to memorize this figure, but not enough time for subjects to reconstrue the picture itself while it is still in view. This latter fact is important, because we wanted to ask whether subjects could *discover* the alternate construal *from their images*. This made it crucial that subjects not know about the alternate construal prior to creating the image.

After 5 seconds, the duck/rabbit picture was removed from view, and subjects were asked to form an image of this shape. Subjects were given as long as they wished to form this image, and then, once they had it, they were asked to try to reconstrue the image, just as they had earlier reconstrued a series of training figures. To help subjects with this task, we gave them a series of hints, urging them, among other things, to try inspecting the "left edge" of their image, the "right edge," and so on. (These are precisely the hints that help subjects reconstrue the figure if an actual duck/rabbit *picture* is in view.) Then, if subjects failed in this task, we simply gave them a blank piece of paper and asked them to draw a picture of the form they had been imaging, and to try reconstruing their own drawings.

The data were clear-cut: Exactly 100 percent of the subjects failed to reconstrue their own image. Just moments later, though, 100 percent of the subjects succeeded in reconstruing their own drawings, drawings presumably based on the image. This implies, among other things, that subjects understood the task, had formed an adequate memory of the figure, and so on.

We have replicated this result with a number of procedural variations, and the result seems reasonably robust. For example, comparable results are obtained if subjects are specifically instructed to make their image a clear and precise copy of the original form—that is, if subjects are specifically warned against biasing their image to make it more "duck-like" or more "rabbit-like." Likewise, compa-

FIGURE 4.1. The duck/rabbit figure (after Jastrow, 1900), used by Chambers and Reisberg (1985), and numerous other studies.

rable results (zero success rates in reversing the image) are obtained if subjects are given practice—first with one image of an ambiguous figure, then with an image of a different ambiguous figure, and so on. As we will discuss below, however, several other researchers have not replicated our zero success rates, but have, instead, documented some apparently successful cases of image reversal. We will have more to say about these cases later, but for now let us simply note that these researchers have confirmed one central result: Reconstruing visual images is, at best, very difficult, and is certainly more difficult (and less frequent) than reconstrual of the comparable visual picture. Hence, to say the least, this seems to be a regard in which visual images are conspicuously not like pictures, and in which the potential for discovery from images seems narrower than the corresponding potential for pictures.

THE UNAMBIGUITY OF AUDITORY IMAGES

Indeed, these claims need not be limited to visual imagery, since we have obtained comparable data with auditory images. This parallel to visual imagery was far from inevitable, for it could have been (for example) that visual imagery and auditory imagery follow rather different principles. Thus, this convergence between the visual and auditory data provides testimony for the robustness and generality of the duck/rabbit results just described.

In our studies of auditory imagery, we have exploited the fact that certain words if repeated aloud yield a sound-stream compatible with more than one segmentation. For example, repetitions of the word LIFE yield a sound-stream that is acoustically indistinguishable from that resulting from repetitions of the word FLY. The difference between these two sound-streams ("life" repeated or "fly" repeated) lies entirely in how the sound-streams are perceptually segmented. Thus, the sound-stream itself is fully ambiguous—it can be segmented in more than one way, with each segmentation yielding an interpretable result (namely, repetitions of one common English word or another). Consistent with this (acoustic) ambiguity, subjects spontaneously report that they perceive these sound-streams as flip-flopping in perceived organization—and so the sound-stream is perceived first as one word, then as another. This obviously resembles the perceptual character of, say, the Necker cube or the duck/rabbit, with the visual information in these cases fully compatible with more than one organization, and spontaneously perceived first in one organization, then in the other.

These observations invite us to ask whether *images* of these auditory "ambiguous figures" resist reconstrual, just as images of visual figures do.[1] Subjects in one of our early studies actually heard repetitions of the stimulus word STRESS (Reisberg, Smith, Baxter, & Sonenshine, 1989). All of these subjects, with short latencies, reported that these repetitions turned into repetitions of DRESS. This was true whether subjects produced these repetitions aloud themselves, or heard the experimenter producing the repetitions, or heard them via tape recording. A different group of subjects was simply asked to *guess* what this stimulus word would turn into if repeated aloud; for these subjects, no mention was made of imagery. These subjects gave every indication of taking their guessing task seriously, and they produced a number of responses, mostly based on letter-rearrangements ("ester," "rests," and so on). However, they rarely produced the DRESS response. (This is not surprising, given the indications that subjects were using letter-arrangements to support their guesses.) This pattern makes the DRESS response a good index of bona fide perceptual reversals—fully compatible with the stimulus information, reliably and quickly perceived, but rarely guessed.

A third group of subjects was asked to imagine that a friend's voice was repeating the stimulus word STRESS over and over. This group reported transformations to DRESS reliably less often than the perceptual group did, but offered the DRESS response reliably *more* often than the guessing group. On the face of it, this implies a striking contrast between visual and auditory imagery: Whereas visual images seemed never to produce reconstruals, auditory images seem to produce reconstruals at an appreciable rate.

However, there is an important control missing here: With auditory imagery, subjects have the option of supplementing their imagery with subvocalization—literally saying the word to themselves. I will say more, later on, about how this might influence performance, but for now let me note simply that this subvocalization is easily controlled: A different group of subjects was asked to imagine a friend's voice repeating the target STRESS, but with this instruction, "We have discovered that it's very important that people's *mouths be occupied while doing this task.* Therefore, while imagining the repetitions, please chew on this piece of candy" (emphasis not in original; note also that the instruction was phrased in a fashion that provided little information about whether chewing would help or hurt performance). Subjects were then supplied with a large piece of chewy candy, and, once they had begun chewing, they were shown the stimulus word so that they could begin the imagined repetitions. This manipulation dropped the rate of DRESS responses to guessing levels. Thus, it seems, auditory images support reconstrual only if the auditory images are somehow supplemented by subvocalization.

This claim has been confirmed in a variety of other procedures. For example, in one study, subjects were instructed to push their tongues up against the roof of the mouth, to clench their teeth, and also to purse their lips. This manipulation, "clamping" the articulators, also succeeded in eliminating reversals of the auditory images (Wilson, Smith, & Reisberg, 1993). However, reconstruals of auditory images have *not* been affected by a variety of control activities. For example, there is no effect if subjects are required to tap rhythmically while imagining the STRESS repetitions (Reisberg et al., 1989). This regular activity should be comparable to chewing in its potential for sheer distraction, and so the non-effect of tapping speaks against a distraction account of our manipulations. Instead, subvocalization seems crucial, and image reconstruals are eliminated when subvocalization is prevented.

We will return to the role of subvocalization below, but for now let us underscore the crucial points: Reversals of the duck/rabbit figure happen routinely, even universally, with *pictures.* Reversals do not happen routinely in mental imagery. Roughly the same can be said for auditory imagery: With subvocalization blocked, we can easily find discoveries that do not happen with imagery, even though comparable discoveries happen routinely with actually perceived stimuli. Therefore, at the least, it seems that we have a clear contrast between images and actual, out-in-the-world stimuli, and therefore one regard in which images are *not* pictorial, and *not* like stimuli.

LIMITS ON LEARNING FROM PERCEPTS

We still need to ask, however, what is going on in these procedures. Why do subjects find it so difficult to make these discoveries from images? As we have already mentioned, we know that subjects can make other sorts of discoveries from images, in other contexts. So what "blocks" the discoveries in the procedures just described? We believe the answer to these questions lies in an analogy to perception, and learning about perceived forms. We begin with an example.

Consider the familiar Necker cube, shown in Figure 4.2A. The *picture* of the

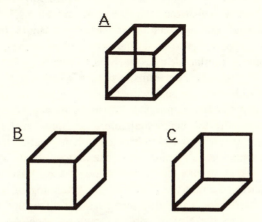

FIGURE 4.2. Panel A shows the standard Necker cube, which can be perceived either as analogous to the (unambiguous) cube shown in B, or the cube shown in C.

Necker cube is of course simply a two-dimensional depiction, and the optical information provided by this picture is ambiguous: Equivalent optical information would be provided either by a cube configured like the one shown in Figure 4.2B, or by a cube configured like the one in 4.2C. Thus, the *picture* of the Necker cube is fully compatible with either of these three-dimensional interpretations. (Of course, the picture is also compatible with a *veridical* two-dimensional interpretation!) Thus, we emphasize, the *picture* is ambiguous—entirely unbiased with regard to interpretation, and fully compatible with more than one interpretation.

The *percept* of the Necker cube, however, is not ambiguous. The cube is perceived as having one configuration in depth or another, or perhaps first one and then the other. The percept is not indifferent or unbiased as to interpretation; instead, the percept specifies an arrangement in three dimensions. The cube is perceived, in brief, as having a particular shape.

This example (and much other evidence) indicates that we need to draw an important contrast between pictures and percepts: Of course, pictures and percepts have a great deal in common—both of these *depict* the to-be-represented scene. A picture, however, depicts in a "neutral" fashion—indifferent with regard to figure/ground organization; indifferent with regard to three-dimensionality, and so on. In these regards, pictures are ambiguous, and these various specifications (figure/ground, 3-D, orientation) need to be imposed on the picture by the perceiver in order to render an ambiguous picture into an unambiguous percept. Percepts are not ambiguous, by virtue of the fact that a figure is perceived as having a particular figure/ground organization, a particular configuration in depth, a particular orientation, and so on.

Percepts are, in this sense, more organized than pictures. As Bruner (1957, 1973) put it many years ago, the percept "goes beyond the information given," by virtue of containing more information, disambiguating information, than is present in the stimulus itself. More recently, Reisberg and Chambers (1991) tried to capture the same notion in claiming that a percept incorporates both depictive information and also a half-dozen "perceptual specifications," detailing how the depiction is to be read. These perceptual specifications would, for example, identify the depiction's top, and also its figure/ground organization, and also its configuration in depth. A similar idea has been put forward by Peterson, Kihlstrom, Rose, and Glisky (1992). In their terms, a percept exists only within the context of a "perceptual reference frame," with the reference frame incorporating the perceptual specifications just mentioned. (Presumably, a similar argument can be applied to audition, with the perceptual reference frame in this case specifying the *temporal* organization—for example, the segment boundaries, and so on.)

The reference frame literally *shapes* the phenomenal form, and this has many consequences. Thus, changing the reference frame can drastically change phenomenal appearance, essentially creating a new psychological stimulus from the same physical stimulus. It is this that underlies the difference between the two percepts engendered by the Necker cube. Likewise, if one changes the assigned orientation of a square, the resulting diamond is a different percept; it looks different (less orthogonal, more elongated), it resembles different forms, and it carries different information.

We have phrased this in terms of phenomenal appearances, but these claims are easy to document. For example, subjects can be asked to detect right angles within a figure; they are likely to yield quicker response times for Figure 4.3A than for Figure 4.3C, even though these forms are geometrically identical (differing only in a 45-degree rotation). Likewise, subjects will provide quicker response times in detecting the symmetry of Figure 4.3D than 4.3B, although, again, these forms are identical except for a rotation. Finally, subjects will judge the resemblance within the A–B pair in Figure 4.3 to be much less than the resemblance within the C–D pair, although the geometric relations are preserved (cf. Goldmeier, 1937/1972; Rock, 1983). In each case, these results seem odd if subjects are basing their judgments purely on stimulus geometry. The results are sensible, though, on the claim that a perceptual reference frame (in this particular case, subjects' understanding of orientation) literally shapes phenomenal appearance.

What a perceived form is seen to resemble and what the perceived form will evoke from memory are also profoundly influenced by the reference frame. The evidence for this assertion will be familiar to most readers, since the evidence is reproduced in many introductory psychology textbooks. For example, we can show subjects the form shown in Figure 4.4, and arrange, by a setting procedure, for them to perceive it as a vase. (This setting procedure can take many forms. We can be as direct as simply telling subjects, "We are about to show you a

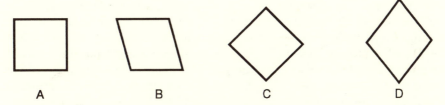

A   B   C   D

FIGURE 4.3. Forms A and B are identical except for a 45-degree rotation; likewise for Forms C and D. However, the differences in orientation have profound impact on phenomenal appearance. (See text for details.)

FIGURE 4.4.   The Rubin vase-profiles

vase," or we can tell them to "look at this white shape," and so on.) Sometime later, we show subjects this same form again, but now, via setting, we arrange for them to perceive it as profiles. (We can, for example, instruct them to "look at the black shape.") Then, with this second presentation, we simply ask subjects whether they have ever seen this figure before. It turns out that subjects will reliably indicate that they have *not* seen this figure before, even though this exact drawing, this exact geometry, was under their view just minutes earlier. Apparently, then, what matters for recognition is not geometry per se, but geometry as understood, geometry as organized by the perceiver *within its reference frame* (in this case, within a reference frame specifying a particular figure/ground organization, and a particular configuration in depth).

The embedded figures task (Gottschaldt, 1926/1967) makes a similar point with regard to parsing. In an embedded figure, we often fail to recognize (even with deliberate searching) the presence of familiar, meaningful figures, presumably because the perceptual context leads us to parse these figures in some unfamiliar way. Here, too, recognition is failing despite familiar geometry, because the geometry is understood with an inappropriate perceptual specification.

As a final example, a number of studies have documented that subjects fail to recognize various figures if the figures are presented in novel orientations: For example, subjects will reliably fail to recognize an outline map of the African continent if the map is depicted with the eastern or western shore at the "top" of the map (rather than the conventional presentation, with the Mediterranean coast at the top). Important for our purposes, it is not the *retinal* orientation that matters: If subjects are shown a map of Africa rotated, say, 90 degrees clockwise, and then are led to turn their heads 90 degrees clockwise (orienting the map "correctly" on the retina), recognition still fails (Goldmeier, 1937/1972; Rock, 1973). What matters then, is not the geometry per se, and not the geometry relative to retinal coordinates, but the geometry *understood as* having a certain "top." That is, recognition is governed by the geometry within a reference frame with, in this case, the reference frame specifying the form's orientation.

In all these cases (and many more cases in the literature, e.g., Davi & Proffitt, 1993), it seems that discoveries about visual inputs are governed by the percept, not by the stimulus. Put differently, discoveries about visual inputs are determined by the stimulus *within its reference frame,* so that discoveries go forward *only if* the discovery is compatible with the stimulus *and* the perceiver's perceptual specifications about that stimulus.

More broadly put, the point here is a familiar one to students of cognition, and it is a point directly relevant to the "mentalism" that is at the heart of most contemporary thinking. The world to which we react, the world that guides our actions, the world that evokes (or fails to evoke) memories, is not the physically specified world; it is not the world as it might be described from some outsider's perspective. Instead, the world to which we react is the world as it is mentally represented. Moreover, this representation is no mere transcription of the stimulus information. In the ways we have already indicated, the mental representation often goes well beyond the information given. In other ways (about which we will see more below) the mental representation can be selective, containing *less* information than the corresponding stimulus. In still other ways, the internal representation can provide an evaluative or interpretive framework, which, again, can heavily influence cognition. This last is clearly in view, for example, in discussions of problem solving (which often depends on how a problem has been "structured") or decision making (heavily guided by how a problem is "framed"), and so on.

These various aspects of mental representation ensure that our mental representations are unambiguous, and thus able to carry meaning (cf. Fodor, 1975). However, this rescue from ambiguity has its price: It simultaneously robs the representation of equipotentiality. This is reflected, for example, in the various perceptual demonstrations just cited, which typically involve *failures* to find some target within a stimulus array. Likewise, demonstrations of "fixedness" within problem solving can be read as making the same point: The problem-solver, fixed on one perspective, fails to see an alternative set of possibilities for the problem setting. One way or another, though, it seems clear that we will make little headway in describing cognition, or action, unless we consider how the world is represented and understood. The "behaviorists' world," so to speak, the objectively defined world, is impressively inconsequential for many psychological purposes.[2]

LIMITS ON LEARNING FROM IMAGES

Returning to the more immediate issues, note that all the cases we have described so far are cases of *perceived* inputs (and, for that matter, perceived *visual* inputs). With pictorial inputs, our reactions and recognitions are guided by stimulus geometry and, it seems, a specification of figure/ground organization, parsing, and orientation. How does all of this apply to mental imagery? Data from Reisberg and Chambers (1991) provide an answer to this question, and the answer is straightforward: Images, just like percepts, seem to exist only within a perceptual reference frame. Discoveries from images, just like those from percepts, must be compatible both with the depicted geometry *and* with the reference frame within which that geometry is understood.

For example, in one of Reisberg and Chambers' studies, subjects were told that we were studying "memory for abstract forms." Subjects were then shown a series of forms, each for 5 seconds. Immediately after each form was removed from view, subjects were asked to form an image of it, and then to imagine that form rotated by a certain amount—sometimes 180 degrees, sometimes 90 degrees, and so on. Subjects were then asked to draw a picture of the form, in its rotated position.

The purpose of all this was simply to prepare subjects for seeing abstract forms, so that we could present the test stimulus (a "sideways" map of the state of Texas), shown in Figure 4.5. This figure was presented, with no special notice, as the tenth figure in the series. As with the other figures, subjects looked at this stimulus for 5 seconds, presumably encoding it as one more abstract shape. Then, as with the training figures, the form was removed from view, and subjects were asked to form an image of it. Subjects were instructed to imagine the form rotated by 90 degrees clockwise, so that subjects were now contemplating an upright map of the "Lone Star State."

At this point, instead of drawing the shape, as they had for all the training figures, subjects were told directly that the shape they were imaging "resembles a familiar geographic form," and subjects were asked simply to identify the form. Subjects were allowed a few minutes to examine their image in answering this question. If they failed to identify the form, they were given a blank piece of paper and asked to draw the form they had just been imaging. Then, with the drawing complete, they were asked to identify the "familiar geographic form" in their own drawing.

What should we expect here? First, it seems likely that subjects will initially understand the side topmost in the original drawing as being the figure's top. This specification of top presumably will not change when subjects imagine the rotation, on the assumption that subjects are imagining the rotation of something like an object-centered form. (That is, we are assuming that imagined rotation is analogous to rotation on the retina—in both cases, the transformation preserves the defined top. In essence, then, the reference frame is "rotated" along with the geometry.) Therefore, at the time of the test, subjects are imaging the "right geometry" for Texas, but with the wrong reference frame (that is, specifying the "wrong" top). Consequently, we should predict that, with the wrong reference frame, this image should not resemble Texas and should not call Texas to mind.

This prediction is borne out. No subjects succeeded in discovering Texas in their image, although, moments later, many subjects were able to recognize Texas in their own drawing. This latter result makes it clear that subjects understood the task, knew what Texas looked like, had adequately encoded the shape, and so on. Even with these assurances, though, there is an obvious concern about this result: Perhaps subjects' failure in this imagery task reflects some other performance limitation. For example, perhaps the Texas form is too complex to image clearly, and so this might be the cause of subjects' failure to make the relevant discovery from imagery. Similarly, perhaps subjects are insufficiently familiar with the Texas form. In this case, a clear and concrete *stimulus* might be enough to evoke the relevant memory, while a less-vivid, less-detailed *image* might not be.

However, we can easily rule out these concerns (and numerous variations on them). On our view, what blocks this discovery from imagery is subjects' inappropriate reference frame. Therefore, all we need do, to change performance, is to change the reference frame. More precisely, all we need do is tell subjects directly to change their understanding of the figure's top. (We know that subjects can easily do this; see Attneave & Reid, 1968; Rock & Leaman, 1963.)

To test these claims, the next procedure parallels the study just described, but with one important change. As before, subjects were told that we were studying memory for abstract forms. They were then shown a series of shapes, each for 5 seconds, and asked to form an image of each one. (In fact, these "setting figures" were the same as those used in the previous study. As before, the purpose of

FIGURE 4.5. The test figure (a sideways map of Texas), employed by Reisberg and Chambers (1991) in Experiments 1 and 2.

these setting figures was simply to lure subjects into encoding the test form as another one of the "abstract shapes.") This time, however, and *unlike* the previous study, we did not tell subjects to imagine each figure rotated by a certain amount. Instead, for each figure we told subjects to think of a particular side as being the form's "new top." This new top was never the top as presented, and the position of this new top varied from trial to trial. (For purposes of control, this sequence was matched to that used in the previous study, so that the top for each figure, explicitly identified in this study, corresponded to the "top" of the figure, after rotation, in the previous study.) Subjects were then asked to draw each figure, with its new top shown at the top of the drawing.

As the tenth figure in the series, subjects were shown the sideways Texas figure, with no particular notice drawn to it, so that, once again, subjects encoded this shape as merely one more abstract form. After 5 seconds, the form was removed from view, subjects formed an image of it, and then subjects were told to think of the left-hand side of the shape as being the figure's top. Consequently, subjects should now be imaging the Texas geometry with an appropriate reference frame—that is, a reference frame matching that of the Texas map.

We are now ready to ask why subjects failed in our initial "Texas" procedure, with the "rotate" instruction. If the problem in this procedure was that this form is too complex to image, then we should again expect failure in this newer task, since the target form has not been changed. Likewise, if some aspect of the task is too hard (e.g., subjects being unfamiliar with U.S. geography), then, again, we should predict failure in the present procedure. However, if the problem from before was subjects' inappropriate reference frame, then we have changed that, and so we should change the pattern of results. This last prediction is correct: In this new procedure, approximately half of the subjects succeeded in identifying Texas in their image, whereas no subjects in the previous experiment had identified Texas in imagery. It would appear, then, that discovery from imagery is indeed bounded by the reference frame. When the reference frame is changed, new discoveries become available.

A variety of other data make this same point. For example, in one study (Reisberg & Chambers, 1991, Experiment 3), subjects were shown a series of training figures, all using the same elements (black on a white background), but with the elements in a different configuration in each training figure. Thus, this sequence gave subjects ample familiarization with the elements themselves. In addition, since the training figures differed from each other only in configuration, they called subjects' attention to the importance of memorizing the elements' exact positions.

The test figure, again presented with no special notice, employed the same elements, but configured as shown in Figure 4.6. Subjects were shown this figure, memorized it, and then were asked to form an image of the figure. At this point, half of the subjects were simply asked what familiar form was depicted here. Other subjects were given a hint: They were told to try thinking of these elements, not as figures themselves, but as the shadows cast by a solid figure.

In this case, the first group, without the hint, was imaging a geometric configuration isomorphic with the numeral "5" but with the wrong reference frame— that is, with the "wrong" figure/ground organization. The second group, with the hint, was presumably imaging the right geometry within the appropriate reference frame. Therefore, by the logic we have already explained, we predicted successful discoveries of the numeral *with* the hint, but not otherwise. That is what the data show: 28 percent of the subjects in the "hint" group detected the target form; zero subjects in the control group detected the target.

It should be noted, of course, that 72 percent of the subjects in the "hint" group did *not* recognize the target form; similarly, half of the subjects in our second "Texas" study failed to recognize Texas, even when led to the appropriate reference frame. On our account, this is unsurprising: In order for discoveries to flow from imagery, the discoveries must be compatible with both the image's reference frame and the depicted geometry. In the cases just mentioned, subjects should have the appropriate reference frame (thanks to our explicit instructions),

FIGURE 4.6. The test figure employed by Reisberg and Chambers (1991) in Experiment 4.

but plainly that will not be enough. They also need the right geometry. Moreover, it seems likely that many subjects will have difficulty in depicting the target form's geometry, since, after all, the Texas form is reasonably complex, as is the form shown in Figure 4.6. Thus, we can see the crucial role of the image's reference frame in the *improvement* in performance, when an appropriate reference frame replaces an inappropriate one. (This is manifest in the "hint" group in the "5" experiment, in comparison to the no-hint group, or in the "redefine top" group in the Texas experiment, in comparison to the "rotate" group.) However, there is no reason to expect that having the appropriate reference frame, by itself, will bring performance to ceiling levels.

There is more to be said about all these data, but it may be useful to summarize where we are thus far: Both images and percepts exist only within the context of a perceptual reference frame, with that frame specifying (among other things) the form's figure/ground organization, its configuration in depth, and its orientation. The reference frame is what makes an image unambiguous, thus making it possible for images to carry meanings (cf. Fodor, 1975). At the same time, the reference frame places substantial limits on imagery function. In the studies we have surveyed so far, subjects have great difficulty in making discoveries from their images if those discoveries are incompatible with the image's current reference frame. However, it also appears that subjects have the option of changing their image's reference frame (typically, with specific instruction), and this leads to a corresponding change in what can be discovered about the image. It is in these ways, therefore, that images can be both unambiguous and also capable of supporting learning and discovery.

THE REFERENCE FRAME AND THE DEPICTION INTERACT

The evidence so far seems to demand a "duplex" conception of imagery, a depiction within a (descriptive) reference frame. The depictive side of imagery, as we mentioned early on, is reflected in the many studies of image scanning, or image rotation, and the like. Indeed, the depictive side of imagery is also evident in our own data: Subjects' *success* in discovering, say, Texas from their image indicates that images really do depict shape, and that we can meaningfully speak of what an image resembles. At the same time, however, subjects' *failure* to discover Texas, given the inappropriate reference frame, implies the influence of, and therefore the presence of, the reference frame. It is this overall pattern—subjects' successes in learning from imagery, and also their failures—that drives us toward the duplex conception: depiction *and* description, geometry *and* reference frame.

In our discussion so far, the reference frame can be understood roughly as a set of instructions for how to *interpret* one's own mental images (or percepts). The reference frame instructs you to think of "this side" as being the image's top; "this aspect" as being figural, and "that aspect" as being ground, and so on. However, I want to argue that the reference frame does more than this: The reference frame and the image depiction *interact* in an important way, such that the reference frame helps determine what is depicted within the imaged geometry itself. I will elaborate on this claim below, but let me first anticipate the direction of the argument.

Let us again consider the duck/rabbit figure (Fig. 4.1). The duck and the rabbit obviously share a common geometry. They also share the more conspicuous elements of the reference frame: Figure and ground are identified in the same way in the duck figure as in the rabbit. The two figures have the same organization in depth, and also the same orientation ("top"). The two figures are perceptually segmented in the same way. Given all this, and given the theory so far, one might expect subjects imaging the duck to discover the rabbit, and vice versa. After all, we have been arguing that discoveries from imagery will be possible whenever an image and the target form share both geometry and reference frame. However, as we have already seen, subjects imaging the duck are *not* reminded of the rabbit, nor vice versa. Thus the duck/rabbit data seem to contradict our claims about when learning from imagery will be possible. In essence, the Chambers and Reisberg (1985) results appear to contradict the Reisberg and Chambers (1991) theory!

To address this concern, we need to elaborate our conception of the perceptual reference frame, and also to clarify the relationship between the reference frame and the depicted material. Broadly put, our claim will be this: An image's reference frame sets "priorities" for what the image must include, and what it must include in detail. Thus, if a subject understands the duck/rabbit form as a duck, this will entail a reference frame that demands clear depiction of the duck's face. I will leave the nature of this "demand" unspecified for the moment; this will, however, be an important point in our subsequent discussion. One way or another, though, the image, understood as a duck image, will specify the duck's face in some detail. At the same time, however, this image, understood as a duck, may be relatively vague about the rabbit's face. Thus, the image is literally missing information needed to support the rabbit construal, and so of course the image will not support the reconstrual. Conversely, the reference frame for the rabbit demands that the rabbit's face be specified in detail in the image, but now the duck's face will be only vaguely depicted, again, making reconstrual difficult.

These various claims are in fact rooted in several arguments already in the literature (and already supported by data); we regard our theoretical proposal, therefore, as relatively modest—largely a knitting together of several prior ideas. In what follows, I will sketch some of the empirical roots for our claims. (My exposition here draws on arguments laid out more fully in Chambers, 1990.) My discussion of these points will carry us some distance from ducks and rabbits, and from issues of image discovery. However, this discussion will lay important groundwork for arguments to be presented later on. In outline, the argument to come is simply this: Both percepts and images are uneven in their levels of specificity and detail; one can easily find areas within these representations that are, at best, vague and unspecified. Several factors determine the location and size of these areas of vagueness; one important factor is *attention:* The deployment of attention plays a pivotal role in determining which aspects of an image are elaborated, and which are left vague. Finally, and crucially, one's construal of an image plays an important role in determining how attention is deployed across the image (and therefore how the image is elaborated). We discuss each of these points in turn, starting, once again, with perception, and then turning to imagery.

IMAGES ARE "NOT EVERYWHERE DENSE"

For most observers, the phenomenally given perceptual world seems uniform in its clarity and detail—one can see a broad section of the visual world, and (it would seem) one can see all of this world equally well. Yet we know this impression to be in some ways illusory: The contrast between foveal and peripheral vision guarantees that we can see some—but not all—aspects of the visual world with clarity and detail. Thanks to the fall-off in acuity, our perception of the visual periphery is necessarily sketchy and imprecise. It is an interesting fact that many people fail to notice their poor acuity in the visual periphery; students in perception classes, for example, are often surprised by their inability to make visual discriminations a mere 10 or 12 degrees away from fixation. However, noticed or not, it is clear that a considerable proportion of our visual field is strikingly unspecific. Our perception of the visual periphery contains skeletal information about the positions and movements of (large) objects, but surprisingly little beyond this.

The "unevenness" of perception is also reflected in a number of experimental findings, documenting that percepts are "not everywhere dense" (Hochberg, 1982; Navon, 1977; Palmer, 1980; Rock, Halper, & Clayton, 1972). For example, Hochberg (1981, 1982) has demonstrated that form percepts are dominated by "local cues," typically cues within foveal vision; the percept is largely uninfluenced by information elsewhere in the stimulus array. This seems a strong argument that the percept does not include all of the details that are visible within a stimulus, but is selective in important ways, including only vague impressions of many aspects of the form. For a concrete case, consider the Necker cube, shown in Figure 4.2. As we earlier discussed, the picture of the Necker cube is ambiguous, and can be understood as either a transparent version of Form B or Form C. Now consider the variant of the Necker cube shown in Figure 4.7. This form is not ambiguous: The intersection marked with an X indicates that one surface of the cube is opaque, and requires that this form (if three-dimensional) be understood as analogous to Figure 4.2B, not 4.2C. Despite this "give-away" cue, Figure 4.7 *is* perceptually ambiguous. If one fixates on the Z in the figure, the form readily reverses, being first aligned with B (in Fig. 4.2), then C, and so on. Apparently, information plainly visible in this stimulus fails to shape the perceived form; this give-away information is, in essence, omitted from the perceived form. As Hochberg (1981, p. 32) puts it, "even with objects before our eyes, perceived structure is schematic, not dense as is physical structure."

A similar point has been made in several studies by Rock (Rock, 1983; Rock et al., 1972). For example, Rock and colleagues showed subjects the form at the top of Figure 4.8 for a few seconds, then removed the form, and immediately

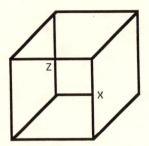

FIGURE 4.7. A modified version of the Necker cube, as discussed by Hochberg (1981, 1982).

FIGURE 4.8. Test stimuli employed by Rock, Halper, and Clayton (1972).

presented the two shapes shown at the bottom of Figure 4.8. The subjects' task was to decide which of these shapes matched the form they had just seen. In this test, despite a lengthy inspection of the first form, and despite a near-zero delay between the inspection and the test, subjects' recognition performance was effectively at chance levels. (The reader can easily confirm this, since, even with the shapes simultaneously in view, the discrimination is not easy.) The problem here is not one of discriminability per se: Subjects in a control procedure were shown just the relevant section of contour, both in training and in test; now recognition performance was near perfect. (Again, the reader can easily confirm this in Fig. 4.9.)

Rock and colleagues account for this result by arguing that the "internal description" that, in their view, constitutes a form percept need not include all details of the stimulus input. That is, "when a given region of a figure is a nonconsequential part of the whole, something is lacking in the perception of it. . . . But when the same physical region of the contour *constitutes* the form, there is no difficulty in perceiving and storing all its nuances" (Rock, 1983, p. 55).

Thus, percepts are not complete transcriptions of an object. We earlier discussed how percepts (and images) go "beyond the information given," by virtue

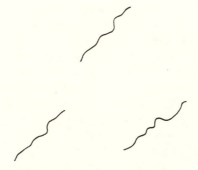

FIGURE 4.9. Control stimuli employed by Rock, Halper, and Clayton (1972).

of incorporating a perceptual reference frame. It now appears that percepts (and, we will argue, images as well) contain *less* than the information given, by virtue of under-representing aspects of the stimulus input, as documented by Hochberg and by Rock.

As an interesting side note, one might ask why these omissions in percepts are so often unnoted. One contribution to this lies in the processes of completion, ordinarily engaged in filling in the portion of the visual field obscured by the blind spot or other scotomata (cf. Ramachandran, 1992, 1993). Similar processes of completion are engaged when one object is partially occluded by another (e.g., Kanizsa, 1979). In either case, the visual system seems adept in filling in the gaps created by missing or partial stimulus information. Perhaps more important, though, is the ephemeral nature of these unspecified regions within the percept. Using Figure 4.7 as our example, when one fixates on Point X, the area identified by Point Z is likely to be unspecified within the percept. However, if one becomes curious about Point Z, one needs to do nothing more than shift one's gaze: If information is missing from the percept, that information can swiftly and easily be supplied, by virtue of reference to the stimulus itself. In effect, the sketchiness within percepts is difficult to detect because the moment one becomes curious about the unspecified region, one draws on the stimulus to flesh out one's perception of this region. As Hochberg notes, this is closely related to what J. S. Mill (1865) referred to more than a century ago as the "permanent possibility of sensations," a possibility that provides an enduring and complete quality to an otherwise partial and transitory percept (cf. Boring, 1942).

Let us return, however, to the case of imagery, because we wish to argue that images, just like percepts, are "not everywhere dense." At the most general level, it seems uncontroversial that images vary enormously in their vividness, clarity, and level of detail. Whether one appeals to experimental evidence or to introspection, it seems plain that some images are akin to "bare-bones" stick figures, containing little more than place-holders for the depicted material: "here a face, here some trees of some sort, here some clothing . . . ," and so on. In contrast, other images seem far richer—with a great deal of detailed visual content, including content often irrelevant to the imager's specific intentions. Thus, for example, one might set out only to image a vase on a table, but end up with an image specifying that the table has a pedestal base, and is surrounded by four Windsor chairs, that the vase is filled with yellow tulips, and so on.

It is far from trivial to assess these differences among images; this is made plain, for example, by the long-standing debate over the validity of measurements of "image vividness." (See, for example, Kosslyn, Brunn, Cave, & Wallach, 1985; Marks, 1983; Reisberg & Heuer, 1988.) What matters for present purposes, though, is simply that images do vary in their specificity, their precision and detail, and their degree of "visual elaboration." Before moving on, however, it may be helpful to note that we will use the term "image" so as to encompass all of these variations—from the stick figure to the near-photographic representation. This terminology derives from our belief that, in important ways, all of these variations *depict,* and this distinguishes them from descriptive representations. In essence, then, we are assuming a definition of depiction that is largely neutral on such matters as "level of detail." To be sure, one of the defining features of imagery is a pattern of "obligatory inclusions," such that *some aspects* of the represented scene or object *must* be represented within the image. (For example, a depiction obligatorily represents a scene as "viewed" from a certain perspective and distance. Likewise, certain spatial relations must be specified within a depiction, and so on.) In this sense, then, there is a "lower boundary" on what must be included in a depiction in order for it to function as a depiction. (For discussion, see Dennett, 1981; Kosslyn, 1983.) However, this still leaves enormous pliability in the level of detail possible within a depiction—that is, pliability in the degree to which one can exceed this "lower boundary"—and it is this pliability with which we are currently concerned. In general, then, we would argue that terms like "depiction" and "image" are best defined with regard to functional criteria other than level of detail (cf. Rey, 1981). For our present purposes, though, relatively little rests on this point; our intent here is merely to be clear about terminology.

Returning to our main argument, we note that these differences in "detailedness," or clarity, or precision are not merely ways in which one image differs from another. Instead, these various levels of precision can be found within a single image: Often some aspects of an image are fully and richly depicted, while other aspects of the same image are depicted only in sketchy terms. This point has been noted by many researchers, often on grounds of introspection (James, 1890; Koffka, 1912, cited in Arnheim, 1969; Titchener, 1926). In fact, Slee (1980) has exploited this (introspective) observation as a measure of image vividness, asking to what extent an individual's images include aspects that would be critical to a picture of an object. For example, if a subject images a cup placed on a table, does the image include the shape of the table, or its color? Slee reports that subjects differ enormously in the level of such detail reported as part of their images. In the same spirit, Dennett (1981) has argued that this "noncommittal" aspect of images is a factor that clearly distinguishes mental representations (e.g., images and percepts) from physical representations (e.g., pictures).

The considerations just mentioned rest largely on introspections about what images do or do not include. As it turns out, however, there is reason to believe that introspective accounts may *under*-represent the degree of "sketchiness" or "vagueness" in images, just as we noted earlier that introspection seems to under-represent the sparse nature of percepts. After all, one presumably fills in those aspects of an image that seem important; consequently, it is the "unimportant" (and probably unattended) aspects of the image that are left vague. This implies that these vague areas may often go unnoticed: These aspects are vague because they are (considered) unimportant, but they are likewise ignored because they are (considered) unimportant.

At least some evidence confirms this suggestion. In an informal experiment by John Kennedy (personal communication), subjects were asked to form an image of a horse. Subjects easily complied with this request, and, when they were asked to scrutinize their image, they noted nothing odd, and, in particular, noted no omissions. Yet, when the subjects were called upon to draw a picture based on this image, subjects quickly realized that they had little idea about how the horse's knees look; in their drawings, the horse often looked (as Kennedy puts it) as if it were wearing pajamas. Thus, apparently, this information was missing from subjects' images, and yet subjects failed to detect this (not small) omission. It was only when the drawing task demanded attention to the knees that the omission was detected.

Introspections aside, though, we can also experimentally document areas of vagueness within imagery. For example, Kosslyn (1980, 1983) reviews a series of studies of *image construction* and *image maintenance*. We will not detail the evidence here, but, in general, the pattern of findings makes it clear that images are not created as entire templates. Instead, images are created in a piecemeal fashion—first an image framework is created, then aspects of the image are elaborated as the task demands, and as the imager wishes. Until these elaborations are created, the image framework contains little more than place-holders, identifying what features can be placed in those positions, if needed. All of this implies that an image will be uneven in its degree of elaboration—consistent with our claims—with some aspects of the image filled in, and other aspects left as place-holders.

In addition, evidence indicates that images begin to fade as soon as they are constructed, but one can maintain the image by a refreshing process linked to mental scanning (Kosslyn, 1980, 1983; also see Hampson & Morris, 1978). Crucially for our purposes, the resources needed for this refreshing process are limited, and so, if the image is large or complex, only some parts of the image can be represented at one time. Again, this leads to the claim that images do not include all aspects of the form they were meant to represent.

Thus, the evidence on image construction and image decay converges with the introspective evidence in arguing that images, like percepts, are not everywhere dense. An image can be clear and detailed on some aspects of a depiction, but largely silent on other aspects. For other aspects of the depicted form, the image may contain only place-holders, which may or may not be filled in at some future point.

All of this leads us to ask: What guides or shapes the pattern of inclusion and exclusion in an image? Why are some aspects specified in detail, while others are not? It seems certain that several factors are relevant here, including how quickly one can refresh the image relative to the speed of fading, the specific task (cf. Kosslyn, 1980, 1983), general visual factors such as the size of foveal view (Hochberg, 1982), and perhaps general knowledge about the scene (cf. Friedman, 1979).

In addition, we wish to argue that the *meaning* of an image plays a pivotal role in determining how the image is elaborated (and, correspondingly, which aspects of the image are left vague). We already know that image elaboration and image maintenance are closely tied to image *scanning* (Kosslyn, 1980). How an image will be scanned in turn depends on how the imager deploys his or her attention. Thus, putting these pieces together, it seems that attended parts of the image will be elaborated while other parts of the image will not be. However, now we need to ask: If image elaboration depends on attention, then what guides attention?

Some years ago, Tsal and Kolbet (1985) provided evidence for a link between attention and a form's meaning for *perceived* forms; we will turn in a moment to our own studies, which document a similar link for *imaged* forms. Ironically, the perceptual evidence comes from studies using the duck/rabbit figure: In one experiment, half of the subjects were shown this figure and asked to think of it as a duck; the remaining subjects were shown the same figure, but asked to think of it as a rabbit. Subjects' sensitivity was then measured to a series of targets superimposed on the figure, with some of the targets appearing roughly on the "rabbit's face," and half on the "duck's face." Tsal and Kolbett report that subjects maintaining a "duck" construal were indeed more sensitive to targets on the duck's face than to targets elsewhere; subjects maintaining a "rabbit" construal were more sensitive to targets on the rabbit's face.

Two further points should be mentioned about this study. First, Tsal and Kolbett argue that this is not an eye-movement effect, since eye movements were controlled during the procedure; instead, it is literally an effect of construal guiding attention. Second, in a subsequent study, Tsal and Kolbett demonstrated the reverse pattern: By means of a target presentation, subjects' attention was directed either to a position close to the rabbit's face, or to a position close to the duck's face; subjects then reported their construal of the figure. In this study, attention predicted construal: Attending to the duck's face made the duck construal more likely; attending to the rabbit's face made the rabbit construal more likely.

The Tsal and Kolbett data, therefore, document that construal of a figure biases attention (and, conversely, that attention can bias construal). It is interesting to ask why this is so—why it is difficult to perceive the figure as, say, a duck, while looking at the "back" of the duck's head. However, we can hold this issue to the side for now. What matters for our present concerns is simply that construal does bias attention, at least for perceptual figures. Can we establish a comparable link for *images?* Moreover, and crucially, can we establish a link between construal and elaboration of an image, or, conversely, between construal and "areas of vagueness" within an image? This latter concern was what led us into this digression about image and percept vagueness; it is now time to return to our main question.

LOCATING "AREAS OF VAGUENESS" WITHIN IMAGES

Before turning to the next round of data, it may be useful to reset the stage, so let us review the argument so far. I have argued that images have a duplex mental representation: a depiction within a perceptual reference frame. The reference frame contains descriptive material, specifying the image's top, its figure/ground organization, and so on. The reference frame renders the image unambiguous, by virtue of specifying how the depiction is to be understood. In addition, the reference frame sets systematic boundaries on learning from images: This learning will go smoothly forward when the sought-after discovery is compatible with *both* the depiction and the reference frame; learning from images is enormously difficult if the sought-after discovery is incompatible with either of these.

This fabric of claims led us to a question about the duck/rabbit (Fig. 4.1), and about the initial Chambers and Reisberg (1985) data: The duck and rabbit obviously share the same geometry; they also seem to share the more conspicuous elements of the perceptual reference frame. Why, therefore, does the duck image fail to evoke the rabbit, and vice versa? We have proposed that this is attributable to one further element of the perceptual reference frame—a specification of what we might call "depictive priorities." These priorities guide how the image is elaborated, and, conversely, they guide what will be left vague within the image.

More specifically, and following the lead of the Tsal and Kolbett data, we propose that one's construal of an image guides how attention is deployed across the image. This will in turn determine how the image is elaborated, given the well-documented link between image-scanning and image maintenance. Thus, with a duck image, one's attention is drawn to the duck's face, and, as a result, the duck's face is clearly depicted, but the back of the duck's head is not. Similarly, with a rabbit image, the rabbit's face is clearly depicted, but the back of the rabbit's head is not. In either case, information needed for the alternate construal is literally missing from the image, and it is for this reason that the image will not support reconstrual.

One further point seems worth mentioning: In imagery, just as in perception, it will be true both that *construal guides attention* and also that *attention guides construal.* To see this point, imagine that we can lead subjects to encode the duck/rabbit shape merely as "an abstract form." Now let us imagine that we draw the subjects' attention to, say, the left side of the figure. Given the link between attention and image elaboration, this will cause the image to be elaborated on the left side, but not on the right. In essence, then, the image will include information needed for the duck construal, and so the imager may well discover the depicted duck. This image will not, however, include information needed for the rabbit construal. Thus, in the previous paragraph, we described a chain of events from image *construal* to *attention* to *image elaboration.* Here we note the equally important chain of events from attention to elaboration to construal.

Chambers and Reisberg (1992) report a series of studies designed to explore and document these various claims. The logic of these studies is easily described, because it builds on the Rock et al. (1972) procedure, which we have already described. Recall that in the Rock et al. task subjects viewed a nonsense figure (the top of Fig. 4.8) for a lengthy inspection period, then, with zero delay, subjects had to choose which of two test figures (the bottom of Fig. 4.8) matched the initially viewed form. As we have already discussed, the data from this procedure (indeed, subjects' near-chance performance) indicate that subjects' percepts were insufficient to support this discrimination, with the strong implication that the relevant information about the contour was literally "missing" from the percept. Note, then, that this study provides several advantages. First, the procedure can be used to determine if something is missing from the perceived form—as revealed by the percept's insufficiency in supporting the relevant discrimination. Second, the procedure can be used to ask *what* is missing from the perceived form—by examining precisely which discriminations the percept will support, and which it will not. In obvious ways, then, this procedure is well-suited to the questions we want to ask about imagery.

In the Chambers and Reisberg (1992) studies, subjects were once again shown the duck/rabbit figure. Half were led to perceive the figure as a duck, with a straightforward instruction: "I am about to show you a picture of a duck. . . ." Half were led to perceive the figure as a rabbit, by means of the comparable manipulation. Subjects were allowed to inspect the figure for 5 seconds, then asked to form an image of this shape, and were allowed to scrutinize this image for a lengthy period. To ensure that subjects did in fact scrutinize their image during this period, we asked them a series of questions, including a request that they rate the image's clarity, using the response scale ordinarily used for Marks' (1972) Vividness of Visual Imagery Questionnaire.

At the end of this inspection period, subjects were shown a pair of pictures and asked which of these pictures more closely resembled the image they were currently holding. One member of this test pair was always the original, unmodified, duck/rabbit itself—i.e., the same figure subjects had been shown just minutes earlier (Fig. 4.10A). The other member of the test pair, for half the subjects, was a figure that we had modified on the duck's face. (Specifically, we had redrawn this figure with a diminished concavity at the top of the bill—Fig. 4.10B.) Thus, these subjects were choosing between the original and a figure modified on the duck's face—we will refer to this as the DFM test pair (for Duck Face Modified).

For the remaining subjects, the test pair included (as before) the standard duck/rabbit outline, and also a figure that we had modified on the rabbit's face. (Specifically we had removed the rabbit's nose—Fig. 4.10C.) These subjects, then, were choosing between the original and a figure modified on the rabbit's face—the RFM test pair (for Rabbit Face Modified).

Overall, therefore, this procedure employs a 2×2 design: Subjects were either imaging the form as a duck, or the same form as a rabbit, and subjects were

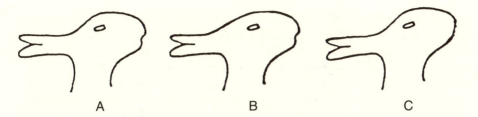

A   B   C

FIGURE 4.10.   Panel A shows the original duck/rabbit figure; B shows the figure modified on the duck's bill, used for Chambers and Reisberg's (1992) DFM pair ; C shows the figure modified on the rabbit's bill, used for their RFM pair.

tested either with the DFM pair or the RFM pair. We hypothesized that subjects imaging the duck would have a clear image of the duck's face. With information about the duck's face thus clearly depicted, the image should support the discrimination between Figure 4.10A and 4.10B. Therefore, these subjects should perform well when choosing within the DFM pair—they should reliably choose the original figure over the modified figure.

In contrast, we expect that these subjects will have only a vague image of the back of the duck's head (that is, the rabbit's face). Therefore, their image is missing the information needed to discriminate between Fig. 4.10A and 4.10C, and so the image should not support discrimination within this pair. Hence, if these subjects are tested with the RFM pair, they should do poorly; in the extreme, they may choose randomly as to whether the original form or Figure 4.10C more closely resembles their image.

This pattern of predictions should of course be precisely reversed for subjects imaging this shape as a rabbit: These subjects should have a clear image of the rabbit's face, and so perform well in choosing between Figure 4.10A and 4.10C. Concretely, they should reliably choose the original figure when tested with the RFM pair. In contrast, these subjects are imaging a shape that is vague with regard to the contour needed for the DFM test pair; in the extreme, these subjects should perform at chance levels if tested with this pair.

As Figure 4.11 shows, these predictions are correct: Subjects imaging the duck reliably chose the original form when choosing within the DFM pair, but were near random in their selections when choosing within the RFM pair. Subjects imaging the rabbit showed the reverse pattern: reliably choosing the original form when choosing within the RFM pair, but near random when choosing within the DFM pair.

There are, however, two problems in interpreting this result. First, it is at least possible that bias is introduced by the test figures themselves. Perhaps Figure 4.10B is just a "less ducky" duck—somehow further from the duck prototype. Likewise, perhaps Figure 4.10C is a "less rabbity" rabbit—again, further from the relevant prototype. In this case a subject merely thinking of the *label* "duck" would be likely to choose Figure 4.10A over 10B (and so on), in accord with the data shown in Figure 4.11. In this way, our study might reveal bias in the test figures, rather than bias in the image itself.

This concern is easily ruled out: In a separate study, subjects were simply shown the two test pairs (the DFM pair and the RFM pair) and asked, within each pair, to select the more prototypical figure. For example, subjects shown the DFM pair were asked to select the more prototypical duck. (These subjects had no prior experience with the duck/rabbit figure, and so had no way of knowing which is the "standard" form.) Subjects in this procedure largely chose randomly, indicating, as we had hoped, no pattern of bias in our test stimuli themselves.

Here is a different concern: Perhaps, at the very outset, subjects expecting to see a duck pay special attention to the duck's face *in the original picture,* that is, while they are initially memorizing the test stimulus. Correspondingly, these subjects, expecting to see a duck, might pay less attention, during this initial (perceptual) encounter, to the rabbit's face. In that case, what we are seeing in Figure 4.11 is not an *imagery* bias; it is instead a bias in the pattern of initial encoding. On this hypothesis, these subjects never encoded the back of the duck's head in the first place, so of course this information was absent from their images!

To address this concern, we ran another study, which starts out as a replication of the study already described: Subjects were led either to image the duck or the rabbit, and were then tested either with the DFM pair or the RFM pair. The results are shown in the left panel of Figure 4.12; as the figure indicates, we replicated the previous finding. At this point in the procedure, however, we lead subjects through one further step: Subjects were told directly, "You know, you're imaging a duck" (or ". . . a rabbit," as appropriate). "But," we told them, "some subjects can also imagine this form as a rabbit" (or, if appropriate, ". . . as a duck"). Subjects were then asked, "Can you image this form as a rabbit?"

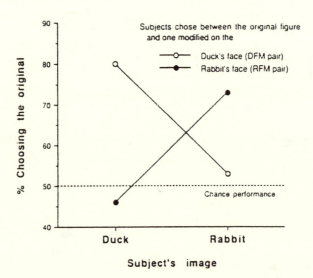

FIGURE 4.11. Results of Chambers and Reisberg's (1992) Experiment 2.

We have already seen that subjects are enormously unlikely to reconstrue this figure on their own—that is, without prior suggestion. However, subjects can often reverse the form if we give them specific instructions, as we are in this procedure. This allows us to *retest* subjects, using the same test pair (DFM or RFM) as before, in order to ask: What predicts performance—the construal that subjects had in mind at the time of encoding, or the construal they have in mind at the time of the test itself?

If subjects' imagery bias is actually arising from *encoding* (that is, if "duck" subjects simply paid more attention to the "duck side" of the picture), then the change in image construal should not change the pattern of results. Subjects (on this hypothesis) began with a biased encoding, and therefore have a biased memory representation, and this should not be reversed by the change in construal. On our view, however, this (deliberately instructed) change in construal will entail a change in the image's reference frame, and, thus, a change in the image's depictive priorities. Therefore, we literally expected that subjects changing the duck image to a rabbit image would be forced to "fill out" the missing detail from the rabbit's face and would simultaneously "let go" of the detail in the duck's face. Likewise, we expected that subjects changing the rabbit image to a duck image would be forced to "fill out" the missing detail from the duck's face, and would "let go" of the detail in the rabbit's face. As a consequence of all this, the pattern of subjects' choosing, with the DFM and RFM pairs, should reverse the pattern of their initial choices: Subjects initially imaging the duck did well with the DFM pair; these same subjects (now imaging the rabbit) should now do poorly with this pair (and likewise for the other combinations of construal and test pair).

The right panel of Figure 4.12 shows that these predictions are correct. Apparently, then, what matters for subjects' discrimination performance is the con-

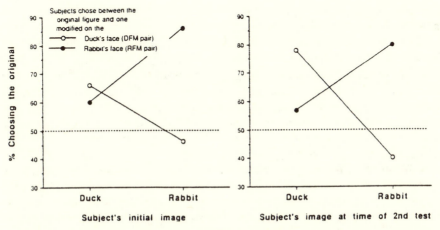

FIGURE 4.12. Results of Chambers and Reisberg's (1992) Experiment 3; the left panel shows subjects' choices before reconstruing the image; the right panel shows choices after reconstrual.

strual they are holding at the time of the discrimination test itself, and not the construal they held during the initial encoding.

However, there is still a concern here. In the procedure just described, subjects actually had two encounters with the stimulus information: Subjects initially encoded the picture, and then were tested. Then, with the picture removed, subjects were led to reconstrue the form and were tested a second time. The initial test in this procedure probed subjects' images, but also provided subjects with an opportunity to re-examine the test figure, and, potentially, to encode more information about the contour than they had on the first encounter. It is not completely clear how this would influence the observed data pattern, but, one way or another, it is relatively easy to rule out the possibility that this repeated encounter with the duck/rabbit picture may have influenced our results. We can do this simply by eliminating the initial test trial.

In the next procedure, therefore, subjects were shown the duck/rabbit figure and were led to perceive it either as a duck or a rabbit. Then the picture was removed, and subjects were led to image the form and to inspect their image. Then, with no testing, and with no re-presentation of the figure, subjects were specifically instructed in how to reconstrue the image. Subjects were then led to scrutinize the image, under this new construal, and, finally, tested, using the same procedures as before.

Figure 4.13 shows the by-now familiar data pattern: What matters is plainly subjects' construal of the image at the time of testing, and not at the time of initial encoding. Subjects imaging the figure as a duck were easily able to make fine discriminations about the duck face, but were unable to make discriminations about the rabbit face (even though these subjects understood the form as a rabbit, during their first and only encounter with the stimulus itself). The reverse was true for subjects imaging the figure as a rabbit.

Finally, we should add that this pattern is generalizable. Details aside, Chambers and Reisberg (1992) report a comparable study, using a "bird/airplane" figure, in place of the duck/rabbit. The results are virtually identical to those just described, providing assurance that there is nothing extraordinary about the duck/rabbit in producing these results.

Before leaving these studies, we should note one further question emerging from the data just described: As we have now seen, when subjects change their construal of an image, they "let go" of aspects of the image that were once clearly specified, and simultaneously "fill in" areas of the image that were previously vague. What information do subjects use in this "filling in"? How do they know what the previously absent contour should be? (Similar questions arise from the Chambers & Reisberg, 1985, studies in which subjects created ambiguous drawings, based on unambiguous images.) One possibility is that subjects merely draw on some generic knowledge about ducks or rabbits (or animal heads), and so, in essence, offer their best guess about the relevant bit of contour. However, Chambers and Reisberg (1992, Experiment 7) provide evidence that this is *not* subjects' strategy; instead, it appears that subjects are drawing on some memory for the specific duck/rabbit contour.

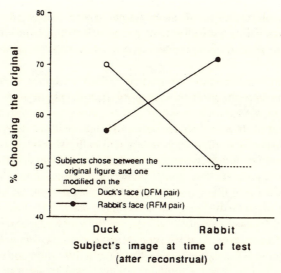

FIGURE 4.13. Results of Chambers and Reisberg's (1992) Experiment 4.

This creates a puzzle. According to the initial recognition test, subjects are plainly missing information about the duck/rabbit contour. Bear in mind that subjects imaging the duck are choosing at near-chance levels with the RFM pair, and likewise for subjects imaging the rabbit, tested with the DFM pair. This implies that subjects know little or nothing about the relevant bit of contour. At the same time, however, subjects apparently *do* remember the full contour because they are able to "reinstate" the missing information, once specifically cued to do so.

Chambers and Reisberg resolve this puzzle by appealing to Kosslyn's (1980, 1983) argument that images are constructed by drawing on information in "image files" in long-term memory. Crucially, image files are not themselves images; they cannot be consulted to "read off" shape information in the same way that one can consult the image itself. Instead, image files provide information (perhaps entirely descriptive information) about how an image might be constructed. Using this information, one can create an "active image" in working memory, which can be consulted for various purposes. In these terms, the Chambers and Reisberg subjects must have had reasonably complete knowledge of the duck/rabbit figure in their image files. However, they could not consult this knowledge directly in making their recognition choices. Instead, these choices were based on their inspection of the active image, which contains less information than is contained in the image files. In particular, the active image contains the face of only one of the animals—the left-most side of the figure for subjects who understand their image as "duck," and the right-most side for subjects who understand their image as "rabbit." In this way, there is no contradiction between chance performance on the recognition test and the ability to reinstate the figure accurately. The former reflects information missing from the active image, whereas the latter reflects information present in the image file. (For further discussion, see Reisberg, 1993.)

DUPLEXES AND REFERENCE FRAMES REVISITED

Again, a brief review of where we are may be useful. We have proposed a duplex conception of images, consisting of a depiction within a perceptual reference frame. The *depiction* in this duplex is revealed in many ways, including the numerous and persuasive studies reviewed by Kosslyn (1980, 1983), Shepard and Cooper (1982), and others. The depiction is also evident in subjects' success in many of the imagery-discovery tasks we have been discussing. The *reference frame* can also be easily documented, by virtue of the fact that the reference frame seems to limit imagery discovery in ways that we have discussed: Learning from images happens routinely if the sought-after discovery is compatible with both the depiction and the reference frame; learning from images seems far less likely if the sought-after discovery is incompatible with either element of the duplex.

In addition, I have argued that the depiction and the reference frame *interact* in an important way: Subjects' construal of the image seems to set what I have called "depictive priorities" for the image. That is, a subject's construal of the image determines what must be specified clearly in the image, and what can be omitted. When the construal changes, this pattern changes: Aspects of the image that were unimportant for the former construal, but important for the new, must be filled in. Conversely, aspects of the image that were important for the previous construal, but not for the new, will be allowed to fade. This pattern of inclusion and exclusion, specification and vagueness, will then have various consequences for imagery function. For example, as we have just seen, this pattern of inclusion and exclusion will determine what *discriminations* the image will support. Similarly, I have argued that the pattern of inclusion and exclusion will determine what *discoveries* the image will support. Indeed, I have argued that this pattern of inclusion and exclusion underlies subjects' failure to discover the duck in a rabbit image, and vice versa: Each of these images is literally missing information needed to support the alternative construal.

Several questions remain, however, about these "depictive priorities." First, is it literally the case that construal determines what is *included* in the depiction? An alternative might be that images (despite my claims) *are* everywhere-dense. On this view, construal simply biases how one scans, or pays attention to, one's own mental images. Thus, a subject imaging a duck might have a complete image of the duck/rabbit figure, but simply neglect the back of the head—that is, fail to pay attention to it. According to this hypothesis, then, construal serves to bias image-scanning, not image content.

Chambers and Reisberg (1992) offer several considerations that speak against this view of their data. In brief, the argument is this: In their data, subjects were effectively at chance in making discriminations about the back of the (imaged) animal's head. Hence, we cannot argue that their attention is merely biased away from the relevant region. Instead, we would have to argue that subjects were, for some reason, completely unable to attend to the relevant region. This is all the more remarkable given that much in the procedure signaled to the subject where the relevant features were located. For example, subjects were urged during the test to direct their "mind's eye" to different aspects of the image. In addition, the stimuli themselves should have cued subjects to scan their images: A subject confronting the RFM pair, for example, can easily see that the test stimuli differ only in the contour of the pictures' right edge. This would presumably lead subjects to inspect the corresponding "edge" of their image in order to make the required comparisons. Finally, and crucially, we know from many results that subjects are able to scan their images, are able to direct their "mind's eye" toward any part of the image they choose (e.g., Kosslyn, 1980, 1983).

All of this, we believe, renders implausible the claim that subjects' images were complete, but that subjects were simply neglecting parts of the image. Subjects can scan their images. The instructions urged subjects to scan. The stimuli signaled where the crucial information was within the image. Despite all this, subjects completely failed to find the sought-after information in their images. We read this as indicating that it is not image inspection that is selective, but the image content itself.

This brings us back to our claim that construal does indeed set depictive priorities: Construal literally determines image content. Attention and scanning play a role in this claim, but it is not a role of determining access to otherwise homogeneous image content. Instead, as we have already discussed, attention and scanning play their role in determining image *maintenance,* and thus image content per se.[3]

I have suggested that these depictive priorities are set by the image's reference frame, but it is important to emphasize the modesty of this specific claim: The evidence indicates that an image's construal does guide image content. I have found it convenient to speak of this in terms of "depictive priorities," but I have little stake in whether these priorities are literally represented, or (more likely) simply manifest in the form of the depiction itself. Likewise, I have little stake (at least for present purposes) in whether these depictive priorities are set in the same way as the other perceptual specifications (orientation, figure/ground organization, and so on) that I have attributed to the image's reference frame.[4] Clearly, these are issues on which further work is needed, with the relevant work likely to include the development of explicit formalisms for representing the relevant information. For now, though, I will use the reference frame notion simply to connote the descriptive information of various sorts that accompanies and shapes a mental image. For present purposes, the strong presumption is that the reference frame merely contains *perceptual* specifications, and does not (for example) specify object-identities, or verbal connotation, or the like. Be that as it may, it is in this modest sense that it seems sensible to speak of the depictive priorities as being part of the image's reference frame.

ESCAPING THE BOUNDARIES ON IMAGE FUNCTION

We have repeatedly spoken of a duplex conception of imagery, but there is one regard in which this terminology may be misleading: The "duplex" term emphasizes the separate identity of the depictive and descriptive elements of mental imagery, and so may imply for some the *separability* of these elements. That is, one might ask whether one can have an image that is a "pure depiction," stripped of the descriptive reference frame. We read the evidence, however, as implying that these elements *cannot* be separated: Both are obligatory elements of any image.

This is a strong claim, but strong claims seem warranted by the pattern of our results. Across a number of studies, we have observed zero success rates in the relevant conditions. No subjects in our studies have succeeded in spontaneously reconstruing the duck/rabbit; no subjects in our studies identified Texas in their image, when they had an inappropriate reference frame; and so on. These are obviously striking patterns of results, and it is these results that invite strongly phrased theory.

However, this seems the appropriate junction at which to sound some cautions about these strong claims. As we noted much earlier, other researchers have not replicated these zero-success rates (e.g., Brandimonte & Gerbino, 1993; Hyman, 1993; Kaufmann & Helstrup, 1993; Peterson et al., 1992). These researchers have certainly obtained data *qualitatively* similar to ours: Conditions we have identified as facilitating image discovery have facilitated discovery in their studies; conditions we have identified as making discovery unlikely have, in fact, made discovery unlikely in their studies. Nonetheless, there is also a clear *quantitative* difference between our results and those obtained in other laboratories, and this needs to be addressed.

As an entry into these issues, it may be helpful to consider when, according to our conception, discovery from images *should* take place. There are several categories of possibilities, and we consider each of these in turn.

1. *Discoveries compatible with the current reference frame:* In many cases, a rich and surprising set of discoveries can be made about an imaged form *without changing* the current reference frame. For example, many of the discoveries described by Finke, Pinker, and Farah (1989) seem of this sort. Consider, as a concrete case, an oft-quoted example from their study: Subjects were invited to imagine a capital-letter "D," then to imagine this "D" rotated, so that it was now lying on its back. Then subjects were invited to imagine a capital letter "J" underneath the reclining "D", such that the top bar of the "J" was joined to the "D" at the "D"'s midpoint. In this procedure, many subjects discovered the resulting umbrella.

This discovery is entirely consistent with our conception of imagery: In this case, subjects understand the D and J in a certain way—that is, within a certain reference frame. The specifications entailed by this reference frame (what is figure, what is ground; how the form is parsed; what orientation is assigned) are all *fully compatible* with the reference frame appropriate for the umbrella shape. Therefore, by virtue of the shared geometry *and* the shared reference frame, the

D + J form should resemble an umbrella, and should, in our view, call the umbrella to mind. This is of course the obtained result.

Notice, though, that the Finke et al. (1989) procedure does require subjects to change how they understand the imaged forms: Subjects initially understood the forms as letters, but come to understand them as object-shapes (umbrella handle, umbrella top, and so on). Why doesn't this change in construal entail a change in reference frame? This question is easily addressed if the reference frame contains *only* the perceptual specifications we have already named (orientation, and so on). In this view, the reference frame is explicit about how a form is (perceptually) understood, but silent on object identity; thus, a change in object identity would not be a reference-frame change.

An argument similar in spirit to this has been offered by Peterson et al. (1992; we note, once again, that the reference-frame terminology is adopted from their paper). These researchers distinguish between "reconstruals" of an image and "reference-frame realignments." They define the latter as a reversal that requires a change in object-centered directions, such as the top/bottom or front/back of the image; they define the former as a reversal that entails assigning a new interpretation to the image components (without a reference-frame change).[5] In their view, the reversals observed by Finke et al. (1989) are predominantly reconstruals (i.e., not requiring reference-frame changes), rather than reference-frame realignments.

In support of their overall conception, Peterson et al. (1992) report a procedure modeled after the Chambers and Reisberg (1985) study. Subjects were briefly shown the duck/rabbit figure, asked to form a "mental picture" of it, and then asked if they could find an alternative interpretation for the image. All of the subjects' responses were recorded, and subsequently coded as either reconstruals or reference-frame reversals. The Peterson et al. (1992) data indicate an interesting contrast between reconstruals (i.e., reinterpretations *compatible* with an image's initial reference frame) and reference-frame realignments. Reconstruals (as they defined them) occurred easily and frequently, and, perhaps more important, occurred without any explicit instructions to subjects. Reference-frame reversals, in contrast, were reliably observed only in those conditions in which subjects were given appropriate hints or teaching examples. This is of course congruent with the points we are making here. However, we still need to explain why, in this study, reference-frame realignments happened *at all,* unlike the zero-rate observed in our own procedures. This is a point addressed in the next sections.

2. *Direct suggestions to the subject concerning changes in reference frame.* We have emphasized that subjects' discoveries from their images seem bounded by the image's reference frame; moreover, we have emphasized the rigidity of this boundary, pointing to the massive difficulties subjects seem to have in imagery tasks if the target form requires a reference-frame switch. However, we also need to understand that this boundary on imagery function is, in a different sense, anything but rigid: A subject's specifications about an image—its figure/ground organization, its orientation, and so on—are, of course, the *subject's* specifications. The specifications are set by the subject, are manifest in how the

subject reads or understands his or her own image, and so these specifications can be changed by the subject.

A number of results confirm that these image specifications can be changed with a little prodding from the experimenter. This is crucial, for example, in the Reisberg and Chambers (1991) experiments described earlier: Subjects asked to imagine a *rotated* map of Texas reliably failed to recognize Texas in their image; however, subjects specifically directed to "redefine" the image (that is, to reset the reference frame) readily discovered Texas in the imaged form. This same point is clear in recent work by Brandimonte and Gerbino (1993) and by Hyman (1993). In both of these latter studies, subjects were specifically instructed to change their understanding of an imaged form (e.g., the duck/rabbit figure); specifically, subjects were urged to reverse what they thought of as the "front" of the figure, and what they thought of as the "back." Prior to this change (that is, when the image was understood "incorrectly"), discoveries from imagery rarely occurred. Subsequent to this change, discoveries routinely occurred. Peterson and colleagues (1992) have obtained similar effects using "teaching examples," rather than specific instructions, as a way of conveying the required change in image specifications.

Thus the overall pattern of these results resembles that of the Reisberg and Chambers (1991) findings—with discoveries governed both by the imaged geometry and by how that geometry is understood, and with new discoveries becoming available once this understanding (the reference frame) is changed. For present purposes, though, these results remind us of an important point, namely that via instruction or example, subjects can easily be led to change the image's reference frame. We emphasize that this is surely no surprise, since, once again, the reference frame is created and maintained solely by the imager, and so open to change by the imager.

One might well ask, however, *why* instructions or examples seem required to bring about these reference-frame changes. After all, nothing prohibits a subject from deciding, on his or her own initiative, to change an image's reference frame. Indeed, these changes would seem quite likely when subjects are specifically urged to explore their images, seeking new forms. If subjects *did* redefine their image's reference frame, this would undermine the impact of the experimenter-defined reference frame. Yet, as we have seen, the experimenter-defined reference frame has a huge effect on the data. We conclude, therefore, that these spontaneous redefinitions of the frame are surprisingly infrequent.

Of course we need to be careful here. We know that some subjects *do* make image discoveries that are "incompatible" with the image's initial frame (cf. Hyman, 1993; Kaufmann & Helstrup, 1993; Peterson et al. (1992); one possibility is that these are the subjects who *have* spontaneously redefined their own images—i.e., have changed the reference frames on their own, without instruction from the experimenter. We are struck, though, by *how few* of these subjects there seem to be. We read this as implying that, despite situational encouragement for this redefinition, subjects are either incapable or inept in this redefinition. With experimenters' instructions, a clear majority of subjects can change their image's reference frame. Without the instructions, only a small minority makes these changes.

A number of hypotheses are available for explaining this contrast, but this surely seems an issue in need of further research. It does seem appropriate, though, to sketch one way this research might unfold. Subjects can, of course, change an image's reference frame if they so choose. In fact, they can change the reference frame *in any way* they choose. They can (for example) define *any* side of the form as the form's top, they can define the figure's configuration in depth in any of a number of ways, and so on. This breadth of options may itself provide something of an obstacle for subjects: Their task might suggest to them that a redefinition of the image would be useful, but subjects have no way of knowing *which* redefinition to choose, from the many that are possible. Conversely, the likelihood of subjects stumbling across the "correct" redefinition (i.e., the one that will lead to the target form) may be small, and this may be the reason why few subjects succeed (without some sort of aid).

On this view, then, the duck/rabbit or "Texas" procedures may be special in two senses. Not only do these procedures require a change in reference frame but they also require a *specific* change, if the sought-after form is to be discovered. Note, however, that one can design tasks without this second requirement—that is, tasks requiring a change in reference frame, but tasks for which any of a number of changes will serve. The implication of our claim is that "creative," unexpected discoveries will be far more likely in tasks of this latter sort. Finke and Slayton's (1988) procedure may provide such a case; likewise for the procedure employed by Anderson and Helstrup (1993; also Finke, 1990).

3. *Stimulus support.* There is one further way in which subjects can escape the boundaries on learning from imagery: They can create a stimulus. In both the Chambers and Reisberg (1985) and Reisberg and Chambers (1991) studies, subjects were able to draw pictures, based on their images, and then to make discoveries from these pictures that they had not made with the corresponding images. Why is this? We have argued elsewhere that some judgments, by their nature, require "stimulus support." That is, these judgments can easily be made about a *stimulus,* but are not easily made with reference to a mental representation (e.g., Reisberg, 1987; Reisberg & Logie, 1993; Reisberg, Smith, & Wilson, 1991). However, this leads to a question: If a judgment requires stimulus support, does that mean the judgment cannot be made with imagery?

An answer to this question is suggested by studies of auditory imagery, which we discussed earlier. Of course, we cannot freely generalize from studies of auditory imagery to claims about visual imagery, nor vice versa: It is entirely possible that each modality of imagery has its own functional profile. Nonetheless, many of our claims about imagery (and about perception) should apply across modalities, and it is reassuring in this regard that auditory images do show some of the same data patterns as visual images. (For a review of auditory imagery research, see Reisberg, 1992.)

More specifically, questions about image ambiguity seem to receive similar answers in these two domains: As we have already seen, visual images seem unambiguous in what they represent: Without specific instructions, imaged ducks seem not to lead to imaged rabbits, nor vice versa. In auditory imagery studies, subjects do seem able to reconstrue their images when subvocalization is possible. When subvocalization is blocked, reconstrual rates drop to guessing levels (Reisberg et al., 1989; Reisberg et al., 1991).

What role does inner speech play in supporting the reversals of auditory images? One possibility is that inner speech provides some kinesthetic cue, crucial for performance. Alternatively, perhaps subjects subvocalize the to-be-imagined event, and then listen with some "inner ear" to find out what they have themselves produced. Note that this latter proposal suggests that subvocalization works in concert with audition. Hence, subjects need both the "inner voice" and the inner ear to perform our imagery tasks. Consequently, blocking use of the inner ear (via irrelevant distractors) should disrupt performance. If, in contrast, subvocalization is providing some sort of kinesthetic cues, then there is no role for audition, and so we should observe no effect of distractor noises.

To assess these claims, subjects were asked to perform the image-reversal task with auditory figures while hearing an irrelevant message through headphones. Control subjects were simply asked to image the target stimulus (and so had access to both the inner voice and the inner ear). In this procedure, 73 percent of the control subjects were able to reconstrue the image. However, when use of the inner ear was blocked by means of the irrelevant message, only 13 percent of the subjects were able to reconstrue the image—comparable to guessing performance. This, in combination with the results already described, suggests that subjects need both the inner voice and the inner ear to perform this task; if denied the use of either, performance drops to guessing levels. The implication is that subjects are literally talking to themselves and then listening to this self-produced stimulus.

Other studies show this to be a widespread pattern in auditory imagery. For example, consider the following task (Wilson et al., 1993). Subjects were visually presented with strings such as "D 2 R," or "N C Q R," and asked what familiar word or phrase would result if these strings were pronounced out loud ("detour" and "insecure"). Some subjects were asked to perform this task while hearing auditory input through headphones, blocking use of the inner ear. Subjects were instructed to ignore this input, and it was in any event irrelevant to their task. Other subjects read the strings while repeating "Tah-Tah-Tah" aloud, blocking use of covert speech. A third group of subjects performed with both the irrelevant auditory input and the concurrent articulation task (both inner ear and inner voice disrupted); a fourth group received neither type of interference.

The results yielded the same pattern as the image-reversal task. When subjects interpreted these strings with no interference (with no auditory distractor and subvocalization possible) they were able to decipher 73 percent of the strings. When subjects were denied use of the inner ear or inner voice, performance declined to 40 percent and 21 percent, respectively, and to 19 percent with both forms of interference present simultaneously. Again, it seems that subjects perform this task by speaking to themselves and then listening to hear what they have said.

An account of this pattern was suggested by Reisberg and colleagues (1991), building on an earlier argument by Besner (1987). More generally, these authors have offered an account of why some judgments about sound seem dependent on subvocalization (and so are disrupted by concurrent articulation), while other judgments are not. We hasten to say that this account is speculative, since relatively few studies bear on this issue directly. Nonetheless, there is a pattern in the available evidence, and the pattern will call our attention back to the issues of main concern here.

In a wide variety of tasks, one must create and then judge some mental representation of sound. For some of these tasks, one needs to do little more than this. That is, one can create these representations of sound as *intact units,* often drawing on some template, so to speak, already in memory. One can then judge the representation without any further analysis—without any reparsing or reorganization. In cases of this sort, the inner voice seems *not* to be needed, and one can simply draw on "pure" auditory imagery. However, other tasks require that one create a mental representation of sound, and then do some postassembly operations on this representation—operations that might include segmentation, or some reparsing, or even mere maintenance. Tasks of this sort seem to require the support of the inner voice, and performance is disrupted if use of subvocalization is prevented.

This pattern obviously fits with the cases we have described so far. The image-reversal task clearly requires that an auditory image be reparsed, and success in this task requires subvocalization. The "D 2 R" task likewise requires reorganization of an image, and also requires the inner voice. As a further example, findings indicate that concurrent articulation disrupts children's spelling, even though it does not disrupt their reading (e.g., Kimura & Bryant, 1983). This again fits with the proposed pattern, on the assumption that spelling, but not reading, requires analysis of phonological codes, requires the creation of and then dissection of auditory images. (For further discussion of evidence compatible with these claims, see Besner, 1987; Reisberg et al., 1991; Wilson et al., 1993.)

This data pattern suggests an important role for subvocalization, and this draws us back to our earlier claims about stimulus support. In general, the key seems to be that some auditory tasks require judgments that are compatible with one's initial understanding of a sound, whereas other tasks require judgments incompatible with this understanding. For tasks of the latter sort, subjects need to set aside their initial understanding to reanalyze or resegment the sound. This is precisely the case in which subjects need something like an actual stimulus, with an existence that is independent of the subjects' thoughts and understanding. With a stimulus, the subject can take a "neutral" stance toward the to-be-judged sound, and so make new discoveries, in essence guided by the sound itself, rather than being guided by the sound-as-initially-understood. Within this context, subvocalization appears to provide a stimulus, albeit a covert one. In essence, subvocalization allows subjects to create an auditory event, and then to "disown" it, to hear the event as a stranger might. In this fashion, subvocalization can aid those auditory tasks requiring stimulus support.

We have pursued the topic of stimulus support largely with reference to auditory imagery; how does all this bear on visual imagery? At one level, the application to visual imagery seems straightforward: As we have seen, discoveries from visual imagery flow easily if the discoveries are compatible with the image's reference frame; discoveries are far less likely if incompatible with the reference frame. Apparently, the same is true for auditory imagery. To make this translation, all we need assume is that the perceptual reference frame for audition includes specifications such as parsing and temporal organization. Thus, the reconstrual of auditory images, or the "D 2 R" task, are discoveries incompatible with an image's initial reference frame. It is these discoveries that seem difficult with "pure" auditory images. Similarly, it is these discoveries that benefit from stimulus support. For these tasks, the subject had one reference frame in mind when creating the stimulus, but, thanks to subvocalization, the subject has the option of setting aside this reference frame and listening with some detachment to the stimulus per se; this creates the opportunity to perceive the stimulus in some new way. In these terms, subvocalization is just the covert analog to drawing a picture, based on one's visual images, and, as we have already seen, subjects routinely make discoveries from these pictures that they were not able, a moment earlier, to make from the image itself.

In a different way, however, the parallel between visual imagery and auditory imagery is less straightforward: It seems useful to distinguish "pure" auditory images (not accompanied by subvocalization) from "enacted" images (accompanied by subvocalization), a distinction first suggested by Reisberg et al. (1989). Discoveries requiring stimulus support (i.e., discoveries requiring a reference-frame change) will be possible with enacted images (or with actual percepts), but not with pure images. Can a similar distinction be made for visual imagery? Reisberg and Logie (1993) have explored the possibility that visual imagery may also have access to some sort of "covert stimulus support," just as auditory imagery has access to subvocalization. Concretely, they explore the possibility that visual imagery can be supported by an "inner scribe," providing input to an "inner eye" (analogous to the inner voice providing input to the inner ear). However, it seems too soon to evaluate this possibility; thus, the prospect of covert stimulus support for visual imagery remains a matter for future research.

ZERO REVERSALS, OR SOME REVERSALS?

In the previous section, I sketched several mechanisms through which subjects can escape the boundaries on image functioning. These various mechanisms allow us to explain many of the apparent challenges to the Chambers and Reisberg position: For example, the discoveries made by Finke et al.'s (1989) subjects are discoveries compatible with an image's initial reference frame. Likewise, the notion of experimenter-cued reference-frame changes allows us to explain various discoveries reported by Brandimonte and Gerbino, by Hyman, or by Peterson and colleagues. Indeed, this notion of experimenter-cued reference-frame changes is needed to explain our own data (e.g., Reisberg & Chambers, 1991).

However, there are other imagery discoveries that seem not to be covered by our discussion so far. In the procedures reported by Brandimonte and Gerbino, by Hyman, or by Peterson et al., subjects in the *experimental* conditions were given instructions (or teaching examples) concerning how they should change their images' reference frames. As we have discussed, these explicit cues clearly facilitated image-based discovery. But what about subjects in the *control* conditions of these just-named studies? Subjects in these control conditions were neither given explicit instructions nor example figures, leading them to specific changes in the reference frame. Likewise, subjects in these control conditions did not have access to stimulus support (did not draw pictures, for example). We might expect, therefore, that these control subjects will reliably fail to make discoveries from their images if the discoveries require a reference-frame change. This is, of course, the result reported by Chambers and Reisberg (1985) and Reisberg and Chambers (1991), with *zero* success rates in the relevant conditions. As we have noted, though, others have not replicated this null success rate. For example, using the duck/rabbit figure, Brandimonte and Gerbino; Hyman; Kaufmann and Helstrup; and Peterson et al. all report reconstrual rates of 15 to 30 percent in their control conditions. This reconstrual rate is amply lower than that achieved by subjects given reference-frame instructions, and amply lower than that achieved by subjects actually perceiving these stimuli (as opposed to imaging them). Nonetheless, this reconstrual rate is plainly not zero.

The theoretical position we have developed is a position strongly phrased. We have argued that images are wholly unambiguous by virtue of being obligatorily created within a reference frame, and inseparable from that reference frame. As we have already seen, these claims are compatible with the fact that discoveries from imagery do occur, but, as discussed in the previous section, these discoveries should occur only under circumscribed circumstances. Thus, we have framed our account in a fashion that tolerates no exceptions. Indeed, in the Reisberg and Chambers study (1991), we went to some lengths to explain a few apparent exceptions to our claims.[6]

How then should we think about the nonzero reversal rates observed by Brandimonte and Gerbino, by Hyman, by Kaufmann and Helstrup, and by Peterson et al? As it turns out, we believe that these reversal rates are open to multiple explanations, most of which are compatible with our position. Thus, in the end, we believe that these results do not pose a challenge for our position. We begin with two accounts of the data pattern that seem, on our view, inadequate. We then turn to accounts that seem more promising.

Kaufmann and Helstrup (1993) have argued, contrary to Chambers and Reiserg, that images *can* exist as pure, uninterpreted icons, amenable to reinterpretation. Why, then, did the Chambers and Reisberg subjects fail to reconstrue their images? Kaufmann and Helstrup suggest that these subjects may have had inadequate imagery prowess: Perhaps image reconstrual is rather difficult, and so is possible only with particularly vivid imagery. If this is the case, then perhaps the

Chambers and Reisberg subjects had imagery not vivid enough to support the reconstrual task.

In support of this position, Kaufmann and Helstrup specifically recruited subjects with particularly vivid imagery. In this procedure, they observed a 15 percent reconstrual rate with the duck/rabbit figure (with no special instructions or training examples). By virtue of the contrast between this success and the zero success rate observed by Chambers and Reisberg, Kaufmann and Helstrup argued that the earlier null result was best attributed to subjects' inadequate imagery.

However, we are skeptical of this account, for several reasons. First, Chambers and Reisberg sought out subjects with particularly vivid imagery, just as Kaufmann and Helstrup did. (Specifically, they recruited architecture and art students, specifically to ensure adequate imagery prowess among their subjects.) In addition, Chambers and Reisberg collected self-report imagery assessments from their subjects; these self-reports make plain that their subjects did (by this measure) have vivid imagery. Thus, there is simply no basis for claiming that the Kaufmann and Helstrup subjects had imagery more vivid than that of the Chambers and Reisberg subjects, and thus it seems unpersuasive to explain the data contrast in these terms. In addition, the success rate observed by Kaufmann and Helstrup, in reversing the imaged duck/rabbit, is rather close to the success rate observed by Hyman (1993) and by Peterson et al., in their control conditions. Yet neither of these latter studies specifically recruited subjects with vivid imagery. Thus, in sum, Kaufmann and Helstrup's subjects had imagery no more vivid than Chambers and Reisberg's subjects, yet the former's subjects performed rather differently from Chambers and Reisberg's subjects. Likewise, it would seem that Kaufmann and Helstrup's subjects did have imagery more vivid than Hyman's or Peterson et al.'s subjects, yet Kaufmann and Helstrup's subjects performed at levels comparable to those of the latter groups. Given this pattern, we see no support for the claim that this contrast among studies can be explained in terms of imagery vividness. (For further discussion of the role of imagery vividness in these tasks, see Chambers & Reisberg, 1992.)

A more plausible account of the data appeals to the *test circumstances* employed in these various studies. In their initial study, Chambers and Reisberg recruited subjects in nonlaboratory settings—in building lounges and so on. Thus subjects were run in a somewhat noisy, largely uncontrolled environment; and these are, recall, the subjects who never succeeded in reconstruing the duck/rabbit image. In contrast, Brandimonte and Gerbino; Hyman; Kaufmann and Helstrup; and Peterson et al. all ran their studies in a laboratory setting—a setting free from distraction and uniform across subjects. These studies observed 15 to 30 percent reconstrual rates from control subjects (again, with no hints or training figures; appreciably higher reversal rates were obtained from the experimental subjects, as we have discussed already).

Why might this difference in setting matter for subjects' performance? As one obvious possibility, perhaps Chambers and Reisberg are simply wrong about the unambiguity of images. In our current terms, perhaps the depiction contained in an image and the reference frame *are* separable, so that the former *can* be contemplated in isolation from the latter. In this case, we might explain the original Chambers and Reisberg results along lines suggested some years ago by Kosslyn (1983), who argued that images are "inherently ambiguous," but that this ambiguity is rarely detected, because of various constraints built into the processes used to inspect images. However, Kosslyn argued, subjects could in principle escape these constraints—that is, subjects could detect the ambiguity if "they made an effort to do so" (Kosslyn, 1983, p. 89). This proposal is easily adapted to our present concern: Perhaps in a noisy, distracting environment, Chambers and Reisberg's subjects were unable to make the relevant "effort" to discover the ambiguity within an image—were unable to make the effort to divorce the image depiction from its reference frame. In contrast, subjects in a quiet environment might be able to accomplish this divorce, and so might be able, in effect, to render their images ambiguous by virtue of stripping their own images of the perceptual reference frame.

At least one study speaks against this distraction hypothesis. In an unpublished study, Kenneth Livingston (personal communication, January 1993) ran a procedure modeled after the original Chambers and Reisberg (1985) study. However, the Livingston procedure also adds a number of desirable controls: Experimenters were blind to the hypotheses (unlike most of the studies in this domain); the stimuli in this study were presented on a computer screen (rather than on index cards, hand-held by the subject, as in the original Chambers and Reisberg study). The computer presentation obviously allows precise timing of stimulus presentations and so on. Crucially, though, all of Livingston's subjects were run in a uniform, distraction-free laboratory environment. If distraction were crucial in producing the Chambers and Reisberg zero-reconstrual rate, we would expect to observe some reconstruals in Livingston's study. This expectation is not confirmed: Livingston reproduced the zero-reconstrual rate originally observed by Chambers and Reisberg, suggesting that the presence or absence of distraction is not the key in understanding this result.

It would obviously be useful to replicate the Livingston procedure—or, better still, to design a procedure that systematically compared image reconstrual rates in noisy and in quiet environments. At least for the moment, though, the evidence we have speaks against this distraction account. This still leaves us, therefore, with our questions unanswered: Why do some authors observe reconstruals, while Chambers and Reisberg (and Livingston) do not? At a more theoretical level, how can the nonzero reversal rates be accommodated by the Chambers and Reisberg position?

Our first suggestion is methodological. In all of the studies under consideration, we wish to ask whether subjects can discover an alternate construal from their image. Therefore, it is crucial that subjects not know the alternate construal prior to creating the image. It is for this reason that subjects are exposed only briefly to the to-be-imaged figure (e.g., the duck/rabbit). Presumably, this brief exposure makes it unlikely that subjects, naïve to this figure, will reconstrue it during the initial stimulus presentation. However, it remains possible that *some* subjects will reconstrue the figure during the initial presentation. If this reconstrual is undetected, then these subjects will appear to have discovered the reconstrual from their image, when, in fact, they knew how to reconstrue the figure prior to creating the image.

Aspects of the Peterson et al. results suggest that this concern may be a serious one. Across their procedures, approximately 25 percent of their subjects were able to reconstrue the duck/rabbit figure during the initial 5-second exposure, i.e., while the picture itself was still in view. (These subjects were replaced by other subjects for the main comparisons.) Moreover, many of the Peterson et al. subjects did not spontaneously report this initial reconstrual; these reconstruals were detected only with specific questioning.

Thus, as we seek to understand image reversals, we must be certain that we are, in fact, discussing *image* reversals, as opposed to reversals discovered during stimulus presentation. We have no easy way of telling to what extent this concern compromises available data, but, at the least, the concern suggests we need to be cautious in interpreting (apparent) reconstruals of mental imagery.

For sake of discussion, though, let us assume (as seems likely) that many of the reversals observed by Brandimonte and Gerbino, by Hyman, and so on *are* reversals from the image itself. How should we explain these? We have already offered one possible account: Our argument throughout has been that subjects' performance in these tasks is limited by an "inappropriate" reference frame. As we earlier noted, though, subjects do have the option of changing their reference frames—the reference frame is, after all, created by, and maintained by, and therefore changeable by, the imager. We have already seen that subjects *can be instructed* to redefine their images in this or that way, but presumably subjects can also change their reference frames without instruction. The suggestion, then, is that the image reversals observed by Brandimonte and Gerbino and others might be attributable to those subjects who, on their own, discover (and implement) this redefinition.

Why does this usually not happen? We earlier noted that subjects have the option of changing their image reference frames in any way they choose, and a huge number of options is available (the image's top can be defined as any compass direction; a variety of configurations in depth can be specified, and so on). It is this range of options that inhibits subjects' performance: With no guidance or cues, subjects have no way of knowing which image redefinition will lead to the target form. Thus, the probability of subjects stumbling across the "correct" redefinition is quite low, and this may be the reason why subjects fail to redefine their images in a fashion that would lead them to the target form.

However, while this probability is low, it need not be zero. It is certainly possible that some small number of subjects will stumble across the correct redefinition of their image, and so will "instruct themselves" in how to redefine the image's reference frame. These subjects would then be led to new image discoveries, just as are subjects who have been explicitly instructed by the experimenter in how to redefine the reference frame.

In fact, this suggestion can be combined with the distraction hypothesis described earlier. We know from Livingston's data that zero reversal rates can be observed even in a quiet, distraction-free laboratory environment. It nonetheless seems plausible that image reversals will be more likely inside of the laboratory than outside. Specifically, a quiet environment, with no distraction, might allow a subject to search systematically through the possible reference-frame changes for an image, in essence trying one reference-frame change after another, until the sought-after target is discovered. This systematic search would obviously increase the likelihood of the subject discovering the change needed for the particular task at hand. In this case, a substantial number of image reversals might be observed if subjects are run in optimal conditions—but not because these conditions allow subjects to strip away the image reference frame. Instead, the image reversals in this setting might reveal the power of reference-frame changes—an effect easily accommodated within the Chambers and Reisberg position.

IMAGE SIZE

In the previous section, I offered two conjectures about the nonzero reversal rates observed by Brandimonte and Gerbino, by Hyman, by Kaufmann and Helstrup, and by Peterson et al. First, these authors may be observing reversals that took place during the stimulus presentation itself, rather than reversals from imagery. Second, these reversals may be attributable to those subjects who discovered, on their own, how to change their image's reference frame—subjects who generated for themselves the instructions provided (for other subjects) by the experimenter.

It should be emphasized that these are conjectures, and they may turn out to be incorrect. Nonetheless, the conjectures are sufficient for my central point: At least for the moment, the nonzero reversal rates observed in various studies are themselves ambiguous, open to multiple interpretations, and thus without theoretical force. Therefore, no conclusions should be drawn from these data (on either side of the debate) until we understand why it is that some studies (including our own) reliably produce no image reconstruals, while other studies do observe reconstruals at a low but nontrivial rate.

In the present section, I wish to underscore this broad point by offering yet another way to think about the extant data. This account will be speculative, but once again I note that speculation is sufficient for my present purposes: The nonzero reversal rates observed by several authors are open to several interpretations.

I have already argued that one's construal of an image sets certain "depictive priorities" for the image: Aspects of the depiction that are crucial for the construal must be specified clearly in the image; aspects that are inconsequential for the construal may be left vague in the image. As we have seen, the Chambers and Reisberg (1992) data speak strongly in favor of this proposal. This proposal in turn can be used to explain the earlier Chambers and Reisberg (1985) data: The duck image literally omits information needed for the rabbit construal, and vice versa.

However, there are actually two different ways to implement these depictive priorities. One possibility is to define these priorities relative to the imaged form, so that (perhaps) one-third of the image might be clearly defined, and the rest vague, or perhaps specified parts of the image would be clear (e.g., the animal's face) and the rest vague, and so on. A different possibility is to define depictive priorities relative to the "medium" in which images are represented. One might argue, for example, that the imagery "medium" contains a region analogous to the retina's fovea, with detail clearly visible for stimuli projected onto the fovea, and detail correspondingly less visible for stimuli projected onto the visual periphery. According to this view, setting one's depictive priorities would be implemented by "positioning" the depiction within the image medium, such that crucial areas of the depiction fell within "foveal view." (Consonant with this view, at least some evidence suggests that imagery is characterized by a gradient of acuity, with a central area providing greater acuity than the periphery—cf. Finke, 1989.)

This latter conception of depictive priorities leads to several testable claims. For example, on this view there should be an interaction between image elaboration and image *size:* Specifically, an object imaged at a small size might fit entirely within the high-acuity region, much as a perceived object of a small visual angle can fit entirely within foveal view. If imaged at a larger size, the same object might "overflow" this high-acuity region within imagery, even though the entire image (or, more precisely, the entire image skeleton) might fit comfortably within the image field itself.

This perspective leads to a suggestion: If an object were to be imaged at a large size, then the imager's depictive priorities would be crucial for determining the pattern of elaboration across the image: Aspects of the image projected onto the high-acuity region would be elaborated, while other aspects would be left vague. If the same object were to be imaged at a smaller size, then the imager's depictive priorities might be irrelevant for image elaboration, since, no matter how the image is positioned, all aspects of the image would fall within the high-acuity area, and thus all aspects of the image would be appropriately elaborated. (By analogy, if one is looking at a large picture, then visual fixation is crucial, since much of the picture will fall outside of foveal view; our specification of the stimulus, therefore, depends critically on locating the foveal view. If one is looking at a smaller picture, visual fixation is less important: No matter where one looks on the picture, all of the picture will fall within foveal view; thus the position of fixation is less important.)

By now, the relevance of this to our present concerns should be clear. We earlier argued that the duck/rabbit image will not support reconstrual because the image is literally missing information needed to support the alternate construal. However, we are now offering the possibility that this will be true only if the duck/rabbit form is imaged at a relatively large size. Otherwise, the entire depiction might fall into the high-acuity region, independent of the imager's depictive priorities. In this case, the entire depiction might be clear and detailed, and so the image would contain information needed for reconstrual.

This leads directly to a testable suggestion: It is possible that the Chambers and Reisberg subjects imaged the duck/rabbit form at a relatively large size, so that the image "overflowed" the image high-acuity region, with the consequences we have discussed. It is possible that subjects in other procedures have imaged the form at a smaller size. More precisely, all we need assume is that 15 to 35 percent of the subjects in these other studies have imaged the form at a smaller size. These subjects would thereby have created an image small enough to fit entirely within the image high-acuity region, and therefore they would have created a uniformly detailed image, and, in particular, an image capable of supporting reconstrual.

This conjecture takes some plausibility from the fact that studies in the literature have, as far as we know, never instructed subjects about the size of the imaged form, and the size of the initially presented *picture* has typically been uncontrolled. (One possible exception to this pattern is a Peterson et al. [1992] study in which subjects were instructed to "build" the duck/rabbit from its constituents. Even in that study, however, the size of the resulting construction was largely uncontrolled.) Thus, we are offering what we take to be a plausible and testable hypothesis about why some studies have yielded a zero-reversal rate, while others have observed some number of reversals.

I close this section as I began it: emphasizing the speculative nature of the comments just offered. I am aware of the risk here. These conjectures (and variations on them) may ultimately render my position untestable, and I will return to this concern below. For the moment, though, these conjectures are subject to disconfirmation, and thus I am comfortable offering the conjectures as plausible accounts of the extant data.

More immediately, the conjectures make it clear that the results described so far can be accommodated within the position Chambers and I have developed. However, let me here emphasize the need for research. We plainly do need an account of why Chambers and Reisberg observed no image reconstruals, while other researchers have observed reconstruals at an appreciable rate. What is at stake, quite clearly, is whether images can be stripped of their reference frames in order to stand as free-standing icons, independent of any interpretive commitments. On the face of things, this is implied by the data by Brandimonte and Gerbino; by Hyman; by Kaufmann and Helstrup; and by Peterson et al.; yet it is precisely this possibility that Chambers and Reisberg wanted to deny. As we have seen, though, the available data do not cut forcefully one way or the other.

THE BRANDIMONTE AND GERBINO STUDY

We turn finally to a different line of recent evidence, which also appears to challenge the Chambers and Reisberg position. Brandimonte and Gerbino (1993) note that studies of image reversal obviously rely on memory: Subjects are briefly shown the to-be-imaged form, and must memorize it. The form is then removed from view, and subjects must generate their image based on what they remember of the form. This leads Brandimonte and Gerbino to ask how imagery might be shaped by subjects' memory strategies and memory codes.

Presumably, subjects draw on some sort of visual representation to encode the to-be-imaged form (e.g., the duck/rabbit). However, Brandimonte and Gerbino note that subjects may also rely (at least in part) on some form of verbal code in memorizing the experimental stimulus. This verbal coding will not eradicate the visual memories; instead, the verbal code will cause some degree of "verbal overshadowing" (cf. Schooler & Engstler-Schooler, 1990), potentially "weakening" the visual code, or rendering the code less accessible, or, as a related option, simply *biasing* the visual code (cf. Carmichael, Hogan, & Walters, 1932).

In any of these cases, verbal overshadowing will leave subjects with a less-available, or a lower-quality, visual image. In this case, subjects' performance in dealing with these images will obviously suffer. It may be for this reason, then, that subjects in the Chambers and Reisberg (1985) procedure (and subjects in a variety of other procedures) have failed to locate the duck in a rabbit image, or vice versa: Because of verbal overshadowing, these subjects simply have a poor quality image.

In support of this position, Brandimonte and Gerbino ran a procedure similar to the original Chambers and Reisberg study, but with one important change: During the initial memorization of the target form (i.e., the duck/rabbit), half of the subjects remained silent. With no overt concurrent verbal task, these subjects were presumably able to engage in covert verbal processing, and so these subjects would be expected to show the (hypothesized) effects of verbal overshadowing. The remaining subjects, while memorizing the target form, were required to repeat "la-la-la" aloud. The concurrent articulation task occupied the mechanisms of speech, and, therefore, presumably left these mechanisms unavailable for other use. Specifically, the concurrent articulation would prevent subjects from using these verbal mechanisms as part of a verbal encoding strategy. Consequently, we would expect that these subjects would not suffer the effects of verbal overshadowing. Instead, these subjects, denied access to verbal coding, would be forced to use a more purely visual code, and so would end up with a clearer, more accessible image. As a result, Brandimonte and Gerbino predicted that these subjects (with concurrent articulation) would be able to reverse the duck/rabbit image, whereas control subjects (with no concurrent articulation) would not.

The results generally confirmed these predictions. For example, in Brandimonte and Gerbino's third experiment, 5 percent of the subjects (1 of 20) in the control group succeeded in reversing the image. Forty percent of the articulatory suppression subjects (8 of 20) succeeded in reversing the image. In addition, Brandimonte and Gerbino replicated the finding that suitable instructions can also facilitate image reversals. As we have already discussed, however, this latter finding is fully consistent with (and, indeed, predicted by) our position; hence, we will not discuss their instruction effects here. (See above for our commentary on this broad class of results—e.g., the section entitled "Escaping the Boundaries on Image Function".)

Two further findings indicate that the effects of articulatory suppression arise during image *encoding*. First, Brandimonte and Gerbino's Experiment 4 required subjects to do concurrent articulation (saying "la-la-la" aloud) while inspecting the image, rather than during the initial encoding of the target form. This manipulation had no effect: Articulatory suppression was only effective during "image loading," not during "image manipulation." (The terms are Brandimonte's and Gerbino's.) Second, articulatory suppression had an effect in these procedures only if subjects' initial exposure to the to-be-remembered, to-be-imaged figure was quite brief. In most of their experiments, the subjects viewed the duck/rabbit picture only for 2 seconds and were aided by articulatory suppression. In their second experiment, however, Brandimonte and Gerbino's subjects viewed the duck/rabbit picture either for 2 seconds or for 5 seconds; all subjects were then identically tested for image reversal. Only the subjects viewing the figure for 2 seconds showed any effect of articulatory suppression. With five-second exposure, performance was identical in the articulatory-suppression and control conditions.

What should we make of all this? On the surface, these results appear to challenge the Chambers and Reisberg claims, inasmuch as the Chambers and Reisberg conception makes no claims about the effect of articulatory suppression, and certainly did not predict a beneficial effect of this suppression. However, we hesitate to draw conclusions from the Brandimonte and Gerbino findings, for several reasons. First, note that the researchers observed no effect of articulatory suppression with a 5-second exposure to the to-be-imaged figure; they conclude that verbal overshadowing does not occur with this exposure duration. (More precisely, verbal overshadowing may occur, but the lengthy exposure affords subjects the opportunity for visual encoding despite the biasing effects of verbal coding.) However, we should bear in mind that Chambers and Reisberg (1985) and others have used a 5-second exposure in their studies—studies that showed subjects unable to reverse the duck/rabbit image. Thus, Brandimonte and Gerbino seem to be saying that the verbal overshadowing hypothesis is inapplicable to just the situation studied by Chambers and Reisberg; hence, according to their argument, we should not interpret the Chambers and Reisberg findings in terms of verbal overshadowing. This leaves Brandimonte and Gerbino without an account of the original Chambers and Reisberg findings. By default, then, the account offered by Chambers and Reisberg themselves seems preferable.

We should perhaps pursue this point for a moment as Brandimonte and Gerbino are somewhat unclear on just this issue. They argue:

> If subjects are shown the picture for a short time . . . . , part of the visual information is lost as a consequence of verbal recoding. . . . If subjects are shown the picture for a longer time (e.g., 5 sec), they learn more visual details by virtue of a double shifting in the use of STM codes. . . . That is, a 5-sec presentation may prompt a process in which the visual input automatically loaded into the visual buffer is readily (e.g., within the first 2 sec) recoded in a verbal form. However, because the stimulus is easily recognizable and nameable, one could use the time left available after recoding to continue its visual analysis. (1993, p. 31)

For emphasis, note the claim that a 5-second exposure will initially invite verbal encoding, but then will still leave sufficient time for further "visual analysis" after the verbal encoding has been completed. This is consistent, of course, with

Brandimonte and Gerbino's own finding of *no effect* of articulatory suppression with 5-second exposures. However, they then go on to argue that their conception predicts "low performance because of verbal overshadowing" in a condition employing a 5-second stimulus presentation, no articulatory suppression, and with no cues or instructions provided. In support of this prediction, they cite (among others) the Chambers and Reisberg (1985) data. We would suggest that there is a contradiction here, with verbal overshadowing claimed to be both relevant and irrelevant to 5-second exposures, leaving Brandimonte and Gerbino with an account that is difficult to interpret and difficult to evaluate.

In addition, we are concerned about the internal logic of their account. At its heart, their account presumes that articulatory suppression disrupts verbal coding; thus, articulatory suppression prevents verbal overshadowing. However, this claim seems at odds with a number of findings in the literature. To be sure, articulatory suppression does disrupt use of certain *rehearsal* mechanisms, with clear implications for memory performance (cf. Baddeley, 1986); likewise, suppression disrupts a number of other tasks apparently requiring use of the inner ear and inner voice (cf. Reisberg et al., 1991). However, articulatory suppression does *not* disrupt verbal coding. We know, for example, that subjects are easily able to read text, even complex text, under circumstances of articulatory suppression. Speech perception is largely untouched by articulatory suppression, as is verbal reasoning. (For reviews of this large literature, see Baddeley, 1986; Besner, 1987.) Thus, as we read the evidence, there is no reason to believe that articulatory suppression blocks verbal coding. Consequently, if Brandimonte and Gerbino's claim about verbal overshadowing were correct, then we might well expect *no effect* of articulatory suppression on verbal overshadowing. On this logic, then, the Brandimonte and Gerbino data do not support their hypothesis. (This concern is amplified by a number of other considerations, including some apparent inconsistencies inside the researchers' results—see, for example, Brandimonte & Gerbino, 1993, p. 32.)

In summary, therefore, I have suggested that the Brandimonte and Gerbino account explains neither their own data nor the original Chambers and Reisberg (1985) findings. However, this still leaves us with the obvious concern: How can we account for the Brandimonte and Gerbino data—specifically, the finding that, with 2-second exposures, and no specific cues given to subjects, articulatory suppression makes image reconstruals possible? (We focus on this result simply because the other Brandimonte and Gerbino results—from procedures using instructions and cues—are readily accommodated within the framework we have developed here.)

In truth, I regard this as a genuine puzzle, and have only conjectures to offer. One such conjecture is provided by Reisberg and Logie (1993), but others are possible. As one broad *family* of accounts, consider the following: Whatever articulatory suppression *actually* does, it seems plausible that subjects will *expect* the suppression to be rather disruptive. In essence, the mere fact of hearing the task instructions may persuade a subject that he or she is heading into a difficult task, in comparison to a control subject, who will anticipate an easier task. It would not be surprising, therefore, if the experimental subjects shifted their strategy, or refocused their efforts, in a fashion different from control subjects. (A similar view of articulatory suppression—and data supporting this view—can be found in Intons-Peterson, 1992.) How this shift in strategy would affect performance remains to be specified, but, in general, one might appeal to mechanisms similar to those already described in discussing the Hyman, the Kaufmann and Helstrup, and the Peterson et al. results.

All of this plainly leaves the Brandimonte and Gerbino results unexplained. My earlier conjectures might be applied to this procedure, but obviously these conjectures remain to be tested. However, these conjectures would allow us to accommodate the Brandimonte and Gerbino findings within the Chambers and Reisberg framework, underscoring my main point: The findings of Brandimonte and Gerbino are equivocal, at least until further data are gathered. Therefore, these data cannot yet be used on either side of the issue under scrutiny here.

FINAL REFLECTIONS

The position offered by Chambers and Reisberg (1985) was motivated largely by philosophical concerns: We were influenced by philosophers as diverse as Casey (1976), Fodor (1975), Husserl (1931), and Wittgenstein (1953), each of whom had sketched properties that mental images would *need to have* if these images were to serve as carriers of meaning. However, none of these philosophers had shown that mental images did in fact have these properties, and therefore none of them had shown that images could have semantic value. Chambers and Reisberg argued that this was (and is) an empirical matter; our initial studies were intended to explore just this issue. The philosophers just mentioned disagree on how exactly images might carry meaning, but they nonetheless share an empirical prediction: To serve as carriers of meaning, mental images must be more than "mere" pictures, and must, in particular, be unambiguous. It was this claim that we set out to test.

In our 1985 paper, we concluded that mental images are, in fact, unambiguous, and are, therefore, eligible to serve as mental representations of meaning. Almost a decade later, we would still endorse these claims. To be sure, our position has expanded somewhat: We have developed our claims so as to explain the undeniable facts that learning from images does occur, that our images can surprise us or remind us and so on. To explain these facts, we have been forced to say more about what it is that renders an image unambiguous. This in turn has led us to a series of empirical claims about when learning from imagery will readily occur, and when it will not, and we believe these claims have fared well in the laboratory. Moreover, these are not the probabilistic claims typically offered by psychologists; rather, they are claims that tolerate no exceptions. Remarkably, even these very strong claims can be sustained in light of the full data pattern: The data remain compatible with the assertion that images are wholly and inextricably unambiguous.

As our conception has grown more elaborate, however, it has also grown more difficult to test, and this is obviously a source for concern. Consider, for example, a subject who makes some discovery from a mental image despite the fact that the discovery is incompatible with the image's initial reference frame. Some have suggested that such a subject has set the image's reference frame aside, and therefore has been able to confront a "pure" uninterpreted depiction. We have suggested, though, that such a subject is instead someone who has spontaneously redefined the image's reference frame, *replacing* an image understood one way with a (new) image understood another way. With this new reference frame in place, the path is open to new discoveries. Are these claims testably different?

In truth, the specific issue just described does *not* strike me as empirically assailable. That is, I see no way to determine directly whether the discovery just described is, in fact, a bona fide reconstrual, or instead a case of image replacement. However, I do not read this as a reflection of obscurity in our position (or that of our critics). Instead, I would suggest that, to no one's surprise, there are some predictions shared by the various theoretical positions, and some facts equally compatible with the various perspectives. Thus, confirmation of these predictions, or documentation of these facts, cannot be used to choose among the positions. This has, in fact, been a theme of the last few sections—that some of the extant data can be equally well explained in more than one way, and so these data are without theoretical force.

Essential here, though, is the fact that we can find *other* grounds on which the positions *can* be empirically distinguished. I have tried to highlight some of these grounds in the last few sections, and my current research is pursuing these points. Hence, it seems that we do still have testable positions in this debate, and questions that can be settled empirically.

While we await further data, though, it may be useful to highlight those claims that seem uncontroversial. I began this chapter with the questions posed in the long-standing "imagery debate." Are images "depictive" or "descriptive"? Is image representation analogical or propositional? I believe the answers to these questions are now clear: Neither the purely "pictorial" nor the purely "descriptive" conception of imagery is compatible with the full pattern of evidence. Images plainly have depictive qualities, and also descriptive qualities, and these interact in defining image function. As a closely related matter, it is now clear that we cannot speak *generally* about discoveries from imagery. There is a category of discoveries that flows easily from imagery, and a category of discoveries that seems far more difficult from imagery. Discoveries of the latter sort are strongly dependent on hints or instructions, in ways that the former discoveries are not. The boundary between these categories can be described in various ways, but, on anyone's account, the boundary depends on factors external to the depiction itself—factors concerned broadly with how the imager understands his or her own depiction.

These seem important points. More, as we promised at the very start, these are points that bear both on the nature of imagery representation and on the nature of imagery function. Thus, to the extent that the debate over image ambiguity has illuminated these issues, the debate has served us well. What then is the issue of disagreement? At its essence, the issue is this: Can one have a image without descriptive properties—in our terms, a depiction without a reference frame? Such an image might well be a desirable thing, given the limits on imagery function that we have described. Such an image would, in short, be able to support discoveries that would otherwise be unavailable. Yet it is just this possibility—of a pure depiction—that one is denying when one asserts that images are necessarily unambiguous. It is on just this issue that further work is needed, in the ways we have already described.

In addition, further work is clearly required on one other front: Research and theorizing about imagery have both benefited from the development of formalisms, describing imagery representation and then operations on that representation. Those formalisms—typically, computational formalisms—have made theorizing more precise, and in several cases have highlighted previously unnoticed issues. However, the available formalism is largely concerned with the depictive aspect of imagery, and so the available formalism is largely unable to address many of the observations discussed in this chapter. It seems clear, then, that further development of formalism is needed. How are the depictive and descriptive aspects of imagery represented? As two separate representations, akin to a "picture" plus a "caption"? Or as some sort of integrated bundle? To what extent is an image reference frame manifest as constraints on how one "reads" a mental image, and to what extent is the reference frame somehow instantiated within the depiction itself? These are questions currently without answers, and they seem crucial questions for research.

NOTES

1. We might mention that these repetitions also lead to a number of other perceived changes, likely to be due to habituation or satiation phenomena (Warren, 1961, 1982; Warren & Gregory, 1958). However, we will not pursue this point here, focusing instead on just those reconstruals of these figures that are fully compatible with the acoustic input.

2. To be historically accurate, many of the behaviorists themselves understood this point, leading to distinctions, for example, between the "nominal" and "functional" stimulus, a distinction in the same spirit as the point being made here.

3. In fact, the claim of "homogeneous images, but biased scanning" may be incompatible with what we know about image maintenance and image decay: Imagine that subjects do have a homogeneous image—detailed on all aspects of the imaged form. Now imagine a pattern of bias in how the image is scanned. Given the relation between scanning and image maintenance, this unevenly scanned image would in fact be unevenly maintained. Thus, even if the image *began* as a homogeneous depiction, it would not remain homogeneous, as the unscanned aspects would decay, while the scanned aspects would be maintained!

4. There are in fact many ways to explicate the "depictive priorities" notion, although some explications seem preferable to me, on the ground that they emphasize the parallels between this notion and the other perceptual specifications: We have already noted that a form has a specified "top," a specified figure/ground organization, and so on. In a similar fashion, one could emphasize the role of a form's "front" and "back," with the presumption that the "front" demands a higher depictive priority than the "back" (cf. McBeath,

Morikawa, & Kaiser, 1992; Peterson et al., 1992). As a closely related alternative, one might argue that a form has a specified "visual center," a term first used, I believe, by the Gestalt psychologist Metzger. Metzger argued that a form's (perceived) center has many consequences, both functional and phenomenal. The visual center can lead to expectations about how a form will move, if it moves; the visual center guides one's attention, as one explores the figure, and so on. Crucially for our purposes, though, Metzger also suggested that a form's center sets one's priorities for what aspects of the stimulus will be perceived with precision and detail, and what aspects will be perceived in a sketchy, vague, noncommittal fashion. Thus, each of these provides a way to talk about depictive priorities: setting them directly, letting them follow from specification of "front," or letting them follow from a specification of "visual center." Which of these is the optimal way to conceive of an image's depictive priorities remains to be seen.

5. There is some risk of terminological confusion here: I have employed the term "reconstrual" in describing all changes-in-interpretation of a perceived or imaged form. In my terms, some reconstruals are compatible with the extant reference frame; some are not. Peterson et al. (1992), in contrast, reserve the term "reconstrual" for those reinterpretations of an image that do not require (in their terms) a reference-frame realignment. In describing the Peterson et al. study, I will use their terms, but I return to my own terminology in what follows.

6. Concretely, we, too, observed nonzero rates of image reinterpretation in a condition in which we had anticipated zero discoveries. However, we offered argument and data in the 1991 paper suggesting that these few cases of reinterpretation were best understood as the result of guessing. Thus, for better or for worse, we clearly have established a precedent of seeking to maintain claims that do not tolerate exceptions.

REFERENCES

Anderson, R. & Helstrup, T. (1993). Visual discovery in mind and on paper. *Memory & Cognition, 21,* 283–293.

Arnheim, R. (1969). *Visual thinking.* Berkeley: University of California Press.

Attneave, F., & Reid, K. (1968). Voluntary control of frame of reference and shape equivalence under head rotation. *Journal of Experimental Psychology, 78,* 153–159.

Baddeley, A. D. (1986). *Working memory.* Oxford: Clarendon Press.

Besner, D. (1987). Phonology, lexical access in reading, and articulatory suppression: A critical review. *Quarterly Journal of Experimental Psychology, 39A,* 467–478.

Boring, E. G. (1942). *Sensation and Perception in the History of Experimental Psychology.* New York: Appleton-Century Co.

Brandimonte, M. A., & Gerbino, W. (1993). Mental image reversal and verbal recoding: When ducks become rabbits. *Memory & Cognition, 21,* 23–33.

Bruner, J. (1957). *Contemporary approaches to cognition.* Cambridge, MA: Harvard University Press.

Bruner, J. S. (1973). *Beyond the information given.* New York: Norton.

Carmichael, L. C., Hogan, H. P., & Walters, A. A. (1932). An experimental study of the effect of language on the reproduction of visually perceived form. *Journal of Experimental Psychology, 15,* 73–86.

Casey, E. (1976). *Imagining: A phenomenological study.* Bloomington,: Indiana University Press.

Chambers, D. (1990). *Images are not everywhere dense.* Unpublished doctoral dissertation, New School for Social Research, New York.

Chambers, D., & Reisberg, D. (1985). Can mental images be ambiguous? *Journal of Experimental Psychology: Human Perception and Performance, 11,* 317–328.

Chambers, D., & Reisberg, D. (1992). What an image depicts depends on what an image means. *Cognitive Psychology, 24,* 145–174.

Davi, M., & Proffitt, D. (1993). Frames of reference and distinctive figural characteristics affect shape perception. *Journal of Experimental Psychology: Human Perception and Performance, 19,* 867–877.

Dennett, D. (1981). The nature of images and the introspective trap. In N. Block (Ed.), *Imagery* (pp. 51–61). Cambridge, MA: MIT Press.

Farah, M. (1988). Is visual imagery really visual? Overlooked evidence from neuropsychology. *Psychological Review, 95,* 307–317.

Finke, R. (1990). *Creative imagery: Discoveries and inventions in visualization.* Hillsdale, NJ: Erlbaum.

Finke, R. (1989). *Principles of mental imagery.* Cambridge, MA: MIT Press.

Finke, R. (1985). Theories relating mental imagery to perception. *Psychological Bulletin, 98,* 236–259.

Finke, R., Pinker, S., & Farah, M. (1989). Reinterpreting visual patterns in mental imagery. *Cognitive Science, 13,* 51–78.

Finke, R., & Slayton, K. (1988). Explorations of creative visual synthesis in mental imagery. *Memory & Cognition, 16,* 252–257.

Fodor, J. (1975). *The language of thought.* New York: Crowell.

Friedman, A. (1979). Framing pictures: The role of knowledge in automatized encoding and memory for gist. *Journal of Experimental Psychology: General, 108,* 316–355.

Goldmeier, E. (1937/1972). Similarities in visually perceived forms. *Psychological Issues, 8,* (entire issue).

Gottschaldt, K. (1967). Gestalt factors and repetition. In W. Ellis (Ed.), *A source book of gestalt psychology.* New York: Humanities Press. (Original work published 1926)

Hampson, P. J., & Morris, P. E. (1978). Some properties of the visual imagery system investigated through backward spelling. *Quarterly Journal of Experimental Psychology, 30,* 655–664.

Hochberg, J. (1981). On cognition in perception: Perceptual coupling and unconscious inference. *Cognition, 10,* 127–134.

Hochberg, J. (1982). How big is a stimulus? In J. Beck (Ed.), *Organization and representation in perception.* Hillsdale, NJ: Erlbaum.

Husserl, E. (1931). *Ideas.* New York: Collier.

Hyman, I. (1993). Imagery, reconstructive memory, and discovery. In B. Roskos-Ewoldsen, M. Intons-Peterson, & R. Anderson (Eds.), *Imagery, creativity and discovery: A cognitive approach.* Amsterdam: Elsevier.

Intons-Peterson, M. (1992). *The role of verbal and visual factors on short-term memory and on a mental subtraction task.* Paper presented December 1992 at the Fourth European Workshop on Imagery and Cognition, Puerto de la Cruz, Tenerife, Canary Islands.

James, W. (1890). *The principles of psychology* (vol. 2). New York: Dover.

Jastrow, J. (1900). *Fact and fable in psychology.* Boston: Houghlin Mifflin.

Kanizsa, G. (1979). *Organization in vision.* New York: Praeger.

Kaufmann, G., & Helstrup, T. (1993). Mental imagery: Fixed or multiple meanings? In B. Roskos-Ewoldsen, M. Intons-Peterson, & R. Anderson (Eds.), *Imagery, creativity and discovery: A cognitive approach.* Amsterdam: Elsevier.

Kimura, Y., & Bryant, P. (1983). Reading and writing in English and Japanese: A cross-cultural study of young children. *British Journal of Developmental Psychology, 1,* 143–154.

Kosslyn, S., Brunn, J., Cave, K., & Wallach, R. (1985). Individual differences in mental imagery ability: A computational analysis. *Cognition, 18,* 195–243.

Kosslyn, S. M. (1976). Can imagery be distinguished from other forms of internal representation? Evidence from studies of information retrieval times. *Memory & Cognition, 4,* 291–297.

Kosslyn, S. M. (1980). *Image and mind.* Cambridge, MA: Harvard University Press.

Kosslyn, S. M. (1983). *Ghosts in the mind's machine.* New York: Norton.

Kosslyn, S. M., Ball, T. M., & Reiser, B. J. (1978). Visual images preserve metric spatial information: Evidence from studies of image scanning. *Journal of Experimental Psychology: Human Perception and Performance, 4,* 1–20.

Marks, D. (1972). Individual differences in the vividness of visual imagery and their effect on function. In P. Sheehan (Ed.), *The function and nature of imagery.* New York: Academic Press.

Marks, D. (1983). Mental imagery and consciousness: A theoretical review. In A. Sheikh (Ed.), *Imagery: Current theory, research and application.* New York: John Wiley.

McBeath, M., Morikawa, K., & Kaiser, M. (1992). Perceptual bias for forward-facing motion. *Psychological Science, 3,* 362–367.

Mill, J. S. (1865). *An examination of Sir William Hamilton's philosophy.* Boston: W. V. Spencer.

Navon, D. (1977). Forest before trees: The precedence of global features in visual perception. *Cognitive Psychology, 9,* 343–383.

Palmer, S. (1980). What makes triangles point: Local and global effects in configuration of ambiguous triangles. *Cognitive Psychology, 12,* 285–305.

Peterson, M., Kihlstrom, J., Rose, P., & Glisky, M. (1992). Mental images can be ambiguous: Reconstruals and reference-frame reversals. *Memory & Cognition, 20,* 107–123.

Ramachandran, V. (1992). Filling in gaps in perception: Part 1. *Current Directions in Psychological Science, 1,* 199–205.

Ramachandran, V. (1993). Filling in gaps in perception: Part II. Scotomas and phantom limbs. *Current Directions in Psychological Science, 2,* 56–65.

Reisberg, D. (1987). External representations and the advantages of externalizing one's thought. In E. Hunt (Ed.), *The Ninth Annual Conference of the Cognitive Science Society.* Hillsdale, NJ: Erlbaum.

Reisberg, D. (Ed.). (1992). *Auditory imagery.* Hillsdale, NJ: Erlbaum.

Reisberg, D. (1993). Equipotential recipes for unambiguous images: Comment on Rollins. *Philosophical Psychology, 7,* 359–366.

Reisberg, D., & Chambers, D. (1991). Neither pictures nor propositions: What can we learn from a mental image? *Canadian Journal of Psychology, 45,* 288–302.

Reisberg, D., & Heuer, F. (1988). Vividness, vagueness, and the quantification of visualizing. *Journal of Mental Imagery, 12,* 89–102.

Reisberg, D., & Logie, R. (1993). The in's and out's of working memory: Escaping the boundaries on imagery function. In B. Roskos-Ewoldsen, M. Intons-Peterson, & R. Anderson (Eds.), *Imagery, creativity and discovery: A cognitive approach.* Amsterdam: Elsevier.

Reisberg, D., Smith, J. D., Baxter, D. A., & Sonenshine, M. (1989). "Enacted" auditory images are ambiguous; "pure" auditory images are not. *Quarterly Journal of Experimental Psychology, 41A,* 619–641.

Reisberg, D., Smith, J. D., & Wilson, M. (1991). Auditory imagery. In R. Logie & M. Denis (Eds.), *Mental images in human cognition* (pp. 59–81). Amsterdam: Elsevier.

Rey, G. (1981). What are mental Images? In N. Block (Ed.), *Readings in the philosophy of psychology* (pp. 117–127). Cambridge, MA: Harvard University Press.

Richardson, J. (1980). *Mental imagery and human memory.* New York: St. Martin's Press.

Rock, I. (1973). *Orientation and form.* New York: Academic Press.

Rock, I. (1983). *The logic of perception.* Cambridge, MA: MIT Press.

Rock, I., Halper, F., & Clayton, T. (1972). The perception and recognition of complex figures. *Cognitive Psychology, 3,* 655–673.

Rock, I., & Leaman, R. (1963). An experimental analysis of visual symmetry. *Acta Psychologica, 21,* 171–183.

Schooler, J., & Engstler-Schooler, T. (1990). Verbal overshadowing of visual memories: Some things are better left unsaid. *Cognitive Psychology, 22,* 36–71.

Shepard, R. N., & Cooper, L. A. (1982). *Mental images and their transformations.* Cambridge, MA: MIT Press.

Slee, J. (1980). Individual differences in visual imagery ability and the retrieval of visual appearances. *Journal of Mental Imagery, 4,* 93–113.

Titchener, E. B. (1926). *Lectures on the experimental psychology of the thought-process.* New York: Macmillan.

Tsal, Y., & Kolbet, L. (1985). Disambiguating ambiguous figures by selective attention. *Quarterly Journal of Experimental Psychology, 37,* 25–37.

Warren, R. (1961). Illusory changes of distinct speech upon repetition—the verbal transformation effect. *British Journal of Psychology, 52,* 249.

Warren, R. (1982). *Auditory perception.* New York: Pergamon.

Warren, R., & Gregory, R. (1958). An auditory analogue of the visual reversible figure. *American Journal of Psychology, 71,* 612–613.

Wilson, M., Smith, J. D., & Reisberg, D. (in press). *The role of subvocalization in auditory imagery. Neuropsychologia.*

Wittgenstein, L. (1953). *Philosophical investigations* (G. E. M. Anscombe, Trans.). Oxford: Basil Blackwell.

CHAPTER 5

Ducks, Rabbits, and Hedgehogs: Resolution, Impasse, or Fostered debate?

**Robert H. Logie, Cesare Cornoldi, Maria A. Brandimonte,
Geir Kaufmann, and Daniel Reisberg**

We took as a starting point a debate about construal and reconstrual of images. Eloquent cases have been made by major proponents on differing sides of the debate. In opening the final discussion for this volume, there might be some merit in trying to establish the current state of agreement or otherwise among the three major contributors to this volume. As the previous chapters have made clear, there are profound disagreements among these authors. Against this backdrop, there are a number of ways in which the debate might progress. It might reach an impasse, with consensus impossible and with the arguments progressing the debate no further. A second outcome can be that the debate is resolved, and the opponents agree, perhaps because of the persuasiveness of one case rather than another, or because some new solution is reached that was not obvious before. Even if we have reached an impasse, however, it is important to be clear as to the purpose of fostering scientific debate. One position to take could be that the debate is itself helpful. It is stimulating intellectually, and it challenges our assumptions, implicit or explicit. This in turn fosters fresh grounds for discussion. Perhaps most important, the debate can—and often does—provoke further research. According to this view, further debate, even if reaching no resolution, is plainly healthy.

If we reflect on the cases made in this volume, we can rapidly dismiss the suggestion that the discussion has reached an impasse. The range of concepts discussed and the body of data on which the authors draw are rich in hints for future research. The next question is whether these hints involve divergent paths, or whether there is sufficient agreement for the discussion to go forward in concert and thus for the research to move us toward resolution. Fortunately, unlike the examples given in our introduction of the Trojan apple, or Gulliver's experiences with the position of eggs, it seems clear that there is mutual respect among the various discussants, and that they are making a genuine effort to understand each other's positions. It is likewise clear that each of the opposing views makes a positive contribution to understanding, yet leaves some tantalizing questions open.

There are promising signs for how the debate will progress. Nonetheless, on the face of things, there do seem indications here of genuine divergence, not convergence, among the research directions. At first blush, the contrasting patterns of data lead to a feeling of "now you can reconstrue," "now you can't," with no clear reasons as to why different laboratories should come up with different results. Like the croquet game in *Alice in Wonderland,* just as you are about to score, your "hedgehog ball" uncurls itself and walks away—hence, the reference to hedgehogs in the title of this chapter. The authors tackle this at two levels. One level is to suggest that the methodology is sufficiently different between different laboratories for different results to obtain. Differences in methodology are not the only focus for the debate, and the second level addresses the more fundamental questions as to the nature of mental representations and the nature of the cognitive architecture supporting those representations.

In hope of furthering these issues, three of the authors for this volume (Brandimonte, Kaufmann, and Reisberg) sat down to discuss these issues in a meeting that took place in Tenerife (Canary Islands) in December 1992, during the fourth European Workshop on Imagery and Cognition. The function of the editors during the discussion was to act primarily as catalysts and mediators for what turned out to be a predictably amicable but very stimulating discourse. We have reproduced here the bulk of that discussion to give readers some of the flavor of the live debate, with direct responses from each of the authors to the others' questions. Such a debate also guarantees that the discussants are addressing each other's true positions, and not setting up straw people.

In producing what follows, there has been very little editing from the original tape recording, other than to add explanatory editorial comments where the context was not clear from the protocol, and occasionally to paraphrase the circumlocutions and false starts that accompany natural spoken language. However, the discussion given here should be read in the light of the arguments and data presented in the substantive chapters in this book. Also, because this discussion took place during a conference, occasionally speakers refer to papers presented at the conference. Some of the material in these papers has been covered in another book in the Counterpoints series (de Vega, Intons-Peterson, Johnson-Laird, Denis & Marschark, in press) although the material in the present volume is designed to be self-contained.

Finally, we should note that this debate represents the authors' views as they were in December 1992. In the intervening months, all of the authors have adjusted their positions somewhat—in part because of the contents of this debate.

The chapters earlier in this volume were, in fact, written more recently than the reproduced discussion. The protocol that follows presents a "live" depiction of the authors' views. However, when the protocol's content differs from that of the chapters, it is the latter that better represent the authors' current thinking.

The convention we have adopted is to place editorial comments in parentheses or as footnotes, while asides by the speaker are prefaced by hyphens. In the main, interjections have been retained.

In the spirit of what we have said above, it was intriguing to note that the debate opened with Dan Reisberg attempting to collate points of consensus, one of which was covered in some depth in Geir Kaufmann's chapter—namely, the picture metaphor of images. But Reisberg very rapidly turns to points of disagreement, most notably the role of articulatory suppression. The putative role of articulatory suppression is a theme that runs through the debate.

THE TENERIFE DEBATE

REISBERG: Can I suggest that it might be useful just to start by trying to be clear about points of agreement among ourselves. Then with those points out in plain view, we can isolate the points on which we disagree. I'll try and list these points of agreement, and please correct me if I say something wrong—i.e., something on which there is disagreement.

It seems to me at this point that there are virtually no scholars in the field, in this room or out, who hold to the strictest of pictorial views. I think Steve Kosslyn has used language which suggested he held a strict pictorial view, but when you read him closely, it is clear that he does not. I would say the same about Ron Finke. In any event, no one holds the strict pictorial view. I do think we can find people who hold the opposite extreme—i.e., a strict descriptive view. There are very few psychologists in this category, but I think we can find philosophers still taking the strong descriptivist stance.

Therefore, by a process of elimination, it seems to me that virtually all research psychologists are now ready to endorse something that looks like a hybrid model; something in which there are undeniably depictive elements; that is, something which looks picture-like, and also some accompanying descriptive information. And then we get to one of the points where I suspect there may still be disagreement, namely what the nature of the accompanying descriptive information is. I've tried to argue that it is purely information about how things should be perceived and not semantics, but that is certainly a point on which, I think, there could still be controversy. A further controversial point is whether the depictive information and descriptive information are in some way separable, because I clearly believe they are not. They are firmly integrated as a package and cannot be pulled from each other.

Beyond that, it seems to me that we are all willing to agree that there is a species of reconstrual that happens easily and effortlessly with images. But there is also a species of reconstrual which happens either with difficulty or with instructions. Here again, though, we find another point of disagreement. We will disagree on what instructions you need or what cues you need to elicit reconstruals in this latter category. I think that this disagreement among us may be linked to the others. For example, Maria [Brandimonte] and Walter [Gerbino] have written that one manipulation that will elicit reconstruals is articulatory suppression.

Of course, I find their data in support of this claim mystifying, quite honestly. Bob [Logie] and I have tried in print to offer various ways those data might be handled, but, one way or another, clearly here's a point of disagreement. In return, from what I understand of your [Brandimonte] position, other of the published data are mysterious for you. So, just as I would be happy to see your data go away, it is not clear to me how in your view one should explain the 1992 Chambers and Reisberg data.

BRANDIMONTE: Mostly we agree. I still think there is disagreement on the point as to whether and how descriptive and depictive aspects of an image can be separated, but I do not think we disagree entirely because, for example, we endorse your conclusion that the centering idea with articulatory suppression might work. However, if we analyze this statement more deeply, it is easy to see that it means that articulatory suppression may weaken the reference frames that you use and that the whole process would be something like: Verbal recoding might prompt some sort of abstract semantic recoding, which in turn overshadows visual memories. That is, this reference frame biases subjects toward a more descriptionalist point of view. Articulatory suppression has the effect of preventing the verbal recoding and therefore preventing the use of this sort of mechanism.

We think that the disagreement is that the image might contain some uninterpreted elements. For example, we completely agree with Geir [Kaufmann] that there is some sort of continuum; that images are both pictures and propositions. (Incidentally, this is the title of one of the articles published by Deborah Chambers and Daniel Reisberg.) Our opinion is that when you adopt articulatory suppression you lead subjects to a more primitive stage of processing, in the sense that you prevent them (the subjects) from recoding the pictures. It is essential that articulatory suppression is present only at the time of learning. If you add articulatory suppression during the imagery phase, you do not get the same effect.

In conclusion, we think it is possible to separate those aspects which are interpreted from those which are not interpreted. There might be aspects in an image which are in a not-yet-analyzed state. In our case, this is an effect of adding articulatory suppression as a means of preventing the interpretation of the whole image. As far as I understand it, your 1985[1] point was that from an image file you take all the characteristics you need to construct an image. The interpreted image is completely unambiguous because it is already interpreted and in this sense we perfectly agree with you. But your point was that in order to have reconstrual, you have to replace one image with another. This means that you have to go back again to this general pool of characteristics that you encoded when you saw the figure—this is what I mean by an image file—take what you need in order to have a different image, and construct a different image that is unambiguous in itself. So you have two unambiguous images and one replaces the other.

Our suggestion is that by adding articulatory suppression—this is a tentative interpretation—you might carry with you something that is not immediately needed for interpretation. (Here, in our opinion, the concept of conscious and unconscious aspects is important. However, we do not wish to take this position at the moment.) So, you have an image that is partially interpreted as a duck, for example, and that is present in your consciousness, but at the same time it contains aspects in a not-yet-analyzed state. When you ask people to look for the other interpretation they might simply direct their mind's eye toward these not-yet-analyzed aspects. Therefore, the problem is, in our view, in the meaning of ambiguity and interpretability of images. In your first paper,[2] it appeared that what is unambiguous necessarily must be interpreted and what is interpreted is necessarily unambiguous. What we are claiming is that what is interpreted might be ambiguous, because if you define ambiguity in terms of presence of not-yet-interpreted, not-yet-analyzed aspects, you might have the seemingly paradoxical situation in which you have interpreted images containing not-yet analyzed aspects which allow you to reinterpret the same image. You do not need to go to the image file, take what you need, and create another image.

REISBERG: May I say several things in response, mostly concerned with this idea of "not-yet-interpreted aspects" within the image. We have no disagreement about the fact that learning from images is possible. Of course, one can make new discoveries about an imaged form. But, if I may, I think you draw the wrong conclusion from this fact. I have repeatedly and consistently argued that it will routinely be the case that there are discoveries and surprises that can be derived from an image without any need to return to the image file, without any need to replace the image. In this sense, then, of course there are "not-yet-interpreted" aspects of the image. These discoveries will, however, uniformly be discoveries that are compatible with the existing reference frame. Therefore, it is going to be crucial for us to distinguish discoveries compatible with the reference frame from discoveries requiring a reference frame switch.

In the 1985 paper we talked about the obvious fact that surely we can learn from images and we need to reconcile that with the apparent unambiguity of the image. I think we described that point in the 1985 paper with considerable clumsiness, which has cost us a lot in subsequent years. In the terms I would now use, though, terms which I think are much clearer, this is the contrast between discoveries compatible with the reference frame, and discoveries not compatible with the reference frame. It's the reference frame that renders the image unambiguous, and it's also the reference frame that sets boundaries on what will be discovered about the image. But having said all that, I have no trouble at all in saying that there are uninterpreted, not yet discovered elements within the image.

Let me now go back to the earlier point. I understand the argument that you are making about articulatory suppression, but it seems to me that there are two very large questions that you need to answer to make certain that you have a coherent position. The questions may have answers, but I do not know what they are. One of them concerns your presumption that articulatory suppression blocks verbal coding. From what we know about articulatory suppression, that is simply a bad argument. We know that articulatory suppression occupies the rehearsal loop in ways that have been well documented in a number of studies. But we also know that it leaves perfectly functioning the central executive component of working memory, which is capable of exquisite and detailed verbal coding. Therefore, the claim "You are getting the data because articulatory suppression blocks verbal coding" cannot, as I have just stated it, be correct.

BRANDIMONTE: It depends . . .

REISBERG: Everything we know about articulatory suppression from the literature on reading, the literature on visual perception, across a variety of literatures, tells that verbal coding happens perfectly well in the presence of articulatory suppression. We need to figure that out, otherwise, I'm sorry, but you just have no position. Maybe there is an answer there, but I just do not see it off hand.[3]

LOGIE: One comment I could make here concerns the assumption that articulatory suppression involves the pure use of the rehearsal loop, and that the rehearsal loop is the only component of the cognitive system that is involved. It is not entirely clear that this is the case. Articulatory suppression can also play the role as a general distracter, causing disruption because of the requirement to carry out a concurrent task, any concurrent task, while imaging. In our own lab, we have been collecting data on the J-D umbrella task[4] showing *disruptive* effects of articulatory suppression on this particular imaging task. There are also disruptive effects of concurrent random generation on this form of mental imagery synthesis. This contrasts with the *improvements* in performance which Maria and Walter have obtained with duck-rabbit reconstruals. Both articulatory suppression and random generation are very much verbal tasks, but with differential demands on the central executive. And so, it may be that there is not so much of an involvement of the articulatory loop in discovery from images, but that it relies heavily on the central executive. The central executive could also be involved in establishing a reference frame, and in the duck-rabbit task, articulatory suppression may have the effect of disrupting the formation of the reference frame in the executive rather than having an effect specifically on verbal recoding.

BRANDIMONTE: Yes, but if I may say this, it is for future research to establish this because there are two positions in my opinion: Either we accept the assumption that if articulatory suppression is performed at a rate that does not go beyond the central executive capacity, it has no effect in terms of distraction (and this is what we did, following the suggestions in the literature). Either we accept this assumption or we cast doubts on it. If we cast doubts on it, why shouldn't I cast doubts on the idea that articulatory suppression may indirectly affect verbal semantic coding?

REISBERG: Because in order to cast doubts on that view, what you need are two things. The first is some control condition to test for general distraction.

BRANDIMONTE: We did it: tapping.

REISBERG: And the data now show?

BRANDIMONTE: That there is no effect. Two people out of 20 reversed [the duck-rabbit figure].

REISBERG: Compared to articulatory suppression, which gave you . . . ?

BRANDIMONTE: Eleven out of 20 [reversed the figure]. Highly significant. I've never used these data before. I ran this condition when Walter [Gerbino] was in the States and wondered whether to add this to the paper. Dan, you and Bob [Logie] suggested an interesting thing[5]: that articulatory suppression makes people able to use the inner scribe—that is, it should have the effect of distracting subjects from verbal coding and from taking advantage of the beneficial effects of having two codes—a dual coding—which would help. In that case, instead of using the verbal code, people use a motoric enactment for the image. Is that your suggestion, Dan?

REISBERG: Right.

BRANDIMONTE: At that point, I said that this was the case. We should see whether this is the effect. We do not have a definite answer to this. Anyway, our opinion is that it is unlikely.

REISBERG: You have never done this kind of experiment?

BRANDIMONTE: No.

LOGIE: Geir: Do you have any comments on this?

KAUFMANN: You [addressing Reisberg] argued that the description is an integral part of the image, is somehow "baked" into it. So you may argue that what subjects do in her [Brandimonte's] experiments is to turn an image into a nonimage, and then you have a reconstrual. In a sense you turn the image into a picture, because you eliminate the integral verbal labeling part of the image.

BRANDIMONTE: This is what I am arguing; that there is more similarity to a picture under articulatory suppression than without articulatory suppression.

KAUFMANN: Yes but you [Reisberg] could make the argument that this really supports your position.

REISBERG: I can?

KAUFMANN: Yes. If the natural imagery phenomenon has this description part baked into it, as an integral part of the image that cannot be separated from the image, when you separate something that cannot be separated, you turn this phenomenon into something else. And then you can have a reconstrual under highly artificial conditions.

BRANDIMONTE: I can't see how you can have a reversal of the duck-rabbit without having depictive aspects of the image and turning it into a description. It is hard for me to understand how to do the imagery task of reversing the duck-rabbit in imagery relying simply on a description or a propositional code. I cannot see this.

KAUFMANN: I think that if we are interested in mental imaging as it naturally occurs, and not as it might occur under some special laboratory conditions, and if you turn this natural imaging phenomenon into something highly artificial, you can show reconstrual under these particular conditions. But this just supports the case that this mental imagery under normal conditions is not like that. There is a description integral to it, and that is what makes it so difficult to reconstrue, not impossible.

BRANDIMONTE: This is interesting, but I have never made this point in terms of natural versus laboratory conditions. My interest was in knowing whether people could reconstrue. The condition—natural or laboratory—does not matter. If you cannot do this [i.e., reconstrue] in one [experimental] condition, and I find another [experimental] condition in which you are able to reconstrue, then this is the most important finding, in my opinion.

KAUFMANN: You can make people do many strange things if you think of the special conditions under which you are working with the subject.

BRANDIMONTE: I have no problem in admitting that articulatory suppression is an artificial technique to induce something which might be either a disruption, or an improvement, as in my case. But if it helps me understand how my mind works when I have to deal with mental images, I will use it.

CORNOLDI: Thinking of Geir's paper suggesting that maybe in some cases not only do we have a dichotomy (yes/no), but also we have intermediate cases. I would like your reactions to some problems related to the perceptual exploration of the pattern. First of all in the automatic processing of the pattern.

This morning, Johnson-Laird suggested an examination of the relationship with language. In the literature on language some data suggest that, although it seems that the word is immediately interpreted, in fact also the other possible meanings of a word are activated. For example, in reading, the context suggests an interpretation of the stimulus—that is, of the word—but other meanings also are activated. In fact, in priming experiments we can find that these other meanings also result in priming effects. I am asking whether it is possible that in the perceptual exploration of an ambiguous pattern, other meanings of the pattern also are activated, although we are not aware of it. This is the first problem.

The second problem is this: When the stimulus is interpreted, do we assume that the interpretation is either yes or no, or do we assume that the subject maintains a certain level of uncertainty as to a number of possible alternative explanation(s). From an experimental point of view this could be examined by asking subjects to indicate their level of certainty about their interpretation of the stimulus. Is it possible that under articulatory suppression, subjects are less certain of their interpretation? Maybe from a subjective point of view, we think we have interpreted the stimulus, but can we have a range of certainty? I mean, can these two aspects, then, affect the reinterpretation of the stimulus?

KAUFMANN: I think we agree that there is a range. What we might disagree on is how wide this range is. You [Reisberg] seem to be holding a more constrained position than we would argue for when you say, in principle at least, that to use this figure/caption analogy of yours allows us to show that you can reinterpret from figure to caption, rather than just from caption to figure. You confirm that that was your position, that there is an asymmetry. I think you are right about describing imagery in the normal case, but I think it stretches wider and that there are cases where you can go from figure to caption.

So I would like to see a model of imagery that is on a continuum from purely description-like images with very few depictive elements, with a range to the other pole with images that are very close to real pictures. You stand outside them, and you look at them, and you discover things from them. That would be the other extreme, but you said that is not proper mental imagery.

REISBERG: Certainly there is a sort of continuum. For example, I can think of a tiger with no pictorial sense of how big it is or the way it is sitting. I can also, if I wish, think of a tiger as a stick figure, which shows little more than the fact that the tiger is pointing to the left and standing up. Or I can imagine the tiger with slightly more pictorial information. I can imagine it being of a particular size and against a particular background. I can in these ways just add more and more visual information, and so I can create a range of mental representations, from one that is purely descriptive—and thus not really an image—to one that is richer and richer in visual detail. There is no question, I think, that this range of possibilities is in place. I also think that the range is anchored, at one end, by a purely descriptive thought, with no pictorial elements. All of that seems uncontroversial

The controversy arises, however, when we confront the possibility that at some point you can get the pictorial information to be rich enough, so that it stands free of the propositional information—a depiction without some sort of attached description. That's the possibility that I'm denying, and so I clearly do want to claim an asymmetry: One can have descriptive thoughts without accompanying depiction, but no depictive thoughts without description. In this regard, Maria [Brandimonte], if your data survive scrutiny, hold up to replication and all the rest, and if we can think through in some detail what is going on—and that is why suppression is having its effects—then your data may refute this claim. Your data, if they hold up, do suggest that with appropriate encoding circumstances you can form the picture, divorced from the propositional information. These data, on the face of things, point us in that direction, but obviously I am not convinced yet.

BRANDIMONTE: Is it your centering idea, Dan?[6]

REISBERG: No, it is not the centering idea, inasmuch as I want to claim that the centering must be specified in some fashion external to the picture. The centering must be specified in some fashion that specifies how to *read* the picture.

BRANDIMONTE: Yes, but what if you force people toward a more neutral representation?

REISBERG: The question is whether you *can* find a reference frame which specifies a neutral center. I shall come back to that in just a moment. Let me first make sure, though, that the context is clear. There is, as I have just sketched, no controversy about there being a continuum which ranges from a bare proposition at one end, to a proposition accompanied by a little pictorial information and then on to a proposition plus a great deal of pictorial information and so on. The question of interest, however, arises when we ask how that continuum—or *if* that continuum—continues, and specifically, whether it is possible eventually to strip away the propositional information.

The fact that there is a continuum of some sort is agreed to in an instant by all of us. The issue is whether there is a point on that continuum when you have just the free-standing picture, and that is clearly a point on which we disagree. Clearly, there are some species of imagery that deserve special treatment.[7] Here is an extreme case: Imagine that I give you an injection of some chemical that causes spontaneous firing of the photoreceptors on the retina. In that case you will have a visual experience in the absence of any external stimulus—you will have the experience of an image. I think there is no question that this particular kind of image will function just like a visual stimulus, and will, for example, be ambiguous, will produce various sensory effects and the like. Indeed, because of the way I have described it just now, this sort of image is, for all practical purposes, a visual stimulus, literally using the neural pathways of vision.

I offer this case merely as the basis for claiming that there are plainly different species of imagery that are possible, some of which are purely, clearly, unambiguously visual. But now that we have opened that door, it forces a very strong conclusion: Once we have admitted that there are different species of imagery, then I think that we have no choice but to say that we do not know in what species dream images belong, in what species hallucinogenic images belong, in what species hypnogogic images belong. The moment we agree that there are multiple species I think we have to take all of those cases, and I am sorry, just push them off the table. We don't know if they are the same variety as ordinary waking images, and thus we can't extrapolate from them to ordinary waking images. If we had reason to believe there was merely one species of image then we would be forced to deal with these more exotic cases. If, for example, they were ambiguous in their depiction, then it would follow that images in general are ambiguous. But the moment we admit that there are multiple species of imagery, then we cannot support that generalization simply because we do not know whether those cases are comparable. Therefore, I think that we are forced to hold them to one side for now.

BRANDIMONTE: I think that this claim was implicit in Kosslyn's model, when he distinguished between loaded images and generated images. For example, in this perspective, loaded images and generated images can be seen, according to the distinction Cesare [Cornoldi] made this morning, as visual memories and visually generated images. Generated images may be more prototypical, while loaded images are more likely to preserve surface characteristics.

LOGIE: Can I just pick up one of the points that Cesare made a few moments ago about the ambiguity in language? Cesare referred to the notion that alternative interpretations of specific linguistic material tend to be primed when that material is presented. For example, when a word is heard or seen, semantic and other associates of the word are activated along with the representation of the word itself. In apparent contrast, research in the context of encoding specificity gave rise to very powerful effects suggesting the converse. That is, if a word is presented along with a specific interpretation of that word, that interpretation later affects the ease of access to the word for retrieval. In a typical experiment, subjects might be presented with the word pair "traffic-jam" in a list of paired associates for subsequent cued recall. At the time of recall it is difficult for subjects to access the alternative meaning for "jam." That is, when later given the word "strawberry" as a cue for recall of a word from the originally presented list, subjects typically fail to retrieve the word *jam* because it had not been thought of in the sense of a fruit preserve. These sorts of ambiguities are ubiquitous in language, but people apparently store presented words on the basis of their initial encoding. And so those sorts of ambiguities and reference frames that provide a particular interpretation of the ambiguity exist in language as well as in imagery. They can affect the way in which we retain and retrieve information. So, there is a precedent in language for having specific, unambiguous interpretations.[8]

BRANDIMONTE: Let me digress a bit from this specific point. Jonathan Schooler and I are planning to use the encoding specificity principle to investigate whether we can prevent verbal overshadowing by using color as a cue, on the assumption that the original visual memories are simply inaccessible, not unavailable. For example, a prediction for image transformations would be that you induce verbal overshadowing (for example, subjects might learn a picture with a specific color and then they might be induced, perhaps by supplying a verbal label for the picture, to verbally recode this picture) and then, at the time of testing, you present the color of the contextual learning experience just before image formation. Color might then work as a cue for restoring the associated visual aspects of the stimulus, and therefore facilitate image transformations.

LOGIE: I am not sure that I would want to take encoding specificity quite so literally. I was using it as an example of a precedent in language demonstrating that people store ambiguous words, along with an interpretation of those words that is in an unambiguous form. Clearly, there is a question within the concept of encoding specificity as to how to predict which particular interpretations and associated cues are going to be encoded and which ones are not. The same could be true with using color. It may not be an effective cue because people simply do not encode it along with the initial stimulus.

BRANDIMONTE: It might not work, I agree. I was just thinking aloud that the encoding specificity principle might be used for an investigation in the visual imagery context as well.

LOGIE: Getting back to you Geir [Kaufmann], I wondered if you had any thoughts on Dan's comments about different species of imagery. Whether we can, in fact, salvage something from what we know about imagery to try to keep these different species on the table and keep them on the agenda. Or should we be more cautious and conclude that they are too difficult to deal with and that they should be kept firmly off the agenda at this stage?

KAUFMANN: There is a danger in defining these phenomena in such a way that you throw out the theory as well. I think you [addressing Reisberg] are doing that, not deliberately, but that is the implication. We can see all the different varieties of mental images coherently falling in one conceptual model, and that would be an alternative to the position where you say that this is mental imagery, but you do not know what the phenomena are, and they are not allowed to play in this game because I have decided on the rules!

REISBERG: No, I don't think that I'm in any sense begging the question. Imagine that we had some data on hypnogogic imagery that spoke against my conception—for example, data showing clear ambiguity, clear potential for reinterpretation, in hypnogogic imagery. In that case, clearly, my attempt to rule these images out of court would be transparently self-serving; indeed, it would be cheating on anybody's account. In other words, I would be hiding embarrassing data. It turns out, however, that we have *no* data about hypnogogic imagery, beyond lots of interesting, intriguing, and inviting phenomenology, but phenomenology nonetheless. Therefore, what I am trying cautiously to push off the table is, in truth, not very much. I am not seeking to hide embarrassing data, or *any* data, because there are no data to exclude.

If at some future point we should uncover some data suggesting that hypnogogic imagery is the same species as waking imagery, these phenomena may be reconsidered. Imagine that we could find relevant neurobiological data, or relevant functional data. If those data come into view, then, at that point, my caution would have been addressed, and at that point we would re-invite those data to the table. I am perfectly willing to greet that day, when it arrives, with a smile. I just don't think that we are close to that day.

KAUFMANN: I think that you can look at mental images on a continuum. There could be cases where the picture is drawn and the description comes afterwards like in hypnogogic images, and maybe that is what you did in your experiment. You created some conditions that somehow come close to this phenomenon. You look at it from a neutral perspective: You look at it as a picture and then you have this pictorially based reconstrual. This would totally support a wider range for defining the phenomena of mental imagery than you are arguing for.

REISBERG: It might be true, but I am not sure what conclusions I would draw from it.

KAUFMANN: There are a whole range of mental-imagery phenomena, and I think that it is possible to deal with this range of phenomena under one conceptual model, if you accept the notion that there is symmetry between the two components.

REISBERG: But now I'm afraid it is you who risk begging the question. It seems to me that you want to presume symmetry—depictions possible without descriptions, descriptions possible without depictions, and all sorts of compromises in between. To be sure, this might, if true, provide us with a wonderful unifying conception. But that surely doesn't mean that it is true. In other words, it's possible that the data simply are not unified and orderly in the way you might want.

KAUFMANN: But then we have two different conceptions and both of them cannot be true. The next step would be to agree on some kinds of experimental conditions that would qualify as a test of two alternatives: one symmetric and one asymmetric. We may be able to frame the question such that we agree on the premises, but we disagree on the expectations that we have from our different conceptions, Dan. For example, I could ask you to look at something resembling a fleeting image that is neutral and for you to label it afterwards. Something like that would be the acid test here, and when we have agreed on the conditions, this would qualify as a test.

LOGIE: One thing that strikes me about much of the discussion thus far is the extent to which it is driven by the nature of the phenomena—i.e., the images. Another approach would be to think about the kind of cognitive architecture that might be involved, that might be the seat for these phenomena. Taking that approach, if we can find evidence to suggest that, say, hypnogogic imagery and imagery manipulation by means of mental rotation, creativity in images, and so on all seem to use the same cognitive architecture, then those are grounds for suggesting that they have something in common. But it seems to me that if the debate is driven solely by the phenomena, there is a danger of cataloguing phenomena in the absence of a coherent explanatory framework. We could end up with enormous numbers of species of phenomena and find ourselves in the position of having to try to find explanations for them all. Allen Newell's[9] paper in the early 1970s pointed out that this may not be a terribly useful way to go. So perhaps one alternative approach is to think of the underlying cognitive architecture, and the extent to which specific components of that might be involved in different kinds of imagery. Of course, that opens the question as to which characterization of the cognitive architecture you are happy to accept. One could simply plunge in at the deep end and say let's take a model off the shelf—for example, Kosslyn's visual buffer and its ancillary components—and investigate the extent to which. . . .

REISBERG: To choose an uncontentious example?

LOGIE: . . . To choose an example—at random! One could then investigate the extent to which that model provides a useful platform. Or to choose another model entirely at random; there is a model of working memory that can be assessed in a similar fashion. In sum then, given that there is this alternative, I wondered whether any of you had comments on an "architecture" or "model-based" approach as a means to avoid the possible dangers of the endeavour becoming too phenomenon driven.

REISBERG: For what it's worth, it was precisely that approach that led us into this swamp in the first place. What actually led us, long ago, to the original Chambers and Reisberg procedure was an interesting argument concerned with the broad architecture, and the broad content, of thought. As it turns out, it's an argument from philosophers, and, interestingly one of the few places in which you find a clear agreement between Husserl and Wittgenstein. It is hard to find many points on which they agree, but this is one.

The notion of cognitive architecture here is one that is less specified than the ones we usually speak of but the argument from Wittgenstein via Fodor is that if images are going to participate in the stream of thought at all, then they must have properties that allow them to carry meaning, and pictorial representation by its very nature cannot carry meaning. Therefore, you have two choices: One choice is either to insist on the pictorial view of imagery, in which case you end up arguing that images cannot participate in the stream of thought; or you have a nonpictorial, or hybrid pictorial view of imagery, in which case we have compromised on the pictorial nature, but at the same time have elevated images in terms of their role.

It seems to me that both of these alternatives are viable, so one needs data to choose between them. In this case, the philosophers' level of analysis cannot resolve the issue, but plainly it does define the issue.

LOGIE: I am not sure that this actually addresses the point, because it then begs questions about what the platforms are for thought, and whether we have a single mechanism involved in mediating thought, or whether we have a variety of mechanisms each having specific functions. There could be a cognitive mechanism, for example, for storing purely visual information, which is available in that store on a temporary basis, and which can be picked out as required. So I am not sure that the approach you outline moves this issue forward.

The other reason I have for setting the question derives from the assumption that we have a common cognitive architecture, a notion that is fairly pervasive in cognitive psychology. It is a notion that also drives the practice of using aggregate data from groups of normal subjects—so we can claim that we obtain overall significance from groups of normal subjects and that this must be telling us something about the way the cognitive architecture operates. Sometimes a large number of individuals in group samples, often a substantial minority of individuals, do not show the group aggregate effect. It is rarely mentioned if, for example 12 out of 20 subjects showed an effect while the remaining 8 did not—although the duck-rabbit debate is a notable exception. Is this pattern of data telling us that the 8 have a different cognitive architecture from the 12 who show the phenomenon? Alternatively, is it something to do with strategy choice, that we all have the same cognitive architecture, but that some people choose to use it in a particular way and this way of using the cognitive architecture results in the appearance of particular phenomena?

REISBERG: It is clear that the conception I sketched is firmly within a particular conception of thought—one which focuses on a symbol-processing view, and that is, of course, itself controversial. But my sense of things was that one needs to grab hold of the bootstraps somewhere, make a number of reasonable assumptions, and see how much trouble you get into.

CORNOLDI: I should like to get back to the question concerning the cognitive structures that are involved in these operations, including image reconstrual. From what I understand, everyone here agrees about the existence of a passive storage of the elements concerning the visual trace and of active operations involved in the manipulation of the elements in the passive trace. Typically when we think of these components, we also consider their capacity limitations. Is it possible that the transformation of an image, like reconstrual, is related to capacity limitations? For example, from an intuitive point of view, the question you have studied—the duck/rabbit—seems different. It seems to be related to the fact that what is interpreted cannot be interpreted again. Maybe we could try to change the question, to see whether in that particular case, sometimes, the operations required to transform the image are beyond the capacity limitations of the systems involved. I would welcome your reactions to this problem.

KAUFMANN: I think my data suggest that we have done something to the subjects to enable them to accomplish the reconstrual in the best possible way. Nevertheless, they had a lot of difficulty with reconstrual. If you look at it from that viewpoint, I was just interested in demonstrating that reconstrual was possible, and we could interpret the difficulty faced by subjects in terms of their capacity limitations. That is, reconstrual may be something which is possible but which is accomplished with the mental functions close to their capacity limits.

BRANDIMONTE: I was thinking that a capacity-limitation explanation could not account for the improvement under articulatory suppression.

REISBERG: It should be the other way round.

BRANDIMONTE: Exactly.

LOGIE: One of the interpretations you alluded to earlier, Maria, and that Dan [Reisberg] and I have toyed with, is the notion that articulatory suppression stops people using a strategy that is commonly used, and it forces them to use a strategy that is actually more efficient, but which is not one that people would commonly choose to use in that particular task. Since the duck-rabbit reconstrual task is artificial, as Geir [Kaufmann] suggested, it confronts the subjects with a task which they have never before encountered in their lives, and certainly not combined with articulatory suppression. They have to react to the demands of the experiment in a sensible way. It seems then that subjects are forced to develop a strategy that allows them to perform rather well using a mechanism that they have not used in that way before, and they suddenly discover that this novel strategy allows them to accede to the task demands. They may not be aware that they are performing better under these conditions, but they are forced to develop some kind of strategy in order to meet the requirements of the experimenter.

In whatever way cognitive capacity may be limited,[10] let us assume that the dual-task requirement in the Brandimonte studies exceeds the capacity of the systems responsible for representing the image. Under suppression, the system that was previously used is therefore no longer available, and subjects are forced to use some other part of their cognitive architecture. Now, of course, this is finessing all of the problems about what articulatory suppression is doing. Maybe, under these circumstances, people do rehearse the verbal labels of the items that they have to manipulate. We can take as an example the experiments by Brandimonte and colleagues, where subjects are shown a picture of something that looks like a wrapped sweet (candy) which they have to image. One end of the image has to be removed, and subjects are then required to report the resulting image, which in this case would resemble a fish.[11] On initial presentation of the picture, subjects may say over to themselves "sweet–sweet–sweet–sweet." This then undermines their ability to subsequently reinterpret the image as a fish when one end of the image is taken away, because the label "sweet" is being covertly rehearsed.[12]

BRANDIMONTE: This is what Margaret Intons-Peterson has done. She has the same opinion that verbal processing is interfering with the initial labeling and final naming.

LOGIE: Yes, but also there is also a storage element associated with verbal processing. In that sense, the interference may be with *retention of* the verbal label, and not because the verbal rehearsal system is normally involved in initially naming objects. We can label objects in the visual scene quite adequately under articulatory suppression. However, if we wish to retain these labels over a period of time, this may involve some form of verbal temporary memory system—e.g., the articulatory loop. The retained label may then be used as a means to retain information about the presented stimulus rather than, or to supplement, the veridical stimulus. If articulation is suppressed then the articulatory code for the label simply is not retained, and subjects have to rely on a more visually based representation.

BRANDIMONTE: The phenomenological experience of people who look at a very simple picture like the duck/rabbit or our other pictures used in the imagery addition/subtraction studies is that they are able to name the pictures while doing articulatory suppression. This is surely true. A problem, I think, may arise because of what it means to give a name. In my opinion, if we think about identification, it is likely that articulatory suppression does not prevent you from knowing what the figure is in terms of simple identification—or, if you like, *naming,* although I am not sure that you could call this naming. What articulatory suppression might do is to block people from carrying out a deeper analysis in terms of how it would have looked if the sweet had been larger or had been real. What I mean is that a deeper semantic analysis might be difficult under articulatory suppression, but I do not think identification would be difficult, in terms of knowing what the item is. It is easy when we look at a picture and we talk or sing a well-learned song to know perfectly well what we are looking at. Therefore, my suggestion is that articulatory suppression might have the effect of leaving absolutely unaltered the ability of naming the picture and identifying it. What is important is that you cannot carry out a deeper analysis of the picture.

REISBERG: I would like to pursue this, because, as I said before, if these data do hold up, the implication will be that I am simply wrong. Therefore, a close examination of these data is very important.

These data come close to documenting the case that Geir [Kaufmann] is hoping for. That is, suppression, on the face of things, makes possible a mental image which stands independent of, or undefined by, any descriptive information. But these data need close scrutiny because it is not at all obvious what lies behind them. As I understand it, there are at least two interpretations of these data on the table, and I am about to add a third. I believe these interpretations are different from each other in important ways, and happily, the differences are testable.

One interpretation, Maria, is of course along the lines you are describing. What articulatory suppression does, in one fashion or another, is to prevent verbal overshadowing, forcing subjects into something closer to a pure pictorial representation. If this interpretation turns out to be right, then so be it, but it is an interpretation that, for obvious reasons, I hope to avoid. And, in fact, I am nervous about this interpretation largely because of the assumptions you need to make about what articulatory suppression is doing in these circumstances. Again, let me note that, despite your claims, there is ample reason to believe that articulatory suppression does not block naming, and this raises real uncertainty about why suppression is having its effect in your studies. That, in turn, makes me rather skeptical about the hypothesis you are offering.

The second proposal on the table is this notion that Bob [Logie] and I have cooked up.[13] That is, we offered the conjecture that subjects typically do not use the inner-scribe strategy; they prefer other strategies. In your procedure, though, since you have blocked subjects from their preferred strategy, they are forced to resort to this less preferred strategy. Ironically, in this case their less preferred strategy actually turns out to be more effective.

This hypothesis still seems to me to be viable, although I must say I was a little troubled, Maria, by your tapping data because, if in fact subjects are resorting to an inner scribe, one might think that tapping should be disruptive, on the simple idea that one can't tap and use the inner scribe, which is motoric in nature, at the same time. So this hypothesis strikes me as being alive, but wounded. [See editorial comments at the end of this discussion.]

Maria, let me therefore offer a third hypothesis about your data, which is in fact close to the one I mentioned in that long letter I sent you, and which I think is testable. Here's a possibility. Deborah Chambers and I have argued in print that the obstacle to reinterpretation of the duck-rabbit lies in the position of the form's visual center. I think in the Cognitive Psychology paper we don't use that terminology, but we should. In essence, the construal—as duck or rabbit—dictates a visual center, specified within the perceptual reference frame, which biases the depiction. Hence, the duck construal leads to a visual center that in turn leads to a depiction that literally favors the duck.

This way of thinking opens up the possibility that one might find a *neutral* position for the visual center, one that is equally compatible with the duck and rabbit depictions. That now allows me to offer the following story about your data. Your manipulation, I will propose, does not force subjects into a *neutral image,* that is to say, your manipulation does not force subjects into an image without a reference frame. I want to continue asserting, at least for now, that an image-without-frame is not possible; a mental image is always, obligatorily, understood within a reference frame. Therefore, what your manipulation is doing instead is to force subjects into an image having a particular reference frame that happens to be compatible with both construals. To put it bluntly, the image is understood within a reference frame, which specifies many things, but which also happens to specify a center that favors neither duck nor rabbit. In this case, both construals are compatible with the reference frame, and that's precisely the setting in which we've argued—that discoveries should flow from the image. Again, as we've said over and over, discoveries from imagery should be easy *if* those discoveries are compatible with the reference frame.

Now if all of this is correct, it should be testable in the following fashion. I've just suggested that your manipulation somehow influences the position of the form's visual center. The position of the visual center is, in turn, crucial for reconstruing the duck-rabbit. However, the position of the visual center is irrelevant for other forms and for other demonstrations in the literature—for example, our sideways Texas experiment. In that particular case, the obstacle to discovery from the image is not the position of the visual center. Instead, the obstacle to image discovery is subjects' understanding where the form's *top* is.

Now we are ready for the predictions: Let us imagine that we ask subjects to form a mental image of Texas, or, for European subjects, of Africa. And, as in our original procedure, the image is initially "misoriented" by 90 degrees, but the subjects are instructed to rotate the image in order to "set it right." And now let us imagine that we include an articulatory suppression condition, so that suppression is on the scene both during image creation, or image maintenance, or both. If you are right about suppression's effects, then this situation will prevent verbal overshadowing, resulting in something like a pure pictorial representation. Therefore, if you are right, with articulatory suppression, subjects should in this situation readily identify the form depicted in their mental image. So you would predict that articulatory suppression should help with this task in the same way it helps with the duck-rabbit.

I, however, would make a different prediction. At least for the moment, I want to entertain the possibility that articulatory suppression forces people into a neutral visual center, which is relevant for the duck-rabbit figure, but irrelevant for Africa. Therefore, I claim that even if articulatory suppression helps with the duck-rabbit, it will not help with Africa. You claim that it should help with both.

FINAL EDITORIAL COMMENTS

One feature of a live debate is that it is prone to curtailment, and this debate is no exception, since at this point the contributors had to return to the main conference program. This then is an apposite point at which to assess the current state of the debate in the light of the various possible outcomes that we considered at the start of this chapter. We have certainly not reached an impasse—far from it. Likewise, we have not reached a consensus on some mutually accepted understanding, but then this is probably overambitious for a 2-hour discussion or even for several chapters in a single volume. What we have done is foster further debate. In this respect it is at the same time unsatisfactory, ironic, and appropriate that the debate has ended with the description of a possible experiment and competing predictions.

It is interesting to speculate about what would have happened had there been no limitations on the time available. Our suspicion is that a similar point would have been reached, perhaps with the participants agreeing on the actual details of an experimental design. Those details could have elaborated the prediction made by Dan Reisberg, or could have pursued the tapping data which Maria Brandimonte mentioned. These data, as we have seen, were taken as a test of whether some form of visuo-spatial working memory system was involved in the image reconstrual task. This seems an important issue: If subjects normally do *not* use a visuo-spatial representation when performing the duck-rabbit task, then adding a secondary tapping task should make no difference. If, on the other hand, articulatory suppression leads subjects toward a visuo-spatial strategy, then we would expect disruption if the subjects were required to do both tapping and articulatory suppression at the same time. The prediction here is that tapping would remove the improvement normally observed under articulatory suppression.

Another possible experimental design is one that tackles the capacity hypothesis, for example, by systematically altering the complexity of the stimuli that are to be considered. It is less clear how to pursue the argument between Dan Reisberg and Geir Kaufmann about the nature of the continuum from a purely pictorial to a wholly interpreted and described representation. For example, one could systematically vary the meaningfulness of the visual stimulus that subjects have to retain, that they have to construe, and that they attempt to reconstrue. However, if we fail to demonstrate that the image is devoid of a reference frame, this could simply be because the task did not sample the extremes of the continuum.

These are just a few examples, and there are numerous other ideas for research within this debate, and indeed within the chapters in this volume. Single experiments, or larger-scale doctorate programm, or even major research endeavours could stem from the range of issues both implicit and explicit in the chapters in these pages.

On reflection, then, there is still a strong sense that the volume, and in particular this discussion, is incomplete. There do seem to be shared starting points, and there is a strong consensus on many issues. Nonetheless, large-scale disagreements remain, with many openings for new work, and new contributions. But then again, the intention of this series of volumes is to highlight contemporary counterpoints in cognition, and we may conclude that the goal here is indeed the debate itself, through which we stimulate critical thinking and provoke further research. We hope that by highlighting these counterpoints we have both pursued and achieved one of the main goals of scientific progress.

NOTES

1. Chambers, D., & Reisberg, D. (1985). Can mental images be ambiguous? *Journal of Experimental Psychology: Human Perception and Performance, 3*, 317–328.

2. Ibid.

3. Note that Reisberg mentioned *"two"* large questions in his previous paragraph, but here considers only one because the flow of conversation moved on. Subsequent to the live discussion, he indicated that his intended second question here concerned the possible role of distraction in the Brandimonte data, a point that was taken up in part by Logie's interjection.

4. Finke, R. Slayton, K. (1988). Explorations of creative visual synthesis in mental imagery. *Memory and Cognition, 16,* 252–257.

5. The reference here is to Reisberg, and Logie, R. (1993). The in's and out's of working memory: Escaping the boundaries on imagery function. In B. Roskos-Ewoldsen, M. Intons-Peterson, & R. Anderson (Eds.), *Imagery, creativity and discovery: A cognitive approach.* Amsterdam: Elsevier.

6. Brandimonte is here referring to a comment Reisberg made earlier, about how articulatory suppression (Brandimonte's manipulation) might influence an aspect of the perceptual reference frame (Reisberg's terminology), which he referred to as the form's "perceptual center." In Reisberg's view, a form's center is specified by the reference frame, which is itself not part of the depicted form: The reference frame specifies how the form is to be (perceptually) understood. For details, see Chapter 4. The idea is also referred to by Brandimonte and Gerbino, Chapter 2.

7. Reisberg's comment here is in response to an earlier remark by Kaufmann, namely that we might gain insight into these broader issues by considering other forms of naturally occurring imagery, i.e., imagery outside of the laboratory. Kaufmann included the possibility of studying dream imagery or hypnogogic imagery. Unfortunately, this early remark by Kaufmann was lost due to a tape recorder malfunction, nonetheless, the debate preserves Reisberg's response to that remark.

8. The implication here is that it is difficult to determine a priori when an alternative

meaning for a word is likely to be activated (and, hence, produce a priming effect), and when it will not (hence, supporting the encoding specificity principle). So too with ambiguous visual stimuli, it could be that some conditions result in the activation of alternative interpretations for the stimulus, while other conditions ensure that only one interpretation is activated. It is of course a separate issue as to how the interpretation of the visual stimulus becomes incorporated into the visual image, or in Reisberg's terms, how the reference frame is determined.

9. Newell, A. (1973). You can't play 20 questions with nature and win. In W. G. Chase (Ed.) *Visual Information Processing*. New York: Academic Press.

10. This refers to the idea that there are a variety of ways in which capacity might be measured or conceived. The most appropriate analogy of capacity limitation may not be that of a tank filling with some fluid. For example, the limitations on the system may be time based (i.e., how long the contents of the system may be retained in the system), or resolution based (i.e., how fine-grained is the representation).

11. See the chapter by Brandimonte and Gerbino.

12. See the Brandimonte and Gerbino chapter for example stimuli.

13. Reisberg & Logie (1993).

Index